Biblical
Authority

Biblical Authority

A Critique of the Rogers/McKim Proposal

John D. Woodbridge

Trinity Evangelical Divinity School

**ZONDERVAN
PUBLISHING HOUSE** OF THE ZONDERVAN CORPORATION
GRAND RAPIDS, MICHIGAN 49506

BIBLICAL AUTHORITY: A CRITIQUE OF THE ROGERS/MCKIM PROPOSAL
Copyright © 1982 by The Zondervan Corporation
Grand Rapids, Michigan

Library of Congress Cataloging in Publication Data

Woodbridge, John D., 1941–
   Biblical authority.

   Includes bibliographical references and index.
   1. Rogers, Jack Bartlett. Authority and interpretation of the Bible. 2. Bible—Criticism,
interpretation, etc.,—History. 3. Bible—Evidences, authority, etc.—History. 4. Theology,
Reformed Church—History. I. Title.

BS500.R633W66 1982   220.1'3   82-8592
ISBN 0-310-44751-8   AACR2

Edited by Ben Chapman
Designed by Louise Bauer

Printed in the United States of America

82 83 84 85 86 87 88 — 10 9 8 7 6 5 4 3 2 1

Contents

Foreword

A battle is raging within evangelical circles today. It is a verbal battle and it is a battle among friends. Although some people think that all such arguments are a useless waste of time—like arguing how many angels can dance on the head of a pin—the battle over the Bible and its authority is worth fighting.

Worthwhile battles need to be fought rightly, and the more important an issue is, the greater is the necessity for strategy. The battleground needs to be chosen carefully. Issues must be sharpened. The style of fighting must be appropriate to those who are wielding the weapons (arguments). A clear delineation of goals is absolutely essential. Well-meaning individuals often enter a battle and take up the cudgels without calculating what they plan to accomplish by their great output of energy. We sincerely hope that this will not be the case in the battle over biblical authority.

Dr. John Woodbridge writes this book as a historian—he is not a polemist. As a careful student of the history of ideas he is deeply committed to setting the record straight. Nevertheless, he enters a pitched battle. He is not unaware of the position of the enemy or of his own commitment to biblical authority. No writer is neutral; everyone brings to the task the baggage of his or her background and personal convictions ("prejudices" to those who do not share them). Happy is the author who, like Dr. Woodbridge, brings to the task the highly honed skills of historical scholarship as well as passionate love for the truth and a deep sense of fairness and intellectual honesty. We have confidence in such authors; we will become wiser by perusing their works. In this volume Dr. Woodbridge shares the fruit of his scholarship in such transparent honesty and deep commitment to the truth that we can rightfully trust, and greatly profit from, the product of his pen.

This volume is a thorough evaluation of the issues raised by Jack Rogers and Donald McKim in their volume *The Authority and Interpretation of the Bible: An Historical Approach* (New York: Harper and Row, 1979). The discussion focuses especially on the history of the doctrine of biblical authority as it relates to such terms as *infallibility* and *inerrancy*. We may well ask what might be accomplished by yet another book on such a well-worn topic. It will help us to answer this question if we first seek to discover the issues being discussed.

Both Jack Rogers and John Woodbridge profess committment to the authority of the Bible as the final and trustworthy guide for faith and practice. Jack Rogers, however, is deeply concerned to free biblical authority from the disrepute brought on it by association with a doctrine of inerrancy. He is impressed by wide agreement that inerrancy is an intellectually impossible position. Emil Brunner argued that belief in inerrance is absolutely incompatible with intellectual honesty (*The Mediator* [New York: Macmillan, 1942], p. 185). Karl Barth declared that to accept a doctrine of verbal inspiration (and inerrancy, which he equated with it) would require a sacrifice of the intellect that he was simply unwilling to make (*Das Christliche Verst ändnis der Offenbarung*. München: Chr. Kaiser, 1948. p. 29). American scholar Millar Burrows documents the consensus with the words, "All wise theologians [have moved] to a better position" (*Outline of Biblical Theology* [Philadelphia: Westminster Press, 1946], pp. 9, 44). Inerrancy, so Dr. Rogers feels, is a stumbling block to faith—a stumbling block with which we would do well to dispense—all the more so because from its earliest period to modern times it has never been the doctrine of the church.

Some stumbling blocks, of course, are necessary: there is a legitimate offense of the Cross. We cannot and ought not to avoid that stumbling block. If inerrancy were truly an aspect of the offense of the Cross, we could only say: "So be it. Such is the tragedy of human sin and pride."

But other offenses are of our own creation and are unnecessary. We must eliminate such false stumbling blocks so that the true offense alone can stand forth unencumbered.

A doctrine of inerrancy, so Dr. Rogers argues, falls into this latter category. He urges Evangelicals, therefore, to remove this false stumbling block so that the offer of the gospel and the complementary doctrine of biblical authority may stand clear and strong.

Dr. Woodbridge and most conservative Evangelicals, on the contrary, are convinced that biblical authority is at stake. Inerrancy means that the Bible tells only the truth—God's truth. If the Bible were not inerrant, the believer would either not know whether anything in the Bible were true or else he would have to have some way of distinguishing between what is true and trustworthy and what is not true and, therefore, is unworthy of our trust. The Christian would be driven to pick and choose from the Bible what comes to us with divine authority.

Of course, Evangelicals do not suggest that inerrancy would solve all problems. The Christian would still have to struggle with interpretation, but we would know that the effort spent in obtaining the meaning of the text would be infinitely worthwhile. This truth is from God—truth that cannot be ignored without peril. This divinely given truth provides us with daily guidance from Christ since the Holy Spirit impresses it upon our hearts and consciences.

The question of inerrancy is nothing less than an issue over the practical means of an objective and usable authority by which the Holy Spirit guides us into His truth and makes effective the practical outworking of the lordship of Christ over His church.

Given the position of these two diverse viewpoints, each guarding doggedly what it deems to be precious truth, Can we hope to accomplish anything through further discussion? Of course, if these alternative stances presented fully contradictory positions, then nothing profitable could be done to reconcile them. We should have only to reckon with the consequences, take our pick, and agree to disagree. Such is far from the case, however. It is essential first to note that this is no mere battle about a word but a battle over an important and very practical aspect of Christian faith—how the Bible is to be viewed in securing guidance and direction from God.

However, if we are to profit from such discussion, those who would defend the inerrancy of Scripture must spell out exactly what is essential and what is not essential to preserve the treasure of biblical authority. Of course, conservative Evangelicals will say that this has been done over and over again. Maybe so. But we have not been heard. Sincere and intelligent people have not grasped the message. We must spell out unequivocally our full commitment to the human authorship and full freedom of the biblical writers as human authors. All disabilities inherent to human language, and the thought forms out of which human language comes must be adequately insisted upon, not just grudgingly acknowledged. No doubt God could have created for the Bible a new and heavenly language of perfection, but He did not choose to do that. In any case who would have understood it and profited from it had He done so? The actual Bible we do possess is a thoroughly human book—as human as any other book.

Accordingly, we find that the Bible is not written in precise language. It does not give us the writing of a modern scientist or a twentieth-century historian. An author writing in the ninth century B.C. or in the first century A.D. may not have meant exactly what we would mean if we used those same words. We must not impose an artificial hermeneutic on the Bible and then find fault with what we have wrongly taken to be its meaning. It is precisely because the Bible is so thoroughly a human book that it can only be rightly understood by drawing its meaning from the way in which those word symbols were used in their historical setting. To some Evangelicals this fact may seem unsettling, but this is the means by which the Bible retains its objective authority. Only in this way can the objective data of grammar, syntax, history, and culture lead us to the meaning of Scripture so that we truly stand under its judgment.

The alternative to this view is to transform the Bible into a subjective authority in which the Holy Spirit simply uses the words of Scripture to create in us individually a private revelation that cannot be tested objectively—or worse yet, a Scripture from which the believer picks and chooses according to his personal whim.

On the other hand, Jack Rogers, Donald McKim, and those who hold similar views cannot rest simply on a case for the full humanity of Scripture. They must also come to grips with the teaching of our Lord and of Holy Scripture itself as to the nature of biblical authority. Certainly the degree to which the Bible is trustworthy is a religious question. It is impossible for anyone to take the dodge that they follow the Bible in its religious and theological teaching but then choose to neglect its teaching regarding its own authority.

In the light of our Lord's teaching and of the Scripture's own teaching about itself, no opponent of inerrancy is likely to win any considerable segment of conservative Evangelicalism to his viewpoint unless he forthrightly clarifies his own ambiguity regarding the full truthfulness of Scripture. Evangelicals do not tend to look favorably on any view that suggests that we must pick and choose what to accept and what not to accept from Scripture. Evangelicals will not accept a subjective authority in which the Holy Spirit simply uses the words of Scripture to create in us individually a private revelation that cannot be tested objectively by an appeal to what stands written in Holy Scripture.

In this volume by John Woodbridge we discover that key figures in the history of the church who played a decisive role at neural points in the formulation of Christian doctrine have clearly and unequivocally taught precisely what conservative Evangelicals today teach about inerrancy. These men have consistently described their view by the term *inerrancy* (or its Latin cognate) and by words and phrases that are precise equivalents of that term.

Even more important for our day than demonstrating that leading theologians of the church have taught a doctrine of inerrancy, this study shows what these seminal thinkers meant by inerrancy. Once for all, this book lays to rest the suspicion that Augustine, Luther, Calvin, and their faithful successors held to a wooden, dehumanized view of Scripture that ignored, slighted, or denied its full human aspect with all that that entails for our understanding of it as God's inerrant word, incarnate in words that are wholly human—one true written Word of God, fully divine and fully human.

KENNETH S. KANTZER

Introduction

Americans still profess a high regard for the Holy Bible. That is the surprising news reported by George Gallup, Jr., one of the respected keepers of the nation's pulse. His pollsters asked the following question in one of their surveys: "Which one of these statements comes closest to your feelings about the Bible? 1. The Bible is a collection of writings representing some of the religious philosophies of ancient man. 2. The Bible is the word of God, but it is sometimes mistaken in its statements and teachings. 3. The Bible is the word of God and is *not* mistaken in its statements and teachings." In *The Search for America's Faith* (Nashville: Abingdon, 1980), p. 136, Gallup indicates that forty-two percent of the general public espoused the third position, the most conservative of the three responses.

Certainly, many of the Americans who make this affirmation have only a vague notion of the Bible's contents. It is also clear that not all of them attempt to live under the Bible's authority. Another important pulse keeper, Daniel Yankelovich, informs us that a large swath of the American public (63%) either regularly or occasionally pursues a self-fulfillment motif. This motif sometimes leads them to ignore or at least to reinterpret Christian teachings about morality and self-sacrifice. Another seventeen percent lives with the self-fulfillment motif *uppermost* in their minds. Only twenty percent of the population functions with the more traditional duty-to-others motif as a life guiding principle. A reading of Yankelovich's *New Rules: Searching for Self-fulfillment in a World Turned Upside Down* (New York: Random House, 1981) cautions us about being too impressed by the tendency toward "orthodoxy" that Gallup sees emerging. We can quietly empty our formal commitment to biblical authority of significance if we deny biblical ethics in day-to-day decision making. Or, we can interpret the Bible so ineptly that its authority is refracted in genuinely disturbing ways.

Nonetheless, the point remains unshaken: there are millions of "Bible believers" among the country's Blacks, Hispanics, Whites, and Orientals, whether they be Roman Catholics, Orthodox, or Protestant, whether they be in the mainline denominations, or in tiny storefront churches. They believe that the Bible is God's Word; its teachings about sin and salvation, about creation and days of final consummation, about money and morality can be ignored only at an individual's or a nation's great loss. For them, the Christ of the Bible is their Christ; He is their Lord and Savior. Many Christians worry about what they assume is a growing disregard, if not outright disdain, for the Bible's authority. Some of them believe that American society is bent on cutting its ties with Judaic-Christian ethical standards. They fear that the United States is lurching pell-mell toward a moral anarchy in which each person does what is right in his or her own eyes. The lyrics of the punk rock record, "No Values," do give one pause.

Another concern has troubled Bible believers within recent years. Respected academics and church persons in the Roman Catholic Church and in Protestant denominations have argued that the Bible, although it relates or even *is* the Word of God, is nonetheless subject to various kinds of "errors." Laypersons, pastors, and theologians alike have been disturbed by this unsettling assessment. It challenges their own understanding of what the Bible teaches about itself. It also contradicts their firm belief that a revelation from God, the author of truth, could be marred by mistakes.

Since Vatican II a new definition of biblical infallibility has gained a certain currency among Roman Catholic scholars. It questions the church's traditional commitment to biblical inerrancy. In *The Truth of the Bible* (New York: Herder and Herder, 1968), Oswald Loretz has proposed that the Bible's infallibility should be interpreted in terms of its capacity to lead us to salvation. He acknowledges that the early church fathers identified biblical infallibility with biblical inerrancy (that is, the Bible teaches truth in every domain upon which it touches). He suggests, however, that the Fathers were simply mistaken. The Bible does contain "errors"; nevertheless it gives faithful, or "infallible," perspectives on salvation. In earlier decades of this century Protestant liberals and neoorthodox writers had questioned the Bible's complete infallibility.

Within the last two decades or so, evangelical Christians have become especially uneasy due to their growing awareness that scholars from their own ranks are proposing that the Bible is infallible for faith and practice but that it is susceptible to "technical mistakes." Not only have the proponents of this stance declared that their view is one that accords with the Bible's own teachings about itself, but unlike Oswald Loretz, several of them have also claimed that their position represents the "central position of the Church."

Jack Rogers and Donald McKim's *The Authority and Interpretation of the Bible: An Historical Approach* (New York: Harper and Row, 1979) represents the most extensive historical apologetic by Protestants to defend these theses. Rogers and McKim portray their lengthy work as setting "the historical record straight." So significant was their ambitious enterprise that external judges for *Eternity* magazine deemed their volume the "Book of the Year" for 1980. Their work continues to evoke both positive and negative commentary.

My own interest in Rogers and McKim's volume was piqued by the authors' stout claim that they were "setting the record straight." For seven or eight years I had been studying the theories about the Bible's authority entertained by Richard Simon, Jean Le Clerc, Baruch Spinoza, and other seventeenth- and eighteenth-century biblical critics I could understand Rogers and McKim's desire to moderate several assertions by Evangelicals who had not been sufficiently judicious in their own claims about "the central tradition of the church." Nonetheless, I found the authors' presentation regarding the issues of biblical infallibility in the seventeenth and eighteenth centuries to be unreliable. I had also studied the beliefs of nineteenth-century American Evangelicals about biblical authority. Rogers and McKim's commentary on these viewpoints appeared to be deficient as well.

In 1980, Donald Carson, editor of the *Trinity Journal*, asked me to write a review of Rogers and McKim's book. What was to be a rather brief review mushroomed into one surpassing seventy pages. The more I analyzed Rogers and McKim's volume, the more I became uncomfortable not only with the methodological problems that hovered behind it, but with the book's central proposal. There was another niggling feature of the volume's presentation: what I would call the "good guys/bad guys" syndrome. The "good guys" were concerned with salvation truths and scholarship, whereas the "bad guys" concentrated on the literary form of the Bible (its inerrancy) and were "scholastic." Whatever one might think about the significance of the biblical authority theme, its terribly complex history does not break down neatly into a world of Platonic good guys fending off scholastic, Aristotelian, bad guys. The *Trinity Journal* review (Volume I NS. No. 2 [Fall 1980]: 165–236) was to become the foundational piece for the present essay.

In the March, 1981, *TSF Bulletin*, Mark Branson, General Secretary of the Theological Students Fellowship, published excerpts of the *Trinity Journal* review. In the April, 1981, *TSF Bulletin*, Donald McKim wrote a response to the review. From McKim's rejoinder I learned how the authors perceived the kinds of criticism I had proferred. Moreover, I gained a better understanding of those points regarding which I may have misinterpreted them. This essay benefits from these insights and correctives.

In June 1981, I attended the conference on "Interpreting an Authoritative Bible," sponsored by Fuller Theological Seminary and the Institute for Christian Studies at Toronto. Jack Rogers and Donald McKim also attended the conference. We had frank discussions with each other. They were held in a spirit of mutual personal respect. I came away from those conversations with Jack Rogers greatly encouraged. I felt that progress had been made toward reconciling our personal differences regarding biblical authority and the history of that concept. Moreover, in a paper delivered at the conference, Rogers offered helpful clarifications of his position.

In the September 4, 1981, *Christianity Today*, Kenneth Kantzer penned a significant editorial. Basing his analysis on conversations with Jack Rogers and upon accounts he had gathered about the Toronto conference, Dr. Kantzer reported that Rogers believed that his view of the complete truth of the Bible was "in agreement with the view of inerrancy set forth in the Chicago Statement on Inerrancy of the International Council of Biblical Inerrancy." Many Evangelicals, one would surmise, were pleased by the irenic tone of Dr. Kantzer's editorial and by its news of a potential breakthrough.

And yet troubling signs continued to dot the theological landscape. In the summer of 1981, Rogers published an essay that echoed some of the major themes of his 1979 volume. He wrote, "In the late seventeenth century, the concept of the Bible's infallibility in religious matters was transmuted into a notion of Scripture's inerrancy in matters of science and history" ("Biblical Authority and Confessional Change," *Journal of Presbyterian History* 59, 2 [Summer 1981]: 133). One could reason, however, that this article had been crafted before the Toronto conference and did not represent Rogers's most recent appraisal. Then, in *Theology Today* (XXXVIII, No. 3 [October 1981]: 344–49), Rogers presented a response written after the Toronto conference in which he left the impression that "verbal inerrancy" was a theological innovation. Nevertheless, one could still interpret Rogers' statements generously and argue that his stress was not upon the innovative quality of the doctrine of inerrancy itself but upon the alleged innovative character of "verbal inerrancy."

On December 7, 1981, Donald Carson and I engaged in lively conversation about these issues with Jack Rogers and Peter Macky of Westminster College, Pennsylvania, during a television taping of the John Ankerberg Show (*Christianity Today*, January 22, 1982). Near the end of the taping, Rogers indicated that when he said that the Bible was without error, he simply meant that the biblical authors did not enter into any purposeful or intentional deceit: "In that book I carefully ... defined error as being deliberate deception from which the Bible is free. So I can say there are no errors in the Bible by that definition of error which I think is a biblical definition of error...." When pressed on this point by Donald Carson, it became clear that Rogers did believe that the biblical authors could make "technical mistakes" and even other kinds of errors. Once again, Rogers was upholding the linchpin premise of *The Authority and Interpretation of the Bible: An Historical Approach* (1979): the Bible's teachings about infallibility and the central tradition of the church allow for "technical mistakes." These teachings and that tradition exclude only "intentional deceits." More recently, Rogers has reportedly declared that the inerrancy posture "distorts our ability to interpret the Bible for our times" (*Chicago Tribune*, March 7, 1982).

The purpose of this essay is to evaluate the Rogers and McKim proposal upon which Rogers depends to sustain his contentions. I shall focus more on the history of "biblical authority" as it relates to the doctrine of infallibility than upon the history of the interpretation of the Bible. Rogers and McKim generally follow this approach also. I shall only incidentally broach the topic of what the Bible's witness to its own authority might be. Moreover I shall not attempt to interact specifically with twentieth-century discussions of biblical authority and hermeneutics. Rogers and McKim do not treat these topics in depth. Anthony C. Thiselton's *The Two Horizons: New Testament Hermeneutics and Philosophical Description* (Grand Rapids: Eerdmans, 1980) provides a marvelous exposition of twentieth-century hermeneutics for readers interested in that subject.

My designs, then, are circumscribed. As specialists will quickly discern, I am not attempting to write a history of the concept of biblical authority. That undertaking is herculean; it clearly exceeds my capabilities. Rather, this essay challenges specifically the basic structure and import of Rogers and McKim's proposal. However, it should also open up vistas on that huge world that is the history of biblical authority. Therefore several of my essay's horizons lie some distance beyond the immediate confines of Rogers and McKim's volume.

I would like to express my thanks to Donald Carson, the present editor of the *Trinity Journal*, for permission to make extensive use of both the Rogers and McKim review and of another article, "History's Lessons and Biblical Inerrancy," *Trinity Journal* VI, 1 (Spring 1977): 73–93 (quoted at length in Chapter 5). Stanley Gundry of the Zondervan Corporation has graciously permitted me to cite portions of an article on Professor Ernest Sandeen's interpretation of the Old Princetonians' attitudes toward Scripture (quoted in chapter 7). This article was coauthored with Randall Balmer who is a Ph.D. student at Princeton University; it appears in a volume entitled *Scripture and Truth* (ed.

D. A. Carson and John Woodbridge [Grand Rapids: Zondervan, 1983]). Many individuals have contributed to my own understanding of matters treated in this volume. I have attempted to acknowledge several of them throughout this volume. My graduate assistants, Dottie Almen and Larry Hoop, have been particularly helpful in ferreting out my errors in documentation. Nonetheless, I take responsibility for those that remain even after their careful sleuthing. Janice Seifrid also contributed much to this project by her good typing.

A wise adage warns: What can be put in a nutshell probably belongs there. I realize that this essay does cram many subjects (some of which are more complex than I have had space to indicate) into a tight nutshell. Whether or not they belong there, others will have to determine.

I trust that this essay will serve to encourage many Americans who already affirm the Bible's complete infallibility. They should know that they are not the proponents of a quirkish new doctrine. At the same time I hope that those Christians who have abandoned their commitments to complete biblical infallibility because they have come to the honest conviction that it was a "scholastic" innovation of rather recent vintage will reconsider their understanding of this important question.

The Bible is God's sure Word to humankind. It was His Word for yesterday; it is for today, and it will be for tomorrow. God, the Holy Spirit, who is its ultimate author and who confirms its authority to us, makes it a living Word to us. Each day Bible believers in this country and elsewhere have drawn strength and comfort from the living, written Word, which speaks of another living Word, Christ. For them, biblical authority is not an abstract concept; they have experienced its life-changing and life-shaping implications firsthand.

Chapter I

The Rogers/McKim Proposal: Preliminary Concerns

Today a number of evangelical scholars are expending considerable energies on a renewed historical quest. They are seeking to ascertain the attitudes of the ancient Christians toward biblical authority.[1] Their enterprise often has an apologetic and very personal impulsion. Some want to demonstrate a concordance between their own beliefs and "the historical position of the church."

Most of the Evangelicals involved in this quest acknowledge formally the principle of *sola Scriptura*. They agree that the Bible's self-attestation about its own authority should play the determinative role in formulating their beliefs. Nonetheless, they also understand that even if Protestants have not historically given authoritative weight to "tradition," as have Roman Catholics, the Orthodox, and Anglicans in a special way, Protestants have frequently attempted to bolster the case for their exegetical and doctrinal formulations by appealing to the witness of Christians of past centuries. From the patristic fathers in the early church, to Luther and other Reformers in the sixteenth century, to French Reformed pastors in the seventeenth, Christian theologians have tended to associate doctrinal innovation with heresy.[2] They have struggled with the problem of determining whether a development in doctrine is a healthy clarification of the biblical data or a dangerous departure from evangelical orthodoxy.[3] If a doctrine has a long history of acceptance by their church, or by "the church," Protestants along with Roman Catholics generally give it serious consideration.[4]

In a similar vein some Evangelicals today believe that their own views on biblical authority will gain more credence in the evangelical community if they can demonstrate that these views have deep and sturdy roots in the rich soil of church history. Therein lies the motivation for their quest.

In *The Authority and Interpretation of the Bible: An Historical*

Approach (New York: Harper and Row, 1979), Jack Rogers of Fuller Theological Seminary and Donald McKim, now of Debuque Theological Seminary, challenge several well-entrenched beliefs among American Evangelicals. Evangelicals have commonly assumed that the biblical writers, inspired by God the Holy Spirit, wrote infallibly. These authors did so, not only for matters of faith and practice, but also in making incidental affirmations concerning history, geography, and the natural world. The contention of Evangelicals is usually based on the internal claims of the writers that what they had written came from God. It is also founded on an a priori premise: God cannot lie. His Word, therefore, contains no admixture of error. Evangelicals have generally affirmed that this perspective represents the historic position of the church. Moreover, Evangelicals have consistently asserted that their stance reflects Christ's teaching about the Bible's authority.[5] Rogers and McKim want to disabuse Evangelicals of these beliefs. One of their goals, therefore, is iconoclastic.

Another one of the authors' goals is more missionary minded. Rogers and McKim seek to persuade Evangelicals and others of the validity of their own interpretation of the Bible's self-attestation. In this regard they argue that the biblical authors wrote infallibly on matters of faith and practice, but that they could and did err on occasion in statements that touched upon scientific, geographical, and historical matters, as judged by modern standards of measurement. Rogers and McKim propose that it is their own analysis that reflects the authentic, "historic" position of the church. They want their readers to join with them in affirming what they believe to be orthodox Reformed teaching concerning biblical authority.

Professors Rogers and McKim should be commended for their willingness to interact with many primary and secondary sources not commonly cited in previous evangelical studies on this subject. They have read widely and adorn their argumentation with copious footnotes. Moreover their writing style is clear and lively. Readers usually encounter little difficulty in understanding what the authors intend to say by their proposals.

The authors should also be commended for their openness to criticism of their work. In the preface of their volume, Rogers and McKim volunteer that they welcome responses and critiques.[6] In that spirit we trust that our own assessment of their interpretation will be instructive and thereby contribute to the ongoing discussion of biblical authority by Evangelicals.

Indeed, analysis should proceed concerning this subject. Competent studies are lacking concerning large tracts of the history of biblical authority. Jacques Le Brun, Professor of Catholic History, Hautes Études (Paris), an expert in the field, recently commented about the multiple gaps in our knowledge for the seventeenth century alone.[7] Several serious studies are presently underway.[8] Nonetheless, a "definitive" survey of the matter seems as elusive as ever. Much of the available literature on the subject is badly dated, conceptually flawed, and thus susceptible to serious revision.[9] Evangelical scholars need to contribute technically reliable essays in this field.[10]

In this chapter we will describe the central proposal that Professors Rogers and McKim set forth. We will also consider several methodological problems associated with their presentation and documentation. We are also interested in how Rogers and McKim do history. In later chapters we will offer several specific criticisms of their proposal. Our criticisms will be forthright. They are, however, designed to advance the discussion and not to inflame it. Hopefully our comments will alert the scholarly community and lay persons to several weaknesses in the approach of Rogers and McKim to writing the history of biblical authority. They should also underscore some of the strengths of their proposal. Throughout our essay we will provide correctives to Rogers and McKim's interpretation and suggest subjects for further research and investigation.

I. THE ROGERS/McKIM PROPOSAL

For Rogers and McKim, the concept of *accommodation* is pivotal for any understanding of biblical authority. God accommodated Himself to our human weakness and limited capacity to understand His thoughts by communicating to us through human words. The central purpose of God's written communication is to reveal salvation truth about Christ. God did not intend that the Scriptures should be read for technically correct information about the world. Indeed, the Hebrew authors of Scripture (for example) thought in word pictures. They did not reflect upon truth with the same categories of Western logic that are familiar to us.[11] They were not concerned to describe historical and "scientific" items with great accuracy. In consequence, what we moderns consider to be the small "errors" committed by the Bible's human authors do not detract from biblical authority, for the Bible's authority is not associated with its form or words but with Christ and His salvation message to which the words point.

How do we know that the Bible is God's Word? In a mysterious way the Holy Spirit witnesses to the believer that the Bible is the Word of God. Rational deductions based on external evidences for the Bible's inspiration play only a secondary, if not minimal, role in this process, for "faith" comes before "reason" in our apperception of biblical authority.

Rogers and McKim argue that scholars with a platonic bent, ranging from Origen and Augustine in patristic times to Luther and Calvin in Reformation days, maintained this biblical perspective on the Scriptures. However, the late seventeenth century (with the emergence of science) witnessed the departure by many Protestants from this stance. Borrowing from the Aristotelian categories of their Roman Catholic opponents, a good number of Protestant theologians forged a theory of biblical authority founded on the words of Scripture (the mere form) rather than upon Christ in the Scripture. In their rationalistic attempt to fend off Catholic apologists, these Protestants extended the concept of "infallibility" to include all the words of the biblical text. Especially the Swiss theologian Francis Turretin (1632–1687), among Reformed thinkers, innovated in this regard. In the nineteenth century, Princeton Seminary professors Archibald Alexander and Charles Hodge advocated Turretin's viewpoint on Scripture in the United States. In the 1880s, the Princetonians A. A. Hodge and B. B. Warfield propounded the thesis that only the original autographs of the Bible are inerrant. The Princetonians were obliged to retreat to this novel idea of inerrancy in the lost autographs because the impact of biblical (higher) criticism and certain developmental theories in science could no longer be ignored. Relying heavily upon Professor Ernest Sandeen's discussion of the Princetonians, Rogers and McKim refer to the Princetonians' position as one of Protestant scholasticism nourished philosophically by Scottish Common Sense Philosophy. They suggest, as does Sandeen, that the Princeton rationalistic theology shaped fundamentalism's perspectives on Scripture and ultimately those of today's conservative Evangelicals.

For present-day Evangelicals to recover a truly Reformed viewpoint on the Scriptures, Rogers and McKim urge them to return to the teachings about Scriptures proposed by the Westminster Confession, Calvin and Luther, and various church fathers (especially Augustine). Evangelicals should understand that their own beliefs about biblical inerrancy are innovative and do not accord with the church's teaching. The "central teaching" of the church has been to affirm that the Bible is infallible for faith and practice, not to propose that the Scriptures are "inerrant." In fact the words *inerrancy* and *infallibility* do not possess similar meanings. Evangelicals should declare that the Bible's purpose is to teach Christ and the Good News about our salvation and not to present infallible data about aspects of human history, geography, science, and the like. If conservative Evangelicals (and particularly a United Presbyterian readership) adopt Rogers and McKim's position, they will be able to interact more serenely with biblical criticism and modern developmental theories in science, while at the same time safeguarding a high view of biblical authority.

This, in brief, is the thrust of Rogers and McKim's argument. It is a carefully construed apologetic, attractively packaged, and apparently well documented. Much indebted to the thinking of the later Berkouwer, this apologetic is designed to justify a particular stance on Scripture from a historical point of view.

II. GENERAL CONSIDERATIONS

Before we begin our critique of several specific issues related to this apologetic, we may be well served to broach several of the larger methodological problems that affect our assessment of the book.

A. The Overly Generous Title of the Volume

A nagging discrepancy exists between the authors' title, *The Authority and Interpretation of the Bible: An Historical Approach*, and the authors' announced purpose for their book: "The intent of this study is to describe the central church tradition regarding the authority and interpretation of the Bible, especially as it has influenced the Reformed tradition of theology" (Introduction, p. xxiii). The broad title suggests that the book encompasses a calm and careful treatment of attitudes toward the Bible by Christians of diverse communions. The real focus of the volume is more parochial. The authors want to justify their own viewpoint on Scripture as opposed to those perspectives that they associate with the Princeton theologians of the nineteenth century and conservative Evangelicals in the twentieth.[12] They presume that the "historic position" of the church feeds into their own particular beliefs. Readers from Anabaptistic, Lutheran, Wesleyan, Roman Catholic, and Eastern Orthodox backgrounds, therefore, may find the book's title curiously misleading and presumptuous, because its expected coverage of their own histories is deficient, if not nonexistent.

B. The Apologetic Cast of the Study

The apologetic variety of history that Rogers and McKim write will make some professional historians wince. Within recent decades many church historians have attempted to salvage a modicum of objectivity for their discipline by forsaking personal briefs for their own communions. Obviously all historians write with their own biases discreetly, or not so discreetly, displayed. Because Rogers and McKim boldly announce that their goal is apologetic, professional historians, particularly European ones, may surmise that the authors' study is a throwback to past centuries of religious controversy.[13] Theoretically speaking, there is no reason why an apologetic historical piece should necessarily encompass bad historical scholarship.[14] But as we shall see, Rogers and McKim's apologetic goal on occasion overwhelms their commitment to an even-handed treatment of the available historical sources. They have a penchant for not citing primary evidence that counters their hypothesis and for minimizing the value of scholarly works that countermand their conclusions.

C. The Arbitrary Selection of Data

Rogers and McKim fail to explain to their readers how they determine who are the faithful representatives of the "central church tradition" on biblical authority. Complex though this issue may be, it is a critically important one for them if their readers are to take their pretensions with any seriousness.[15] Some historians may judge that the arbitrary character of the authors' selections constitutes a fatal wound for the study. We will note how this important methodological oversight jeopardizes the value of the authors' findings.

D. The Doubtful Documentation

Upon first glance, the footnotes that Rogers and McKim have assembled to support their contentions appear impressive, but a careful appraisal reveals that they are less reliable than we might first suppose. First, the authors rely heavily upon secondary literature rather than interacting with primary sources (a major exception being their treatment of the Westminster Assembly). Thus the quality of their study can rise only as high as its secondary sources. Second, Rogers and McKim frequently do not take great pains in their citation of sources; this is one of the most disturbing features of the volume. Third, the authors on occasion ignore the conclusions of noted specialists who disagree with their line of argument. Often, they do so without justifying their own interpretation. Readers should examine the footnotes and citation of sources with a critical eye.

E. The Limiting Optic of the Authors' Concerns

Due to the fact that Rogers and McKim are so intent to prove that their own definition of biblical infallibility is the "historical position of the Church," the authors frequently give short shrift to the full orbed meaning of their volume's theme, namely, biblical authority. What "biblical authority" meant for the patristic Fathers only becomes evident in the context of what the same Fathers thought about the "rule of faith," tradition, Christian experience, and church authority.[16] Rogers and McKim largely pass by these concerns, which are so important if one is to do justice to Roman Catholic perceptions of *authority*. The full significance of biblical authority for seventeenth-century Calvinists only becomes apparent when their philosophical presuppositions are carefully examined. Rogers and McKim do attempt to sort out some of these philosophical presuppositions, but their own categories of analysis are rigid and lack nuance (reason vs. faith, Aristotelian vs. Platonic, et al.). These juxtapositions do not lend themselves to capturing the complex philosophical currents that swirled through Reformed circles during the seventeenth century. Some Dutch theologians, for example, joined Ramist and Aristotelian principles in their own thought. This is an intellectual linkage that Rogers and McKim's categories of analysis cannot countenance. In fact Rogers and McKim assume incorrectly that Ramist logic was diametrically opposed to Aristotelian categories. Moreover, the authors do not seek to elucidate the relationship between biblical authority, Christian experience, tradition, and reason in Methodist church history. Their optic, then, is quite limited.

F. The Propensity for Facile Labeling

As we have already noted, Rogers and McKim are given to speaking about the "historic position of the church." Another one of their habitual expressions is *scholastic*, a term that both they and Professor Brian Armstrong acknowledge is difficult to define.[17] Nonetheless Aquinas, most continental Calvinist and Lutheran theologians of the seventeenth century, the nineteenth-century Princetonians, and twentieth-century conservative Evangelicals are all dubbed "scholastic." Professional historians know the danger of using this expression and other ones like it (Pietist, Romantic, Enlightenment figure, Renaissance man).[18] Facile labels have all the trappings of false concreteness. Rogers and McKim's consistent use of such labels harks back to an outmoded method of doing intellectual history, when historians grouped individuals from different ages together without sufficient regard for the different cultural contexts in which their subjects lived. Facile labeling is often a short cut for doing careful historical research. A label with little specificity does not greatly aid us in understanding the richness of an individual's theology, its evolution or devolution in time, or its meaning when placed against the social, intellectual, and cultural tapistry of a particular age.

G. The Inappropriate "Historical Disjunctions"

In logic, a disjunction is a proposition in which two (or more) alternatives are asserted, only one of which can be true. In their study Rogers and McKim work with a whole series of what we might coin "historical disjunctions." They assume that certain correct assertions about an individual's thought logically disallow other ones from being true.[19] Their assumption is sometimes accurate, if the thoughts being compared directly contradict each other.[20] However in their historical disjunctions the authors create disjunctions between propositions that are not mutually exclusive. They engage in an empty form of deductive, historical speculation that assumes much without sufficient proof.

A partial listing of the authors' more important "historical disjunctions" would include these: because a thinker believes the central purpose of Scripture is to reveal salvation history, it is assumed that he or she does not endorse complete biblical infallibility; because a thinker speaks of God accommodating Himself to us in the words of Scripture, it is assumed that he or she does not believe in complete biblical infallibility; because a thinker indicates that the Bible is the infallible rule of faith and practice, it is assumed that he or she does not believe in complete biblical infallibility; because a thinker engages in the critical study of biblical texts, it is assumed that he or she does not uphold complete biblical infallibility; because a Christian with Platonist leanings believes that reality consists of forms or ideals, it is assumed that he or she does not think that biblical revelation can be perfect even though God the Holy Spirit is its primary author;[21] because a thinker emphasizes the Christic content of Scripture, it is assumed that he or she does not also believe in complete biblical infallibility; because a thinker stresses the fact that the authority of the Scriptures is confirmed to an individual through the internal witness of the Holy Spirit, it is assumed that he or she does not also believe in complete biblical infallibility. Fostering a kind of history based upon deductions, these historical disjunctions cut the nerve of careful historical research. Only scrupulous and open-minded historical investigation can perhaps reveal if a person adheres to limited or complete biblical infallibility. Unfortunately, historical disjunctions play too determinative a role in Rogers and McKim's analysis. Once the authors have posited a premise, they sometimes fail to demonstrate the historical accuracy of their conclusions based on the premise.

H. The Dated Models of Conceptualization

Rogers and McKim do not give much evidence of an acquaintance with recent developments in what Peter Gay of Yale University has called the social history of ideas.[22] For many decades some intellectual historians assumed that they had captured the beliefs of a movement by explicating what its founder, or its principal spokesmen, or its creeds affirmed. Rogers and McKim do the same. This form of elitist history is based on a misleading extrapolation. An example of it goes something like this: if Luther thought A, Lutherans think A. Today, scholars are much more sensitive to the disparities of belief and practice that commonly exist among clergy and laypersons from the same communion even within fifty miles of each other. European scholars like Emmanual Le Roy Ladurie have written brilliant essays in which they have examined the particularities of a religious community in a narrowly circumscribed geographical locale.[23] The bevy of books on "popular religion" has also revealed remarkable variations of religious belief and practice even in countries with a state religion.[24] Moreover a good number of scholars have a growing appreciation for the difficulties that exist in adequately describing one person's thought. They understand the complexity of tracing their subject's changing opinions in time. To do this, they must study the individual's correspondence, printed works, and unpublished manuscripts (and now videotapes and cassettes). Moreover, they are obliged to take stock of the individual's thought in the categories of his or her era. A smaller group of historians, who are experts in the book trade (Robert Darnton of Princeton University, Henri-Jean Martin of Hautes Études [Paris], Raymond Birn of the University of Oregon) have challenged the old-fashioned "influence histories" from another direction.[25] They want to establish roughly how many books of a given author were published, who bought or borrowed these books, and who read them, before these scholars are prepared to pronounce upon the author's influence through the printed word. Their studies are presently transforming historians' perceptions of the relative popularity of writers in a given age. Their methods can help us track the dissemination of ideas about biblical authority through pamphlets, books, and other printed media.

Unfortunately, Rogers and McKim's awareness of these helpful new tools and models of conceptualization appears limited. As a result, their study is surprisingly dated, even though it was recently published. Writing good history is a far more difficult task than the authors imagine.[26]

I. The Confusing Infallibility vs. Inerrancy Motif

Rogers and McKim argue that the Bible is infallible but that this does not mean that it is "inerrant." Although the human authors of Scripture never deliberately lied or knowingly told an untruth, their product contains "technical errors." These are due to the authors' humanness and limited knowledge. The biblical authors, for example, incorporated into their texts the imperfect knowledge of their contemporaries about the natural world. Christian spokespersons who represent the "central" tradition of the church recognized the presence of "technical errors" in Holy Writ. Rogers and McKim summarize John Calvin's alleged thinking on this point: "For Calvin, technical errors in the Bible that were the result of human slips of memory, limited knowledge, or the use of texts for different purposes than the original were all part of the normal human means of communication" (pp. 110–11). Moreover Calvin did not expect the Bible to afford him with "technically accurate information on language or history" or with "data [with which] to question the findings of science" (p. 111). For Rogers and McKim, it is the Bible's saving function that is infallible, not its words (or form). The authors offer to us an "infallible" but "technically errant" Bible. "Errors" crop up especially in its historical, geographical, and scientific domains. How an infallible "message" (delimited to "faith and practice" issues) is carried by an errant text, Rogers and McKim never fully explain.

In our study it will be important to determine if the Christian spokespersons whom they cite as representative of the "central church tradition" did define infallibility in the way the authors propose, or whether these individuals propounded the view that the Bible does not wander from the truth in anything it affirms or says (biblical inerrancy).

J. The Dubious Presuppositions Concerning the History of Science

Rogers and McKim apparently work with a set of dubious presuppositions regarding the history of "science." The authors evidently assume that the ancients were not of a mindset to describe historical events, geographical details, or the natural world in "precise" terms; they did not have at their disposal categories of measurement that could mesh in a meaningful way with those employed by participants in the "new science" (post-1650?). Living as they did, bereft of these concerns and capabilities, the biblical authors and church fathers by this fact alone could not have been "inerrantists." For the word *inerrancy* is a post-1650 term; it connotes scientific precision. In his doctoral thesis, *Scripture in the Westminster Confession: A Problem of Historical Interpretation for American Presbyterianism* (1967), Professor Rogers goes so far as to argue that the Westminster Divines did not address the question of inerrancy because they lived in a "prescientific" era (p. 306).

Rogers and McKim have posited too radical a paradigmatic break between "modern science" and an unspecified "prescientific" period. Even the most enthusiastic disciples of the noted advocate of "paradigmatic" analysis, Thomas Kuhn (if they follow their mentor's latest revisions), acknowledge that there are some commensurable features shared by "paradigms"; if such do not exist, members of one paradigm could never understand the culture of individuals living in another.[27] In this context Ian Barbour writes about continuity in the history of science:

> ...there is in the history of science more continuity than one would expect from Feyerabend or from Kuhn's earlier work, in which truth is entirely relative to a succession of self-contained language systems dominated by diverse paradigms. I have argued that observations and basic laws are retained through paradigm-shifts, at least as limiting cases under specifiable circumstances; a new theory usually explains why the older theory was as good as it was and why its limitations became evident.[28]

Pierre Duhem's remarkable studies concerning medieval science give indications of its richness and promise for future "scientific" endeavors.[29] As Marshall Clagett observes, one can accept the essential continuity of Western thought without doing injustice to the novelty of scientific activity of the seventeenth century.[30]

Obviously scientists of the twentieth century can measure and portray the external world with more precision than the ancients. Nonetheless the ancients could describe aspects of that same world with what we today would recognize as adequate precision. In his *The Exact Sciences in Antiquity*, O. Neugebauer dispels the misconception that the ancients were so intellectually retrograde that they were obliged to be hopelessly "inexact" in their measurements or mathematical calculations.[31]

It is true that, like us, the biblical writers occasionally use phenomenological and everyday language (the sun rises in the morning) in their descriptions of the external world. Given the purport of this "language-game," we do not need to say that we or they necessarily "err" when employing it.[32] From certain vantage points the sun does appear to rise in the morning over the eastern horizon. Our description accurately relates that phenomenon from our perspective.

Nor does the use of this kind of language by a biblical writer imply that he is unconcerned about minor details, or elsewhere will not describe things in a more equivalent fashion.[33]

This being the case, we should seek to determine what we are reading in the Bible.[34] For example, if we recognize metaphors and figurative speech in a text, we do more justice to the author's intention by seeking what truth the metaphors and figurative language bear, than if we interpreted the passage in a wooden, literalistic manner.

Nor will it do to focus upon the first English reference to the word *inerrant* (1652; p. 235) as a clue to the dating of the concept's origins. Rogers and McKim associate this first usage with the emergence of the "new science" and "precise" measuring. Locating the birth of an idea does not generally result from easy appeals to first uses in dictionaries or theological tomes. Savants who are acquainted with the polemics surrounding the history of the concept of transubstantiation know this only too well.[35] Dictionary definitions can represent verbal and intellectual thought patterns centuries old. In addition, the first entrance of a word into the dictionaries of one language may tell us nothing about the history of words that denote the same concept in another language. Or a word in one language may have been represented earlier by another one in the same language with close conceptual ties. An illustration related to our discussion is particularly pertinent: in middle English (mid-fifteenth century) the primary meaning of the word *infallible* was apparently "incapable of error."[36] The study of the connotations associated with a word demands far more sophisticated etymological procedures than Rogers and McKim have demonstrated.

The history of "science" is complex and multifaceted. Skewed by several dubious presuppositions, Rogers and McKim's treatment of it needs thoughtful revision.

Alerted to these general methodological problems we turn to our next chapters where we will suggest several specific criticisms of the Rogers and McKim proposal. Due to our genuine reluctance to comment about fields of scholarship where our own expertise is limited, our task will be a modest one. We will restrict ourselves to an assessment of several select points in their argument. On certain topics where our knowledge is restricted, we will merely indicate how Rogers and McKim exploited their secondary sources. In other areas where our footing is more sure, we will as well provide our own interpretation. Even with these limitations, the chapters should provide needed correctives to the Rogers and McKim proposal as it relates to biblical infallibility, which is one of their foremost concerns.[37] They should also furnish pointers to the worlds of scholarly literature that Rogers and McKim were obliged to glide by in their whirlwind journey through two thousand years of Christian thinking about the Bible. And finally, it may prompt other scholars to launch carefully delimited and technically competent studies to supplement and revise Rogers and McKim's interpretation. For, as we shall see, even our cursory study reveals that it is built upon shaky pillars.

Chapter II

The Patristic Period and Middle Ages

Beginning church history students learn rapidly that expressions such as the church "taught" or the church "believed" are awkward ones, especially as applied to the first four centuries. Our sources of information are painfully sparse for various Christian communities throughout the Roman world. We know little about the lives of certain of the men and women who followed Christ in many towns and villages scattered around the Mediterranean basin.[1] Moreover Christians disputed with each other. Various schools of thought existed among sincere believers concerning wide-ranging theological issues.[2]

And yet common traits of agreement did apparently exist among many Christians regarding biblical authority.[3] Based on a survey of the extant patristic literature that bears on the subject, we know that the Fathers apparently concurred that God is the primary author of Holy Scripture.[4] They did, however, debate the way God used human authors as His instruments in the writing of the inscripturated Word.[5] Professor Geoffrey Bromiley observes:

> Emphasis on the divine authorship of Holy Scripture could lead sometimes to a certain depreciation of the role of the human writers. Athenagoras is perhaps the best known representative of this tendency with his reference to the ecstatic nature of prophesying and his comparison of the Holy Spirit to a flutist. . . . Nevertheless, the early church hesitated to commit itself to a theory of divine inspiration by ecstasy or dictation.[6]

Moreover it is fair to say that the Fathers generally assumed that because God is the author of truth, His Word cannot mislead or deceive in any way (whether in salvation truth, or in historical, "scientific," or geographical detail).

Professor Bruce Vawter, whose authority Rogers and McKim repeatedly invoke, frankly acknowledges the Fathers' commitment to biblical infallibility extended beyond salvation truths to matters of "natural science" and history:

> It would be pointless to call into question that biblical inerrancy in a rather absolute form was a common persuasion from the beginning of Christian times, and from Jewish times before that. For both the Fathers and the rabbis generally, the ascription of any error to the Bible was unthinkable;... if the word was God's it must be true, regardless of whether it made known a mystery of divine revelation or commented on a datum of natural science, whether it derived from human observation or chronicled an event of history.[7]

Vawter's analysis appears well founded. Clement of Rome's *First Letter to the Church at Corinth* (first century) lends some support to it:

> You have studied Scripture [O.T.] which contains the truth and is inspired by the Holy Spirit. You realize that there is nothing wrong or misleading in it.[8]

In his *Dialogue with Trypho* (second century), Justin Martyr, an apologist with Platonic leanings, is more specific:

> ...but if (you have done so) because you imagined that you could throw doubt on the passage, in order that I might say the Scriptures contradicted each other, you have erred. But I shall not venture to suppose or to say such a thing; and if a Scripture which appears to be of such a kind be brought forward, and if there be a pretext (for saying) that it is contrary (to some other), since I am entirely convinced that no Scripture contradicts another, I shall admit rather that I do not understand what is recorded, and shall strive to persuade those who imagine that the Scriptures are contradictory, to be rather of the same opinion as myself.[9]

The great Irenaeus (second century) commented about the truthfulness of Luke's reporting:

> Now if any man set Luke aside, as one who did not know the truth, he will (by so acting), manifestly reject that Gospel of which he claims to be a disciple.... It follows then, as of course, that these men must either receive the rest of his narrative, or else reject these parts also. For no person of common sense can permit them to receive some things recounted by Luke as being true, and to set others aside, as if he had not known the truth.[10]

In addressing the non-Christian Autolycus, Theophilus of Antioch (second century) spoke directly about the accurate quality of the prophets' writings:

> Moreover, it is said that among your writers there were prophets and prognosticators, and that those wrote accurately who were informed by them. How much more, then, shall *we* know the truth who are instructed

by the holy prophets, who were possessed by the Holy Spirit of God! On this account all the prophets spoke harmoniously and in agreement with one another, and foretold the things that would come to pass in all the world. For the very accomplishment of predicted and already consummated events should demonstrate to those who are fond of information, yea rather, who are lovers of truth, that those things are really true which they declared concerning the epochs and eras before the deluge: to wit, how the years have run on since the world was created until now, so as to manifest the ridiculous mendacity of your authors, and show that their statements are not true.[11]

These statements and others like them should be carefully weighed in their contexts. When this is accomplished, their meaning is quite clear.

Nevertheless, Rogers and McKim propound the thesis that the church fathers did not hold to complete biblical infallibility. How do they attempt to establish this perspective in the face of much evidence to the contrary, and against the verdict of notable scholars such as Vawter, J. N. D. Kelley, and others?[12] On the one hand, authors Rogers and McKim simply do not allude to Clement of Rome, Justin Martyr, Irenaeus, Theophilus of Antioch, or other church fathers who make statements that counter their hypothesis. On the other hand, they suggest that the writings of Clement of Alexandria, Origen, Chrysostom, and Augustine support their contentions. Professor David Wells points out that the first three authors were Greek and the "fourth dallied with Greek philosophy."[13] Thus Rogers and McKim largely ignore the Roman, legal, and western tradition among the Fathers. Their selection, therefore, is constricted and not felicitous.

Be that as it may, let us review briefly segments of the argumentation Rogers and McKim propose for their interpretation of Origen, Chrysostom, and Augustine. Rogers and McKim base much of their case on the principle that God accommodated Himself to our weakness and frailty by communicating to us through the human words of Scripture. They cite an important passage of Origen (p. 12):

He condescends and lowers himself, accommodating himself to our weakness, like a schoolmaster talking a "little language" to his children, like a father caring for his own children and adopting their ways.

Because Origen knew that the words of Scripture were the result of God's accommodating activity, Origen "acknowledged that the New Testament evangelists and Paul expressed their own opinions, and that they could have erred when speaking on their own authority" (p. 11).

The content of Rogers and McKim's judgment about Origen's recognition of errancy is based principally on page 26 of Bruce Vawter's *Biblical Inspiration*.[14] It is intriguing to note, however, that the authors do not cite Vawter's continuing discussion on page 27. After indicating that on occasion Origen wrote as if he did not believe in inerrancy when making a pragmatic response to an exegetical or apologetic difficulty, Vawter declares:

> It seems to be clear enough that, in company with most of the other Christian commentators of the age, he most often acted on the unexpressed assumption that the Scripture is a divine composition through and through, and for this reason infallibly true in all its parts. He could say, in fact, that the Biblical texts were not the works of men but of the Holy Spirit (*De princ.* 4.9, PG 11:360), and that from this it followed that they were filled with the wisdom and truth of God down to the very least letter. He could therefore entertain a notion of verbal inspiration. . . .

Rogers and McKim's selective use of Vawter's scholarship is quite disappointing.

In reality, as Vawter proposes, a good case can be made for Origen the inerrantist. Origen's recognition of the principle of accommodation has no ultimate bearing on the subject. The principle of accommodation carries with it no logical concomitant to an errant biblical text.[15] God does not necessarily mislead us in any detail of the Scriptures because He speaks to us through human words.[16] A father, particularly an omnipotent and omniscient One, can speak truly though simply.

R. P. C. Hanson, a respected Origen scholar whom Rogers and McKim cite frequently, argues that the Alexandrian believed in biblical inerrancy and employed the principle of accommodation for the purpose of guarding that doctrine:

> Origen then recognizes that in spite of the inerrancy and inspiration of the Scriptures they do display a gradation of revelation, and that they contain a number of features which demand skilful and sometimes embarrassingly complicated explanations. To account for these phenomena, which sometimes look painfully like imperfections in the book, Origen produces a principle which exhibits at once the remarkable flexibility and the strength of his thought, the principle of accommodation.[17]

We recall that Rogers and McKim affirm that Origen on the contrary relied on the principle to help explain why the Bible *does* contain errors. As we shall see, they consistently break ranks with their own secondary authorities and misread their representatives of the "central church tradition" regarding the meaning and significance of accommodation.[18]

It is correct to observe that Origen, a sensitive moralist, shaped malleable allegorical interpretations of the Scriptures to help him smooth out the rough edges of what he thought were rather unsavory historical incidents in Holy Writ or passages whose inerrant meaning lay in a "spiritual" rather than in a literal exegesis. Hanson observes:

> But the most usual resort which Origen uses in order to reconcile incon-
> sistencies in the Bible is to abandon the literal meaning of portions of the
> passages which cause the difficulty and to represent them as composed
> partly of literal and partly of purely allegorical meanings.[19]

Origen believed that the use of allegory was prescribed by Scripture.[20]

But Origen was also capable of doing fastidious harmonization work regarding "historical" texts. While falling back on allegorical interpretations in *Contra Celsum*, the Alexandrian more generally argued point by point with Celsus who had evidently scorned the historical reliability of many biblical accounts.[21]

Whether or not Origen was an inerrantist (however inconsistent in practice), is not our concern at this juncture.[22] Open-minded scholars have differed about the matter. What concerns us more is the disconcerting discovery that Rogers and McKim do not interact even-handedly with their documentation in sorting out Origen's attitudes on the question.

The authors' treatment of Chrysostom is just as perplexing. A splendid preacher and practical theologian, Chrysostom (347?–407) fashioned marvelous homilies and sermons.[23] His eloquence, spiritual counsel, and disciplined lifestyle gained for him a sterling reputation that traversed the centuries. The story goes that the learned Aquinas was once approaching the fair city of Paris. A student companion, perhaps somewhat sycophantic, remarked to the great man that he would like to give the city to him. Aquinas whose mind was ever busy with writing projects replied: "At the moment I would really much rather have Chrysostom's homilies on St. Matthew."[24]

Rogers and McKim do not pronounce directly upon Chrysostom's stance concerning biblical infallibility. But they relate his thinking about the principle of accommodation in some detail. They write: "Although he attributed the content or message to God, Chrysostom understood the form of the writing to be human, in accordance with his doctrine of accommodation" (p. 20). True to their pattern, they leave the distinct impression that Chrysostom would have allowed for "technical errors" in Scripture due to its human element.

In fact, Chrysostom apparently believed in biblical infallibility extended to every detail. He does not set forth a comprehensive discussion of the subject, but scholars who have surveyed the corpus of his work usually affirm that this is the case. In their analysis of Chrysostom's attitude toward accommodation, Rogers and McKim (p. 59, n. 75) refer to his fifteenth homily on Genesis as quoted in one of their important sources, Luis Alonso-Schökel's *The Inspired Word* (New York: Herder and Herder, 1966), p. 137. In introducing this homily, Schökel remarks that the accommodated character of biblical language did not produce an errant text:

Or to look at it the other way, the very fact that God has chosen all of language as His medium of communication proves that He desires to make a personal revelation; "...the words of God expressed in human language, are made like to human speech in every respect, except error."

The authors also recommend that their readers consult another of their principal sources, Chrysostomus Baur's, *John Chrysostom and His Time...* (Westminster, Maryland: The Newman Press, 1959), I, pp. 318–19, for more information concerning Chrysostom and the humanness of Scripture. Interestingly enough, Baur declares in these pages that Chrysostom believed in biblical infallibility that extended to history, science, and the like:

The inspiration of God extends into the collected thought content of the Holy Scripture, not merely in dogmatic and moral theology, but also in matters of scientific and historical learning, dates, lists of names, forms of salutations, inscriptions, and similar things. He also says repeatedly that in the Holy Scripture there is nothing without purpose, not a syllable, not an iota, not the smallest dash.... Chrysostom understood very well that, because of Divine inspiration, it is impossible for the Holy Scriptures to contain errors. Therefore, in his eyes, Scripture proofs are stronger and surer than proofs founded on reason. One must also admit that he has honestly endeavored to find a reasonable means of agreement for contradictions appearing in the Bible, especially in the Evangelists; he traces them back to mere variations, which he neither contradicts nor corrects.

Thus, two of Rogers and McKim's most prominent authorities counter their inferences concerning Chrysostom and biblical infallibility.

Chrysostom's own words allow us better to understand his sentiments:

It was not without reason these points came in for mention, not in vain I spoke to you about them. My reason, in fact, was that some men are like robots: when they take hold of the divine books, and find in their pages a heap of dates or litany of names, they pass them by without a thought, meeting any objection with the remark: They are only names, nothing useful in them. Do not utter such infamy. God speaks, and you have the effrontery to say, Nothing useful in what is said. I mean, if you merely have the chance of laying your eyes on an inscription come to light—tell me, do you not eagerly pore over it and examine the wealth it contains? But why talk of dates and names and inscriptions? Note the force of the addition of one single syllable, and stop despising whole names. Our patriarch Abraham (he belongs to us, you know, rather than to the Jews) was originally called Abram which has the meaning "migrant." But later his name was changed to Abraham and with this he became father of all nations; and it was the addition of one syllable that entrusted this upright man with such a glorious destiny. In other words, just as kings hand out to their officials golden ledgers as a sign of their authority, so God on that occasion gave that just man for sign of his importance a syllable.[25]

He summarized his efforts at harmonizing the accounts of the Evangelists with these words:

> The harmony between them we will establish, both by the whole world, which hath received their statements, and by the very enemies of the Truth.[26]

Chrysostom emphasizes Christ as the pilot to help us in our understanding of Scripture. At the same time he avers that the Bible is completely reliable in every detail.[27]

The manner in which Rogers and McKim treat St. Augustine is also instructive concerning how they do history. Upon a prima facie reading of several of St. Augustine's comments, we would conclude that the influential Latin believed in complete biblical infallibility:

> For it seems to me that the most disastrous consequences must follow upon our believing that anything false is found in the sacred books.... For if you once admit into such a high sanctuary of authority one false statement, as made in the way of duty, there will not be left a single sentence of these books which, if appearing to any one difficult in practice or hard to believe, may not by the same fatal rule be explained away, as a statement in which, intentionally, and under a sense of duty, the author declared what was not true.[28]

Again he declared:

> The authority of the Divine Scriptures becomes unsettled ... if this be once admitted, that the men by whom these things have been delivered unto us, could in their writings state some things which were not true from considerations of duty; unless, perchance, you [St. Jerome] purpose to furnish us with certain rules by which we may know when a falsehood might or might not become a duty.[29]

Augustine also noted:

> I have learned to yield this respect and honor only to the canonical books of Scripture: of these alone do I most firmly believe that the authors were completely free from error.[30]

Or elsewhere, Augustine wrote:

> Therefore everything written in Scripture must be believed absolutely.[31]

With this type of statement in mind, Professor A. D. R. Polman, whose book, *Word of God According to St. Augustine*, Rogers and McKim repeatedly cite, observes that for St. Augustine, "not even the universal council of the Church is infallible, for infallibility is the exclusive prerogative of Holy Writ."[32] And he states: "He [St. Augustine] thought it inconceivable that the Holy Spirit, the real author of Holy Scripture, should have contradicted Himself."[33] Even Oswald Loretz who shares with Rogers and McKim similar perspectives about the nature of biblical truth admits that St. Augustine and many other church fathers advocated "biblical inerrancy."[34]

In attempting to neutralize the import of St. Augustine's statements, which apparently teach that the Bishop of Hippo held to complete biblical infallibility, Rogers and McKim proffer this explanation (p. 31):

> Error, for Augustine, had to do with the deliberate and deceitful telling of that which the author knew to be untrue. It was in that context of ethical seriousness that he declared that the biblical "authors were completely free from error." He did not apply the concept of error to problems that arose from the human limitations of knowledge, various perspectives in reporting events, or historical or cultural conditioning of the authors.

Thus the biblical authors may have made inadvertent errors due to their limited understanding and humanness.[35] Nor did they teach authoritatively concerning science, so subject were they to the social conditioning of their times and the imperfect viewpoints of the natural world that their contemporaries entertained.

St. Augustine did not perceive the writers in this fashion. When they wrote under the inspiration of the Holy Spirit, they could describe the external world as it was. For example, Augustine indicates that the biblical writers knew truths about astronomy that they did not reveal in Holy Writ. In his *De Genesi ad Litteram*, he commented concerning their knowledge of the heavens:

> For myself it matters little, whether the sky as spherical in form completely encloses the earth, suspended as it is in the midst of the universe, or whether it only partially covers it as a vault from above. But inasmuch as this question bears on the truth of Scripture, I will discuss it. For lest anyone, not rightly understanding the words of Scripture, (since in matters of this kind one may either have found or heard that there is in our Scriptures something which seems to be opposed to the conclusions of reason), should entirely refuse to believe them when they set forth useful instruction, narrations or declarations on other matters, I feel in duty bound to say that our authors knew the truth of the matter concerning the form of the heavens, but the Spirit of God, who spoke by them, did not intend to teach men these things in no way profitable for salvation.[36]

For Augustine, the biblical writers did not write a scientific textbook, but the phenomenological language they sometimes employed, if properly interpreted, was truthful. And when they made incidental comments about the world, they wrote infallibly and were not bound by "human limitations of knowledge" in the sense of being "paradigm dependent" upon the values and beliefs of their own cultures.[37]

St. Augustine was not prepared to say that the Bible has *no* bearing on science as Rogers and McKim infer. He declared:

Whatever, they [the men of physical science] can readily demonstrate to be true of physical nature, we must show to be capable of reconciliation with our Scriptures; and whatever they assert in their treatises to be contrary to these Scriptures of ours, that is, to Catholic faith, we must either prove it as well as we can to be entirely false, or at all events, we must without the smallest hesitation believe it to be so.[38]

Rogers and McKim have badly misinterpreted St. Augustine on this important point. Their repeated claim that the Augustinian tradition precludes the Bible from speaking to science is not justified.

In attempting to demonstrate that St. Augustine did not believe the Bible was infallible in matters of science when properly interpreted, the authors cite a passage in which they believe St. Augustine warned Christians "not to take their 'science'" from the Bible (pp. 26–27):

Many non-Christians happen to be well-versed in knowledge of the earth, the heaven, of all the other elements of the world.... It is therefore deplorable that Christians, even though they *ostensibly* [italics mine] base their dicta on the Bible, should utter so much nonsense that they expose themselves to ridicule. While ridicule is all they deserve, they also give the impression that the Biblical authors are responsible for their mutterings, thus discrediting Christianity before the world, which is led to assume that the authors of the Scriptures were ignorant fools also. Whenever any Christian is confounded and shown to be an idle chatterer, his chatter is attributed to our Holy Books....

By referring to this statement, Rogers and McKim imply that St. Augustine believed the Bible to be unreliable in scientific matters. But that is not the gist of St. Augustine's remark. He was warning poorly trained Christians who *ostensibly* base their discussions on the Bible to cease from their speculations. They were engaged in a form of chattering not biblically derived. Rogers and McKim, who borrow this quotation from Polman, fail to take note of Polman's introductory commentary on the citation:

St. Augustine remembered vividly how many telling blows he himself had delivered during his Manichean days, against those Christians who lacking thorough instruction yet tried to defend their faith with all their might. Hence he warned the pious not to try to cover up their ignorance of fact by discussing scientific questions with an easy appeal to Scriptures.[39]

As Polman indicated, St. Augustine was arguing that the interpretations of poorly instructed Christians might be in error. He was not indicating that the Bible itself erred in its incidental teachings about the natural world, nor that the Bible's statements had no bearing on that world. Polman puts the matter this way: "Whenever, therefore, the nature of things is discovered by reliable investigation, these discoveries will always be capable of being reconciled with the Scripture."[40]

In addition, Rogers and McKim insist that St. Augustine's commitment to the principle of accommodation permitted him to think that variant readings in the text were of no ultimate concern (pp. 29–30):

> Augustine could take account of all the human techniques used by the writers of Scripture while affirming the divine truth of what they said. Variant readings concerning the same event were not an ultimate problem for Augustine because he saw them as the work of the Holy Spirit who permitted this pluriformity of perspectives in order to whet people's spiritual appetites for understanding.

Rogers and McKim document this last statement by alluding once again to Bruce Vawter's *Biblical Authority*, pp. 38–39.[41] Vawter indicates that St. Augustine believed that on rare occasions the Holy Spirit "permitted" a biblical writer to pen what was "in apparent variance with other Scripture." But St. Augustine was embarrassed by what appeared to be a transgression of his formal principle of "no discordance in the sacred word" (p. 38). Contrary to the impression Rogers and McKim give of his thought, Vawter writes:

> For Augustine and the Fathers in general all the "difficulties" of Scripture—and these included, besides the *cruces* of exegesis that have remained difficulties for their successors, the numerous instances where they felt the need to harmonize variant passages, to bring the Bible into accord with natural science, profane history, etc. . . .—were first of all divinely intended, meant to stimulate the spiritual appetite. . . .[42]

From Vawter's perspective, Augustine and most of the Fathers were quite intent to harmonize the biblical data with history, natural science, and the like.

Whereas Vawter's analysis is astute, Rogers and McKim's is misleading (p. 28):

> Scripture was a divine unity for Augustine. He did not allow that discordancy of any kind could exist. Yet the unity of Scripture was in the consistency of its message, not in a formal harmony of all its verbal forms, in which God's message was expressed.

Harnessing this kind of form/function dichotomy (verbal statements vs. salvation truths) to Augustine is inappropriate. In *The Harmony of the Gospels* (I, 7, 10) St. Augustine sets forth his design to confute those unbelievers who deny the harmony of the four Gospels in their attempts to discredit the Christian faith:

> And in order to carry out this design to a successful conclusion, we must prove that the writers in question do not stand in any antagonism to each

other. For those adversaries are in the habit of adducing this as the palmary allegation in all their vain objections, namely that the evangelists are not in harmony with each other.

Then in what becomes almost painful harmonization work St. Augustine adduces explanation after explanation to prove that no "contradictory accounts" (I, 35, 54) exist in the Evangelists' verbal statements when properly interpreted. In treating the problems surrounding Matthew's reference to Jeremiah rather than Zechariah in Matthew 27:9, he proposes several intricate solutions: he suggests that some interpreters may prefer to see the problem as emerging from a copyist mistake (III, 7, 29), though he himself did not like this solution to this particular textual question; or, he notes that since the prophets spoke with one voice, for Matthew to cite Jeremiah would be the same as for him to cite Zechariah (and thus the "discrepancy" disappears, III, 7, 30).

> The same consideration might also fitly suggest the duty of accepting unhesitatingly whatever the Holy Spirit has given expression to through the agency of these prophets, and of looking upon their individual communications as also those of the whole body, and on their collective communications as also those of each separately.

Or, he propounds the possibility that the Evangelist had some kind of mystical meaning in mind that clarified his reference to Jeremiah (III, 7, 31). Even if we are not happy with St. Augustine's projected solutions to the textual problem, we can gain an appreciation from them for his concern that not one word should create a real contradiction in Holy Writ. St. Augustine's desire to harmonize the Gospel accounts was closely associated with his belief that the Bible was God's Word; it should not be impugned with error of any kind (even concerning the word *Jeremiah*).

We have seen, however, that Rogers and McKim leave the distinct impression that the Bishop of Hippo thought that there were genuine disagreements in the "form" (human verbal constructions) in Scripture, but that the saving "message" was true. They attempt to sustain their interpretation with this commentary and a citation from St. Augustine (pp. 28–29):

> Augustine never wavered in his belief that the message conveyed in the Bible was true. But he was quite aware of disagreements in form between the accounts offered by different biblical writers. When discussing the order in which a narrative about Peter's mother-in-law was introduced, Augustine wrote: "It is quite probable that each evangelist believed it to have been his duty to recount what he had to in that order in which it pleased God to suggest it to his memory—in those things at least in which the order, whether it be this or that, detracts in nothing from the truth and authority of the Gospel. But why the Holy Spirit, who apportions individ-

ually to each one as he wills (I Cor. 12:11), and who therefore undoubtedly also governed and ruled the minds of the holy writers in recalling what they were to write because of the preeminent authority which the books were to enjoy, permitted one to compile his narrative in this way, and another in that, anyone with pious diligence may seek the reason and with divine aid will be able to find it." For Augustine, God "permitted" variant forms in order to accomplish his single saving purpose.[43]

Once again our authors have misinterpreted their sources. In the citation in question St. Augustine was merely stating that if we cannot identify the time frame of a particular reference made by an Evangelist, then it matters little in what order the reference occurs in the text. Without a knowledge of its temporal locus, we cannot indicate that it creates a contradiction. Rogers and McKim fail to quote St. Augustine's continuing statement in which he notes that if the time sequences of events described by the Evangelists are known, then the interpreter should attempt to reconcile any potential "time sequence" problems:

> For this reason, therefore, when the order of times is not apparent, we ought not to feel it a matter of any consequence what order any of them may have adopted in relating the events. But whenever the order is apparent, if the evangelist then presents anything which seems to be inconsistent with his own statements, or with those of another, we must certainly take the passage into consideration, and endeavour to clear up the difficulty.

As we shall see, our authors frequently present citations without the context that permits us to understand them. In this particular instance our authors' attempt to establish a form/function dichotomy in Augustine's thought is less than successful.

It is noteworthy that St. Augustine, rather than speaking about the words of Scripture as "imperfect forms," describes them as "pure" in his famous *Confessions* (Book VII). Before his conversion, he had wondered about the coherence of the Scriptures:

> With great eagerness, then, I fastened upon the venerable writings of thy Spirit and principally upon the apostle Paul. I had thought that he sometimes contradicted himself and that the text of his teachings did not agree with the testimonies of the Law and the Prophets; but now all these doubts vanished away. And I saw that those pure words had but one face, and I learned to rejoice with trembling.

Augustine does not appear to have had that tolerance for the "imperfect form" of words that Rogers and McKim suggest. Supposed verbal contradictions had constituted a hindrance for him as he had contemplated the faith.[44] Speaking about how he came to the conviction that Jesus Christ was the "Word made flesh," Augustine declared (*Confessions*, Book VIII):

And if these things were falsely written about him, all the rest would risk the imputation of falsehood, and there would remain in those books no saving faith for the human race.

Therefore, because they were written truthfully, I acknowledged a perfect man to be in Christ—not the body of a man only, nor, in the body, an animal soul without a rational one as well, but a true man.

For Augustine, if the Scriptures' records were not true, then no hope of salvation for humankind remained.

St. Augustine insisted that Jesus Christ was the "Truth."[45] But he also believed that the words of Scripture that point to Christ, when properly interpreted, relate the truth. In a very real sense these words belonged to God the Father, God the Son, and God the Holy Spirit. No individual word of Scripture belonged solely to its human author.[46]

Nor should any word or group of words be permitted to constitute a genuine contradiction in the Bible ("the venerable writings of thy Spirit"). Like John Calvin after him, St. Augustine expended great energies demonstrating the harmony of the texts. Trained as a rhetorician, he believed that the Bible often exemplified high standards of rhetoric and that it could relate truth by using many different words to recount the same event.[47] He was fearful that unbelievers would exploit alleged contradictions and stylistic infelicities in their efforts to cast aspersions on the veracity of the Christian faith itself.[48]

But we recall that Rogers and McKim see things differently. They limit Augustine's conception of error to "the deliberate and deceitful telling of that which the author knew to be untrue" (p. 31). Rogers and McKim base their interpretation upon St. Augustine's "shocked dismay that Jerome in his *Commentary on Galatians* represented Paul as having deliberately lied about his confrontation with Peter for the sake of expediency" (p. 30).[49] In his correspondence with Jerome (in which he indicated that the Bible has "no errors"), did not St. Augustine propose that if Paul lied for a good purpose, then the truthfulness of the Bible itself would be put in jeopardy?[50] Does this not prove that when he declared that the Bible had "no errors" within it, he only meant that the biblical writers do not tell any purposeful lies? The core of Rogers and McKim's argumentation for the "Augustinian conception of error" is bared by these two questions.

We respond that in his correspondence with St. Jerome, the Bishop of Hippo did not limit the Bible's concept of error to the question of the deliberate and deceitful telling of that which an author knew to be untrue. In letter 82 (A.D. 405), which continues the discussion with St. Jerome about the propriety of St. Paul's remarks, St. Augustine affirms his commitment to the complete infallibility of the Bible and does so without placing Rogers and McKim's delimitation upon the concept of error (82, 3):

For I confess to your Charity that I have learned to yield this respect and honour only to the canonical books of Scripture: of these alone do I most firmly believe that the authors were completely free from error. And if in these writings I am perplexed by anything which appears to me opposed to truth, I do not hesitate to suppose that either the MS. is faulty, or the translator has not caught the meaning of what was said, or I myself have failed to understand it. As to all other writings, in reading them, however great the superiority of the authors to myself in sanctity and learning, I do not accept their teaching as true on the mere ground of the opinion being held by them; but only because they have succeeded in convincing my judgment of its truth either by means of these canonical writings themselves, or by arguments addressed to my reason. I believe, my brother, that this is your own opinion as well as mine. I do not need to say that I do not suppose you to wish your books to be read like those of prophets or of apostles, concerning which it would be wrong to doubt that they are free from error. Far be such arrogance from that humble piety and just estimate of yourself which I know you to have. . . .

It should be noted that in this passage Augustine suggests to Jerome that the latter would not like his own works to be considered "free from error"; they were not like the "errorless" Scriptures. If Augustine had limited the concept of error to the deliberate and deceitful telling of what an author knew to be untrue, then his comment encompassed a wicked slap at the sensitive Jerome's moral character. Augustine would have been saying that Jerome's works, since they contain "errors," were marked by purposeful deceits and lies that the famous translator knew to be untrue. In point of fact, St. Augustine was attempting to reestablish better personal relations with the older scholar in his letter. He continues his remarks by saying (82, 4):

Now if, knowing as I do your life and conversation, I do not believe in regard to you that you have spoken anything with an intention of dissimulation and deceit, how much more reasonable is it for me to believe, in regard to the Apostle Paul, that he did not think one thing and affirm another when he wrote of Peter and Barnabas. . . .

Although St. Augustine had suggested to St. Jerome that his works contain genuine "errors," he does not claim that Jerome himself was deceitful. It is apparent, then, that Augustine does not limit errors to "willful deceits" when he propounds the thesis that the Bible is "free from error."[51] For him, infallibility meant freedom from error; the Bible always relates the truth when properly interpreted.

Rogers and McKim's definition of Augustine's concept of error is not well founded. It is based on a misreading of the Augustine/Jerome correspondence. It does not accord at all with the biblical scholar's attempts to resolve "contradictions" in the biblical texts whose origins Augustine does not suspect to stem from purposeful deceit by the biblical authors.[52] Nor does it mesh with his repeated claims about the Bible's freedom from error in passages other than the Augustine/Jerome correspondence.

As a Christian, St. Augustine urged that the Scriptures should be approached with reverence and awe. A person understands them more fully if he or she is spiritually regenerated and seeks the Holy Spirit's illumination in studying them. Because the Bible teaches faith, hope, and love, the goal of exegesis is to teach faith, hope, and love.[53] In his important work on hermeneutics, *On Christian Doctrine* (III, X), he declares that the "Scripture teaches nothing but charity...." Then he clarifies this statement: "It is a history of past things, an announcement of future things, and an explanation of present things; but all these things are of value in nourishing and supporting charity and in conquering and extirpating cupidity." Augustine was convinced that the proper study of the Word would stimulate *charitas* in the Christian community. Moreover, he was generous to those who interpreted passages of the Bible differently than he did.[54] After all, were there not difficult portions of Scripture to exegete, deep and significant meanings of the text to ferret out, and various rules to apply in crafting proper understandings of figurative language in the text?[55] Might not Christians arrive at different but helpful interpretations of the text on occasion?[56]

Although St. Augustine wanted to preserve peace and foster love within the church, he was nonetheless prepared to challenge politely the venerable St. Jerome whom he feared might be making allowance for genuine errors within the text. But he also rejoiced when St. Jerome apparently reversed his interpretation of St. Paul's discussion of Peter. Couched in gracious prose, St. Augustine's repeated solicitations may have influenced the learned Jerome's decision.[57]

St. Augustine's commitment to harmonization efforts and to the complete infallibility of the Bible influenced many Christian theologians during the Middle Ages. Hans Küng, himself no friendly partisan of biblical inerrancy, describes St. Augustine's impact in these terms:

> ... it was above all St. Augustine who, under the influence of Hellenist theories of inspiration, regarded man as merely the instrument of the Holy Spirit; the Spirit alone decided the content and form of the biblical writings, with the result that the whole Bible was free of contradictions, mistakes and errors, or had to be kept free by harmonizing, allegorizing, or mysticizing. St. Augustine's influence in regard to inspiration and inerrancy prevailed throughout the Middle Ages and right into the modern age.[58]

Küng founds this judgment on the research and conclusions of Herman Sasse.[59] Although Küng, Oswald Loretz, and several post-Vatican II scholars dislike St. Augustine's commitment to complete biblical infallibility and sometimes attribute it to his alleged adoption of a "mantic" theory of inspiration, they do acknowledge that he held that stance.[60] Their evaluation on this point accords with the perception of St. Augustine by scholars ranging from Richard Simon (1638–1712), one of the first modern biblical critics, to A. D. R. Polman, Charles J. Costello, and other twentieth-century analysts.[61]

Our brief review of Rogers and McKim's treatment of the thought of several select Fathers reveals that, despite several helpful insights, their interpretation is marred by serious flaws. Their application of a form/function conceptual framework (apparently imported from contemporary social sciences), their proposal that the Fathers excluded science from the purview of the Bible's teachings, and their presentation of St. Augustine's definition of "error" are inappropriate and misleading. And unfortunately, our authors pyramid their misunderstanding of St. Augustine and other Fathers into the Middle Ages, the Reformation, and beyond. For example, in discussing St. Thomas Aquinas, they write (p. 46):

> In Thomas's teaching, the concept of error shifted somewhat. The early church theologians like Augustine had understood error in the biblical sense of willful intent to deceive, and they were quick to affirm that the Bible never erred in that sense. But Augustine did not apply the concept of error to limited scientific knowledge on the part of the biblical writers. Thomas moved in a different direction when he introduced the quote from Augustine: "Only those books or writings which are called canonical have I learnt to pay such honour that I firmly believe that none of their authors have erred in composing them."

Or, in analyzing John Calvin's thought, they aver (p. 111):

> Calvin's attitude toward error was equivalent to Augustine's approach, as discussed earlier. Both theologians rejected the notion that the biblical writers had ever intentionally told untruths in communicating the saving message entrusted to them. That was a completely different matter, for both Augustine and Calvin, than the fact that the biblical writers were limited and conditioned by their historical context and that they made *technical mistakes* [our emphasis] in writing as all normal human beings do. Augustine and Calvin were both rhetoricians who concentrated on the saving function of Scripture as the locus of its authority.

Because their standard for discerning the "Augustinian tradition" regarding these issues is misshapen, they unwittingly venture into unfortunate interpretative culs-de-sac. They press down their restricted conception of what an error might be on historical personages who in fact espoused a wider Augustinian definition of error. This procedure throws the validity of their volume's basic proposal into serious doubt.

We shall leave to others to assess our authors' interpretation of biblical authority in the Middle Ages.[62] We do not have sufficient knowledge of this vast subject matter to make pertinent remarks.[63] Moreover Professor Rogers, in the face of criticism from the Roman Catholic scholar Avery Dulles, has already indicated that the authors' interpretation of Aquinas's view of the faith/reason relationship should be reconsidered.[64] We surmise that other misinterpretations may exist in their analysis of medieval and Renaissance figures. They misread their secondary sources when they comment on the thought of pre-Reformer John Wycliffe (pp. 73–75). They write (p. 74):

> Wycliffe declared: "The Bible is therefore the only source of doctrine that will insure the health of the Church and the salvation of the faithful." With this understanding that the purpose of Scripture was salvation and guidance for the life of faith, Wycliffe could say "any part of Holy Scripture is true according to the excellence of the Divine Word."

This judgment is based essentially on pages 50–51 of William Mallard's article, "John Wyclif and the Tradition of Biblical Authority," *Church History* 30 (March 1961): 50–60. In reality, the first quotation they attribute to Wycliffe was made by the author Mallard (p. 51). Moreover, just below it, Mallard wrote:

> He [Wycliffe] is thoroughly scornful of theologians who slight Holy Scripture. If any such persons find contradictions or errors in the Bible, their own ignorance is at fault rather than the sacred text.

Then, on the next page of his essay (p. 52), Mallard outlined what the scope of biblical authority included for Wycliffe:

> According to the most learned doctors of the tradition, Holy Scripture contained not only all Christian doctrine, but all truth generally. It was a "divine encyclopedia," a *summa* of the wisdom of God. The Bible included mathematics, philosophy, and natural history. Although the core of Scripture could be grasped by the simplest peasant, the most learned scholar could use all his knowledge in penetrating the hidden truths. Wycliffe supported the idea of the "divine encyclopedia."

Wycliffe's use of allegory in interpretation was based on his presupposition that the words of Scripture were utterly reliable.[65] Rogers and McKim's suggestion that Wycliffe limited infallibility to truths related to "salvation and guidance for the life of faith" is simply unfounded, as judged by their own principal (secondary) source.[66] But, to repeat, we demur to more competent students of medieval exegesis and biblical authority to assess Rogers and McKim's interpretation of these topics.[67]

For our part, we shall turn to the Reformation of the sixteenth century and Martin Luther and John Calvin. These biblical scholars were very much indebted to St. Augustine and John Chrysostom in matters regarding biblical infallibility and biblical exegesis. On the other hand, their appreciation of Origen was quite circumscribed, whereas Erasmus, one of their multitalented contemporaries, found in the Alexandrian much stimulation for some of his innovative proposals.[68]

Chapter III

The Reformation: Luther and Calvin

For Rogers and McKim, the testimonies of Luther and Calvin about biblical authority are critical for their interpretation. What Luther, Calvin, and to a lesser extent Zwingli believed constitutes a standard of Reformation orthodoxy.[1] If we would be the theological children of the Reformation, our perspectives about biblical authority should concur with those of these Reformers. The authors omit any sampling of the thought of representatives of the Anabaptist movement.[2]

Rogers and McKim give a competent analysis of Luther's and Calvin's stress upon the Bible's essential function of revealing salvation truths.[3] They correctly emphasize the role of Christ, the incarnated Word of God, in sustaining the authority of the written Word, the Bible. They rightly note the importance of the Holy Spirit in confirming the authority of Scripture for the believer. They also understand that for Luther and Calvin, doing theology should bear practical fruit in the Christian's life. Readers can benefit from these insights.

Rogers and McKim are less successful in drafting an overall context with which to understand the Reformers' thought. Their commitment to several of the "historical disjunctions" to which we referred earlier throws their basic interpretation askew. Rogers and McKim assume almost mechanically that Luther and Calvin did not believe in complete biblical infallibility. This assumption is made because the Reformers acknowledged the principle of accommodation, because they indicated that the Bible's chief function is to reveal salvation truths, and because they engaged in forms of biblical criticism. Our authors propose that Luther and Calvin viewed the locus of the Bible's authority in its "infallible" saving function.

Due to their basic, fallacious assumption about Luther and Calvin, the authors cannot adequately account for those many statements where Luther and Calvin affirm a commitment to complete biblical infallibility. The authors' either/or historical disjunctions do not mesh with the reality of Luther and Calvin's both/and categories. Nor does their definition of error (purposeful deceit) accord with the Reformers' definition.

THE MISSING REFORMATION "PARADIGM" IN THE ROGERS/McKIM PROPOSAL

When the former defenders of the pope, Martin Luther and John Calvin, broke away from the Roman Catholic Church, they refused henceforth to accept the ultimate authority of councils, papal pronouncements, church traditions, and diverse ecclesiastical dicta. They would submit themselves to the authority of Holy Scripture alone (sola Scriptura). Luther put the matter in a straightforward way: "It is the Word of God that is to determine an article of faith—nothing else, not even an angel."

The Reformers' emphasis upon the authority of the Bible involved no simplistic substitution of the authority of a paper pope for that of a sumptuously garbed Renaissance bishop of Rome.[4] They acknowledged a decree of a council or a tradition of the church only if it had scriptural warrant. And in their debates with Roman Catholic disputants, the Reformers demonstrated an impressive grasp of patristic literature and incorporated aspects from it into their worship practices.[5]

Roman Catholics shared a general commitment to biblical authority with the Reformers, but they placed that authority into a different theological matrix. Luther and Calvin associated the essential authority of the words of Scripture with the incarnated Word, Christ. They emphasized the witness of the Holy Spirit in confirming the Bible's authority for the believer.[6] Stressing the principle that Scripture should interpret Scripture, they affirmed that the Bible was a sufficient rule for determining faith and practice. Roman Catholics on occasion inferred that the Church had a role in validating biblical authority and in establishing the canon. They maintained that the Church's teachings (papal pronouncements, tradition) should also be used in making judgments about faith and practice and in interpreting the Bible.[7] In a word, the Bible belonged to the Roman Catholic Church, and her representatives were its only legitimate interpreters.

Not only did Calvin and Luther declare that the Bible alone was their authority but they also claimed that Holy Writ was infallible. At this point Roman Catholics generally agreed with Protestants. In his debate with Luther on the subject of free will, Erasmus, a humanist who remained within the Roman Catholic camp, explained the common ground he and Luther shared:

> The Holy Spirit can not contradict himself. The canonical books of Holy Scripture originated under his inspiration. Their inviolable sublimity is acknowledged and affirmed by both parties in the dispute. Therefore one must find an interpretation which resolves this seeming contradiction.[8]

At least formally, Erasmus followed the traditional premise that God does not contradict Himself in His Word. As a result, Erasmus argued that the differences in opinion between Luther and himself proceeded from the fact that one of them had formulated a mistaken interpretation of the text. Neither viewed the text itself as at fault. Erasmus believed that Luther erred in his interpretation because he relied on his own private judgment in determining an interpretation of the text. The sage from Rotterdam claimed that church teaching had helped him to arrive at a proper understanding.[9]

In an important published letter (to Martin Dorp; May, 1515), Erasmus had earlier set forth his designs for textual criticism. He wanted to go behind Jerome's Vulgate and to reestablish as much as possible the infallible originals of Holy Writ:

> I ask you, most learned Dorp, if what you write is true, why is it that Jerome, Augustine, and Ambrose had different readings from the ones that we have? Why did Jerome expressly censure and correct many readings which are still contained in this edition? What will you do in the face of such converging testimony, that is when the Greek codices offer a different reading from ours, when Jerome in making citations uses that reading, when the most ancient Latin texts have the same reading, when its meaning fits better into the context? Are you going to disregard all these facts and still follow your own codex, which might have been corrupted by a copyist? Certainly no one is stating that there are mistakes in the Divine Writings (something you seemed to have suggested); nor is there any question here of that dispute Augustine had with Jerome. The solution to the problem almost stares us in the face, for it would be clear even to a blind man, as they say, that the Greek was often poorly translated because of the ignorance or laziness of a translator, that often the authentic and true text has been corrupted by ignorant copyists (something we see happening every day) or even changed by unskilled or inattentive ones. Who is more indulgent to error: the one who corrects and restores the mistakes, or the one who would sooner see a blunder added than removed, especially since it is the nature of mistakes that one causes another?[10]

It should be noticed that Erasmus did not limit his definition of *mistakes* to "purposeful deceits." Moreover he generally attributed mistakes to the deficient work of translators and copyists. Several scholars have doubted Erasmus's own commitment to biblical infallibility, but his perception of the "paradigm," or common set of beliefs, out of which the Reformers debated Roman Catholics is sound. In the sixteenth century, Protestants and Roman Catholics debated principles of interpretation but both parties (in which there were many sub-groupings) generally assumed that the Bible was completely infallible.

LUTHER AND BIBLICAL AUTHORITY

In a significant essay, *"Sola Scriptura:* Luther on Biblical Author-ity," Professor David Lotz of Union Theological Seminary (New York City) attempts to establish the ultimate grounds upon which Luther stakes out his reforming claim to *sola Scriptura.*[11] Lotz believes that these grounds were ultimately christological:

> While it is not mistaken to hold that Luther asserted the sole normative authority of the Bible over, and if need be against, ecclesiastical traditions and the teaching authority of popes and councils, such a view is too restricted. Nor does it say what is decisive. By urging Scripture alone Luther was in fact urging Christ alone. *Solus Christus* is the presupposi-tion and ground of *sola Scriptura.*[12]

Lotz's efforts to identify the strands with which Luther weaves to-gether his complex doctrine of biblical authority are salutary. Often Luther's views have suffered distortion through oversimplification. On the one hand, Lotz highlights the import of Scripture's christological concentration for Luther; on the other hand, he cautions us that Luther does not separate the Word of God from the Bible:

> Scripture for Luther *is* God's Word since it has God the Holy Spirit as its ultimate author.... One may not invoke Luther's authority in defense of such familiar formulas as "Scripture witnesses to the Word of God," or "Scripture becomes God's Word when heard in faith," or "Scripture is the record of God's revelation"—*if* such formulas are taken to mean that for Luther himself Scripture is only a fallible, human word which first be-comes an infallible, divine Word when "animated" by the Spirit of Christ, or that Scripture is not as such God's true Word and authentic revelation. These formulas have their provenance in modern theology, chiefly in Protestant neo-Orthodoxy. They can be attributed to Luther only by read-ing them back into his theology in an anachronistic, hence erroneous, fashion.[13]

Although they will be disturbing to some, Lotz's observations merit careful consideration.

Professor Lotz has rightfully emphasized Luther's existential en-counter with the Christ of the Bible and sorted out what impact that encounter had in shaping the Reformer's views of biblical authority.[14] But at another level, he has probably played down too much Luther's association of the Bible's authority with its infallibility.[15] In an apt summary of Luther's statements about biblical infallibility, the distin-guished German scholar Paul Althaus describes that association:

We may trust unconditionally only in the Word of God and not in the teaching of the fathers; for the teachers of the church can err and have erred. Scripture never errs. Therefore it alone has unconditional authority.[16]

For Luther, Christ the living Word undoubtedly gives to the Bible, the written Word, its authority. But in another sense it is fair to say that the Bible is authoritative because it is infallible; it sits in judgment over popes, councils, and all worldly wisdom.[17] The truthful God is its ultimate author.

LUTHER AND BIBLICAL INFALLIBILITY

For Luther, no inconsistency existed between affirming that the Bible communicates the Good News of salvation, and holding the belief that the Bible is completely infallible. Nor did he distinguish between the Bible's infallibility for matters of faith and practice, and its supposed capacity to err in historical, geographical, and scientific matters.

It is impossible that Scripture should contradict itself; it only appears so to senseless and obstinate hypocrites.[18]

But everyone, indeed, knows that at times they [the fathers] have erred as men will; therefore I am ready to trust them only when they prove their opinions from Scripture, which has never erred.[19]

Whoever is so bold that he ventures to accuse God of fraud and deception in a single word and does so willfully again and again after he has been warned and instructed once or twice will likewise certainly venture to accuse God of fraud and deception in all of His words. Therefore it is true, absolutely and without exception, that everything is believed or nothing is believed. The Holy Spirit does not suffer Himself to be separated or divided so that He should teach and cause to be believed one doctrine rightly and another falsely.[20]

"It is certain that Scripture cannot disagree with itself."[21] Nor did Luther think it odd to search for the meaning of biblical passages in what they tell us about Christ (John 5:39), while at the same time recognizing the authority of the words of Scripture:

One letter, even a single tittle of Scripture, means more to us than heaven and earth. Therefore we cannot permit even the most minute change.[22]

Or elsewhere:

Consequently, we must remain content with them [words], and cling to them as the perfectly clear, certain, sure words of God which can never deceive us or allow us to err.[23]

Martin Luther's commitment to the verbal plenary inspiration and to the infallibility of the Scriptures appears to be clearly documented in these statements and in others like them.

Rogers and McKim view Luther's perspective on biblical infallibility otherwise. They write that Luther did not (p. 87)

> hold to the theory of the scientific and historical inerrancy of the original manuscripts of Scripture that began to develop in the post-Reformation period.... For Luther, the Bible was infallible in accomplishing its purpose of proclaiming the salvation which the Father had wrought in His Son Jesus Christ.

Upon what kind of arguments do the authors stake their claims? In the first place, they do not cite many of Luther's unambiguous statements on the subject. In the second place, they resort to historical disjunctions. They intimate, for example, that because Luther held to the principle of accommodation he obviously did not believe in complete biblical infallibility.[24] We have already noted that this type of argument is not convincing. In the third place, they present a brief listing of Luther's "critical opinions" concerning textual matters (p. 87):

> ...his [Luther's] statements regarding the authorship of Genesis, Ecclesiastes, and Jude; the propriety of the canonicity of Esther, Hebrews, James and Revelation; the "errors" of the prophets, the trustworthiness of Kings vis-à-vis Chronicles, and the value of the Gospel accounts.

The authors have compiled this list from one page (p. 300) of Reinhold Seeberg's *History of Doctrines*.[25] In his survey text, which dates from the last years of the nineteenth century, Seeberg gives proof texts for these "critical opinions" of Luther with little commentary, and his analysis has not gone unchallenged. In 1944 the Lutheran scholar, M. Reu, published a massively documented book entitled *Luther and the Scripture*.[26] Reu evaluated disputed passages in Luther after placing the Reformer's suspect quotations back into their contexts. Let us consider one purported critical problem that Rogers and McKim raise following Seeberg's lead; it is what they call "the trustworthiness of Kings vis-à-vis Chronicles." In *Table Talk*, Luther is quoted as having said: "The Books of Kings are more trustworthy than the Books of Chronicles." Not hiding behind the possibility that this reminiscence about what Luther spoke may have been incorrectly reported, Reu comments:

> We shall only give the entire sentence from which the quotation has been taken. That will suffice to show with what little right anyone may use this as a proof for Luther's liberalism. The sentence reads: "The writer of Chronicles noted only the summary and chief stories and events. Whatever is less important and immaterial he passed by. For this reason the Books of the Kings are more credible than the Chronicles." What more does this state than that the Chronicles pass by many things and condense others which the Books of Kings include or offer in detail? In view of the different plan followed by these two Biblical books the value of

Chronicles as a historical source is less than that of Kings. But there is not a word about errors in it.[27]

In more lengthy discussions Reu analyzes the context for other "critical opinions" Luther had concerning the Scriptures. He concludes that a fair assessment of these texts reveals that the Reformer did not admit the reality of any genuine discrepancy in the Holy Writ, although he acknowledged his own inability to resolve some apparent problem passages.[28] This observation concurs with Luther's statements about the infallibility of the Bible. Moreover it accords with his thoughtful attempts to harmonize biblical texts.

As Reu points out, Luther assumed biblical infallibility only for the original documents. His textual critical work was designed to remove errors in copies and versions so that the original documents might be more closely approached. Although to our knowledge he does not speak about the original autographs as such, his practice makes it clear that he, with humanists of his day, desired to establish better texts (whether classical or biblical) that would reflect as much as possible the original texts of antiquity. In commenting about Acts 13:20, Luther appended this gloss:

> Some texts have 400 (altogether 450) but the histories and reckoning of the years do not permit it. It is an error of a scribe, who wrote four instead of three, which could easily happen in Greek.[29]

Many such remarks are found in Luther's glosses and in his other writings where he deals with the harmonization of the biblical texts. They reflect the Reformer's awareness of copyists' errors and his desire to restore the infallible originals.

Rather than interacting even-handedly with the arguments and evidence in Reu's significant study, Rogers and McKim dismiss the work *in toto*, but do so in a most unsatisfactory fashion. They appeal to authority. In note 115, page 133, they cite a negative judgment of Otto Heick concerning Reu's study. They fail to observe that Heick, a church historian with pronounced neoorthodox leanings, may have found Reu's exhaustively documented essay disconcerting.[30] And then, in what can only be judged as an awkward attempt to bolster the authority of Seeberg's list of "critical opinions," they cite J. Theodore Mueller's assessment of the quality of Seeberg's scholarship. Mueller's evaluation is found in a collection of essays, *Inspiration & Interpretation*, written by Evangelicals and edited by John Walvoord.[31] The authors misquote Mueller in a very significant way. They have Mueller declaring that Seeberg's *The History of Doctrines* "represents a most scholarly and reliable treatise *on Luther's views of Scripture*" [italics mine] (n. 114, p. 133), as if the author approved all of Seeberg's commentary upon Luther's views of Scripture. In truth, Mueller actually declared that Seeberg's *Dogmengeschichte* "represents a most scholarly and reliable treatise *on this point* [italics mine] . . ." (p. 94). What is the point to which Mueller alludes? It is apparently Seeberg's recognition that Luther believed in the full authority of Scripture and that he did not associate the Reformer with any "mechanical inspiration theory" (pp. 93–94). Mueller, however, disagreed categorically with Seeberg on other aspects of his analysis. For example, he wrote:

> It is indeed very significant that Seeberg does not admit Luther's identification of God's Word with Holy Scripture, that is, his manifest teaching that the Bible, as a whole and in all its parts, is the very word of God. The claim which Seeberg here makes, is that of modern liberalism which ignores the evident historical facts (p. 95).

Rogers and McKim's treatment of Reu and Mueller does little to enhance an open-minded reader's confidence in the reliability of their documentation or in their manner of doing history.

CALVIN AND BIBLICAL AUTHORITY

Those acquainted with the literature on Calvin's view of biblical authority know its vast dimensions. The nonspecialist finds it difficult to sort out the relative merits of a given analysis or to establish its niche in the complex Calvin historiography that exists.[32] Added difficulties emerge because Christians from many backgrounds, in a spirit of triumphalism, have claimed Calvin as their own. They tend to elevate one aspect of Calvin's thought that coincides with their own theological preferences, while minimizing if not denying other teachings by the Reformer.

Rogers and McKim base portions of their interpretation concerning Calvin's attitudes about Scripture on a well-respected historiography including studies by Ford Lewis Battles, John McNeill, T. H. L. Parker, François Wendel, and others. But this particular historiography is on occasion the tributary of neoorthodox presuppositions.[33]

Rogers and McKim argue that Calvin believed that the central purpose of the Bible is to communicate salvation truths about Christ, and that its authority is made known to believers through the internal witness of the Holy Spirit.[34] On these points most Calvin scholars concur. In the *Institutes of the Christian Religion* Calvin declares (III, ii. 7):

> Therefore our mind must be otherwise illumined and our heart strengthened, that the Word of God may obtain full faith among us. Now we shall possess a right definition of faith if we call it a firm and certain knowledge of God's benevolence toward us, founded upon the truth of the freely given promise in Christ, both revealed to our minds and sealed upon our hearts through the Holy Spirit.

Richard Muller comments well about Calvin's doctrine of Scripture:

> Scripture is produced by the inspiration of the Spirit who testifies to our hearts of the truth and authority of his words. By the Spirit we recognize Scripture to be the Word and Wisdom of God the Father given *to us* in a form that we can apprehend; and by the Spirit we are drawn to find in Scripture the Gospel of Christ, the essential Word of the Father given *for us*.[35]

Calvin joins the authority of Christ, the living Word, with that of the Bible, the written Word; he highlights the role of the Holy Spirit in confirming biblical authority to us. The Bible is also authoritative because God, the source of truth, is its principal author.

CALVIN AND BIBLICAL INFALLIBILITY

But when Rogers and McKim indicate that Calvin held a belief in biblical infallibility limited to faith and practice, then many Reformation scholars from diverse theological backgrounds balk. They include experts who are not themselves proponents of biblical inerrancy. In his *Knowledge of God in Calvin's Theology* (Columbia University Press, 1952), Edward Dowey, a very knowledgeable Calvin scholar, writes:

> To Calvin the theologian an error in Scripture is unthinkable. Hence the endless harmonizing, the explaining and interpreting of passages that seem to contradict or to be inaccurate. But Calvin the critical scholar recognizes mistakes with a disarming ingeniousness. The mistake or the gloss is simply a blunder made by an ignorant copyist (p. 104).
>
> If he [Calvin] betrays his position at all, it is in apparently assuming a priori that no errors can be allowed to reflect upon the inerrancy of the original documents (p. 105).

Or Brian Gerrish, in his 1957 *Scottish Journal of Theology* article "Biblical Authority and the Continental Reformation," notes:

> Perhaps even more important is the corollary that Calvin is obliged by his view of inspiration to think of the Scriptures as inerrant, and he exercises much ingenuity in reconciling alleged contradictions, and explaining apparent errors.... And the other method of explanation, which he uses against apparent errors of historical fact, is to attribute the error to a copyist, hence enabling himself to hold to the inerrancy of a hypothetical "original document."[36]

H. Jackson Forstman, in his *Word and Spirit: Calvin's Doctrine of Biblical Authority* (Stanford University Press, 1962) puts the matter this way:

> Those who do not interpret Calvin as a literalist make much of his emphasis on Christ, the promises, and faith. Their point cannot be denied. Insofar as the knowledge of faith is concerned, Calvin does not need and does not use a theory of verbal inspiration. Neither can we deny or explain away the strong emphasis on the totality of scripture and particu-

larly on all its individual parts. So we must also say: insofar as the wider knowledge is concerned, Calvin both needs and is forced to use scripture in such a way as to emphasize its literal inerrancy.[37]

Rogers and McKim flatly disagree with these judgments, even though they come from noted Reformation scholars whose studies they rely upon for other arguments.

Calvin's own statements about biblical inspiration do not lend support to Rogers and McKim's interpretation. Regarding the classic "inspiration" passage, 2 Timothy 3:16, Calvin writes:

> This is the principle which distinguishes our religion from all others, that we know that God hath spoken to us, and are fully convinced that the prophets did not speak at their own suggestion, but that, being organs of the Holy Spirit, they only uttered what they had been commissioned from heaven to declare. Whoever then wishes to profit in the Scriptures, let him, first of all, lay down this as a settled point, that the Law and the Prophets are not a doctrine delivered according to the will and pleasure of men, but dictated by the Holy Spirit.[38]

Notice how he describes the inspiration of the Evangelists:

> The Spirit of God, who appointed the Evangelists to be his clerks, appears purposely to have regulated their style in such a manner, that they all wrote one and the same history, with the most perfect agreement, but in different ways. It was intended, that the truth of God should more clearly and strikingly appear, when it was manifest that his witnesses did not speak by a preconcerted plan, but that each of them separately, without paying any attention to another, wrote freely and honestly what the Holy Spirit dictated.[39]

Calvin's own efforts at harmonizing the Scriptures were based on the premise that the "truth of God" undergirded what the biblical writers penned under the influence of the Holy Spirit.

CALVIN AND THE CONCEPT OF ERROR

Nonetheless, Rogers and McKim boldly state that Calvin "was unconcerned with normal, human inaccuracies in minor matters" in Scripture (p. 109). They point to several comments made by Calvin in an attempt to substantiate their contention. Their list of problem passages, if rearranged, bears a striking resemblance to a list found in John McNeill's influential *Church History* article of 1959, "The Significance of the Word of God for Calvin." In his essay, McNeill, a distinguished Calvin scholar, attempted to demonstrate that Calvin did not believe in biblical inerrancy.[40] He misconstrued his argument, however. He assumed that if he could prove that Calvin did not maintain a complete mechanical dictation theory, then the Reformer did not affirm biblical inerrancy. Obviously, Calvin does not hold such a theory in its crassest configuration.[41] But McNeill won only a Pyrrhic victory. It does not follow that because the Bible's human authors were not automatons in their writing of Scripture the resultant product was errant. Such a stance limits dramatically the power of God to protect His Word. Rogers and McKim tend to approve McNeill's premise, and they too assume that Calvin admitted the existence of errors in the original biblical documents. These "errors" were allegedly due to the humanness of the biblical authors.

Let us examine examples of the strongest evidence they muster for their case. Since John Calvin's thinking is so pivotal to Rogers and McKim's interpretation, we will assess this evidence in some detail. The authors write (p. 109):

> ... Calvin noted that Paul misquoted Psalm 51:4 in Romans 3:4. Calvin generalized about such inaccuracies: "We know that, in quoting Scripture the apostles often used freer language than the original, since they were content if what they quoted applied to their subject, and therefore they were not over-careful in their use of words."

Rogers and McKim's suggestion that Calvin thought Paul "misquoted" Psalm 51:4 is not an appropriate evaluation. A few lines before the passage Rogers and McKim cite, Calvin declared: "And that Paul has quoted this passage according to the proper and real meaning of David is clear from the objection that is immediately added ... (Rom. 3:5)."[42] The apostles did not "misquote" Scripture because they expressed the meaning of Old Testament passages with other words. Rogers and McKim declare (p. 109):

> Similarly in Calvin's commentary on Hebrews 10:6, he affirmed that the saving purpose of the biblical message was adequately communicated through an imperfect form of words: "They (the apostles) were not over-scrupulous in quoting words provided that they did not misuse Scripture for their convenience. We must always look at the purpose for which quotations are made ... but as far as the words are concerned, as in other things which are not relevant to the present purpose, they allow themselves some indulgence."

The commentary warrants several observations. First, the passage Rogers and McKim cite comes from Calvin's commentary on Hebrews 10:5, not Hebrews 10:6. Second, Calvin does not refer to the "saving purpose of the biblical message" in the passage. Third, the authors exclude an important statement from their quotation: "We must always look at the purpose for which quotations are made *because they have careful regard for the main object so as not to turn Scripture to a false meaning.*"[43] In this deleted sentence Calvin is apparently arguing that the apostles did not intend to betray the meaning of Scripture by creating misquotations. He does not say anything about the "imperfect form of words" in this passage.[44] Rogers and McKim note (pp. 109–10): "In his commentary on Hebrews 2:7, Calvin acknowledges that some felt that the phrase, 'a little lower than the angels' was not used by the author of Hebrews in the same sense as David had meant it in Psalm 8." The authors do not cite Calvin's continuing comment on this passage: "David's meaning is this: ... The apostle has no intention of overthrowing this meaning or of giving it a different turn; ..."[45] Rogers and McKim notice Calvin's counter to those who questioned Paul's propriety in applying the words, "Say not in thy heart, Who shall ascend?" (Deut. 30:12), to the death and resurrection of Christ (Rom. 10:6) (p. 110):

> If it is alleged that this interpretation is too forced and subtle, we should understand that the object of the Apostle was not to explain this passage exactly, but only to apply it to his treatment of the subject at hand. He does not, therefore, repeat what Moses has said syllable by syllable, but employs a gloss, by which he adapts the testimony of Moses more closely to his own purpose.

The authors fail to note Calvin's continuing commentary where he denies that Paul misused Moses' words:

> ... If, therefore, we take these statements of Paul as having been made by way of amplification or as a gloss, we shall not be able to say that he has done violence to or distorted the words of Moses.[46]

Rogers and McKim's inference about this passage, "Calvin understood Paul to be a preacher of the Good News of Christ, not an historian or linguist concerned with transmitting a past document with minute accuracy" is misleading indeed (p. 110). The authors claim that Calvin the scholar "discerned technical inaccuracies in the humanly written text" (p. 110).

> In his commentary on Acts 7:16, Calvin declared that Luke had "made a manifest error" as comparison with the text of Genesis 23:9 showed.

Calvin actually wrote:

> And whereas he [Luke] saith afterward, they were laid in the sepulchre which Abraham had bought of the sons of Hemor, it is manifest that there is a fault (mistake) in the word Abraham. ... Wherefore this place must be amended.[47]

Calvin does not tell us to whom the error should be attributed; "it is manifest that" is the language of an observation, not an attribution. It is probable that the Reformer believed that a copyist had made the error. Just two verses earlier (Acts 7:14) Calvin had handled a textual problem by referring to an error on the part of copyists.[48] Rogers and McKim refer to Calvin's comments on Matthew 27:9 (p. 110):

How the name of Jeremiah crept in, I confess that I do not know, nor do I give myself much trouble to inquire. The passage itself plainly shows that the name of Jeremiah has been put down by mistake, instead of Zechariah (xi. 13) for in *Jeremiah* we find nothing of this sort, not anything that even approaches it.

In this passage Calvin does not admit, as Rogers and McKim propose, that due to a human lapse the original text contained a genuine error. Rather Calvin's observation, "How the name of Jeremiah crept in" exhibits a verb that is logically associated with problems of textual transmission. Errors creep into texts during the process of copying.

Rogers and McKim write that Calvin did not believe Moses "knew any more or thought any differently about the natural order than other people of his time and culture" (p. 112). They imply that Calvin knew that Moses had made a mistake in affirming that the moon and sun were the two great lights. For did not Calvin point out that astronomers had discovered that Saturn was larger than the moon?[49] In fact, Calvin does not acknowledge that Moses erred. According to the Reformer, Moses in accommodating himself to his audience's perspective, used phenomenological language and thereby made an accurate observation. The moon and sun are the largest lights in the sky as viewed by the naked eye from the earth. Calvin writes: "Had he [Moses] spoken of things generally unknown, the uneducated might have pleaded in excuse that such subjects were beyond their capacity." The next line of Calvin's quotation is very important, but Rogers and McKim omit it: "Lastly, since the Spirit of God here opens a common school for all, it is not surprising that he should chiefly choose these subjects which would be intelligible to all."[50] To accuse Moses of making an error here would be tantamount to accusing the Holy Spirit of the same fault, according to Calvin. Rogers and McKim fail to mention this. We can learn from Calvin how important it is to try to ascertain a biblical author's intent before we interpret his words. Elsewhere in his commentary on Genesis 1 and 2, Calvin accepts at face value Moses' comments about the creation of the natural world and man. Nowhere does Calvin indicate that any of Moses' remarks about the natural world were inaccurate when properly interpreted.[51] The Reformer does not hesitate to seek some form of accord between the science of his day and Holy Writ.[52] We will refer again to Calvin's attitudes toward this issue in a later section.

Following the lead of Professor John McNeill, Rogers and McKim refer to Calvin's comments on Romans 5:15 to document their contention that he perceived "defects in the discourse" of Paul's *original text*.[53] What does Calvin actually propose in his commentary?

We shall add what he [Paul] omits to say in his explanation. Although he frequently mentions the difference between Adam and Christ, all his repeated statements lack a balancing clause, or at least are elliptical. These, it is true, are faults in his language, but in no way do they detract from the majesty of the heavenly wisdom which is delivered to us by the apostle. On the contrary, the singular providence of God has passed on to us these profound mysteries in the garb of a poor style, so that our faith might not depend on the power of human eloquence, but on the efficacy of the Spirit alone.[54]

Rogers and McKim have misunderstood Calvin's attempt to defend the Scripture against the charge that it lacks elegance and grace, a common charge by the Bible's detractors in his day.[55] Calvin avers that Paul apparently violated rules of rhetoric and style, not that he propagated factual errors in the original text.

Rogers and McKim refer to 1 Corinthians 10:8, where Paul mentions 23,000 being killed instead of 24,000 (Num. 25:9), as a type of discrepancy that Calvin countenanced due to his concept of accommodated language (p. 142, n. 252). In fact, Calvin reveals a deep concern to reconcile these figures in his commentary on 1 Corinthians 10:8:

> *Neither let us commit fornication.* Paul now turns to fornication. From historical records it is clear that the Corinthians indulged in this freely, and it is easy for us to gather from earlier chapters, that those who had given their allegiance to Christ were not yet free from this vice by any means. The punishment for this sin ought to make us afraid, and remind us how much God hates filthy and lustful passions, for in one day twenty-three thousand, or, according to Moses, twenty-four thousand, of them perished. But although they differ about the number, it is easy to reconcile their statements. For it is not unheard of, when there is no intention of making an exact count of individuals to give an approximate number. For example, there were those whom the Romans called the *Centumviri,* The Hundred, when in fact there were one hundred and two of them. Therefore, since about twenty-four thousand were destroyed by the hand of the Lord, in other words, over twenty-three thousand, Moses gives the upper limit, Paul the lower, and there is really no discrepancy. This story is to be found in Numbers 25:9.[56]

Rogers and McKim would have us believe that for Calvin a minor mistake in number was unimportant. In reality, the Reformer goes to ingenious lengths to demonstrate that both writers were correct in their assertions. His commitment to biblical harmonization cannot be gainsaid.

Rogers and McKim's attempt to defend the thesis that Calvin allowed for "technical errors" in the text and that he limited biblical infallibility to matters of faith and practice falters badly. It encounters the heavy opposition of Calvin's formal statements, a few of which Professor Dowey places back to back in this fashion:

"...we see that the Spirit is not less diligent in narrating burials than the principal mysteries of faith." We "ought to embrace with mild docility, and *without any exception, whatever* is delivered in the Holy Scriptures." "For Scripture is the school of the Holy Spirit in which as *nothing useful and necessary is omitted, so nothing is taught which is not profitable to know.*"[57]

This kind of statement could be duplicated tenfold. Moreover, Calvin's extraordinary efforts at harmonizing biblical texts countermands the thesis completely. Rupert Davies, the learned Reformation scholar, who earlier notes that Emile Doumergue's list of Calvin's "admitted" errors has questionable validity, summarizes well Calvin's attitude to Scripture:

And the instances quoted by Doumergue of Calvin's recognition of errors in the Bible are but drops in a bucket of unquestioning reverence for the words of Holy Scripture, and indicate at most that he was very occasionally in a long career untrue to one of his dearly-cherished ideas.[58]

THE REFORMERS' ATTITUDE TOWARD "SCIENCE"

Rogers and McKim propose that Luther and other Reformers did not rely on the Bible's incidental statements about the natural world in their assessment of contemporary scientific theories (p. 87). The Reformers understood that these statements could err due to their status as accommodated language. According to the authors' interpretation, it was seventeenth-century Protestant "scholastics" (along with Roman Catholic scholastics) who began to use the words of Scripture as a basis for establishing their viewpoints on science: "For Voetius and other Protestant scholastics the issue was clear. When the findings of science contradicted the apparent literal text of the Bible—the findings of science had to be rejected" (p. 167). Rogers and McKim do not think Calvin and Luther reacted against scientific findings in a similar fashion.

The authors are quick to discount the implications of a passage from Luther's *Table Talk* (which they only partially cite) according to which the Reformer turned his back on Copernicus's heliocentric theory because it contradicted a biblical passage:

There was mention of a certain new astrologer who wanted to prove that the earth moves and not the sky, the sun, and the moon ... [Luther remarked]: "So it goes now. Whoever wants to be clever must agree with nothing that others esteem. He must do something of his own. This is what that fellow does who wishes to turn the whole of astronomy upside down. Even in these things that are thrown into disorder I believe the Holy Scriptures, for Joshua commanded the sun to stand still and not the earth (Josh. 10:12)."[59]

Rogers and McKim contend that this was "likely just a common sense remark," made "from the memory of one of his guests," "printed ... twenty-seven years afterwards (1566)."[60] In other words, Luther did not really interact with the Copernican revolution on the basis of a passage in Joshua.

It is true that one can minimize the impact of this *Table Talk* remark by suspecting its authenticity. But the criteria that Rogers and McKim use so confidently to dismiss the comment have the earmarks of special pleading. If followed, they minimize too drastically the historical value of Luther's *Table Talk*, which authors Rogers and McKim themselves use as a source of one of Luther's "admitted errors": "the trustworthiness of Kings vis-à-vis Chronicles."

Alexandre Koyré, the renowned historian of science, observes that Melanchthon adjudged Copernicus's attempt "to give motion to the Earth and bring the sun to a standstill" as absurd and worthy of censure by a wise government.[61] Melanchthon, Luther's close associate, made this comment in a letter of 1541 to Bernardus Mithobius, only two years after Luther had allegedly uttered his disputed remark.[62] After surveying the textual problems associated with Aurifaber's *Table Talk* and Lauterbach's *Journal* (where Luther's remark is reported in another format), Koyré concludes that Luther did in fact oppose Copernicus's scientific formulation: "Luther takes Copernicus to task for his inordinate desire for originality; Melanchthon did the same, and also accused him of copying the Ancients, especially Aristarchus of Samos."[63] There is a strong possibility that Luther did reject the Copernican proposal with Joshua 10:12 in mind.[64]

Rogers and McKim take some of their details about the creation of Luther's statement from John Dillenberger's *Protestant Thought and Natural Science* (Nashville: Abingdon, 1960), pp. 38–39. Dillenberger asserts that Luther and Calvin did not defend their scientific views of the world based on their commitment to the biblical inerrancy of Scripture (p. 39). But he does acknowledge that the Reformers held to a complete biblical infallibility (p. 31):

> It is true of course that the Reformers were creatures of their day with respect to accepting the total words of the Bible as true. It would not have occurred to them to suggest that the hermeneutical principle freed them from what we today call the notion of the infallibility of the text. But it is important to note that the text free from error (except for linguistic or copy errors) was not the centre of their attention.

Rogers and McKim feel quite comfortable to use Dillenberger's comments for one phase of their analysis, but they appear reluctant to cite other significant statements he made.

Much debate has centered upon the attitudes of Calvin toward

Copernicus. In heated interchanges found in the *Journal of the History of Ideas* (1960, 1961), Professors Edward Rosen and Joseph Ratner discuss Calvin's position extensively.[65] More recently, Richard Stauffer, Hautes Études (Paris), has brought new materials into the debate concerning Calvin's potential references to Copernicus.[66] Then again, scholars have seriously challenged the authenticity of a remark ascribed to Calvin: "Who will venture to place the authority of Copernicus above that of the Holy Spirit?"[67] Rogers and McKim give no hint of this long-standing debate in the text of their volume.[68] As they dismiss the import of Luther's reported remark about Copernicus out of hand, so they declare categorically that "Calvin never mentioned Copernicus . . ." (p. 166), a remarkable supposition to be attributed to so widely read a man as Calvin.[69]

The authors contrast Calvin's openness to natural science with the stance of Melanchthon who "stood firmly in the Aristotelian/Ptolemaic schema" (p. 166). They fail to notice that in several of Calvin's commentaries written thirteen and sixteen years after Copernicus's writing of 1543, the Reformer shows himself to be a partisan of the old cosmology: "We are indeed not ignorant that the circuit of the heavens is finite and the earth, like a little ball, is located in the middle."[70] He in fact held to the same general cosmology as Melanchthon. Rogers and McKim do not mention this.

Did some sixteenth-century theologians evaluate the Copernican hypothesis with an eye to its bearing upon biblical teaching? In his *Science and Change 1500–1700*, Hugh Kearney, whose authority Rogers and McKim invoke, follows the lead of Edward Rosen by citing individuals in the sixteenth century ranging from Luther (his *Table Talk* remark) and Melanchthon, to Tycho Brahe (1546–1601) who reacted against the Copernican hypothesis due in part to their interpretation of the Bible's teachings. Brahe's statement is particularly straightforward:

> What need is there without any justification to imagine the earth, a dark, dense and inert mass, to be a heavenly body undergoing even more numerous revolutions than the others, that is to say, subject to a triple motion, in negation not only of all physical truth, but also of the authority of the Holy Scripture which ought to be paramount?[71]

Brahe's correspondence with Rothmann in 1589 reveals the important role of Scripture in his thought processes.[72] In England, several scholars responded favorably to the Copernican hypothesis, but others rejected aspects of it on biblical grounds. Thomas Blundeville published a popular treatise on arithmetic and cosmology, entitled *M. Blundeville His Exercises* (1594), a volume that passed through seven editions (until 1638). In it, he scored the Copernican hypothesis for both philosophical and theological reasons:

Some also deny that the earth is in the middest of the world, and some affirme that it is moueable, as also *Copernicus* by way of supposition, and not for that he thought so in deede; ... But *Ptolomie, Aristotle*, and all other olde writers affirme the earth to be in the middest and to remaine immoueable and to be the very Center of the world, prooving the same with many most strong reasons not needefull here to be rehearsed, because I thinke fewe or none do doubt thereof, and specially the holy Scripture affirming the foundations of the earth to be layd so sure, that it neuer should mooue at any time: Againe you shall finde in the selfe same Psalme these words, Hee appointed the Moone for certaine seasons, and the Sunne knoweth his going downe, whereby it appeareth that the Sunne mooueth and not the earth.[73]

In Poland, opposition against the thesis of the native son remained strong deep into the eighteenth century. Kearney comments about the widespread reaction against Copernicus in the sixteenth century:

The truth is that within the general range of religious opinion, Catholic, Lutheran and Calvinist alike, the Copernican view was dismissed as an absurdity. All the accepted authorities were against it. The Bible contradicted it expressly. The weight of common sense acted as an additional obstacle.[74]

Writing in the first third of the sixteenth century, Copernicus himself suspected that his theory might encounter opposition based on his contemporaries' reading of the Bible:

Perhaps there will be babblers who, although completely ignorant of mathematics, nevertheless take it upon themselves to pass judgment on mathematical questions and, badly distorting some passage of Scripture to their purpose, will dare to find fault with my understanding and censure it.[75]

Copernicus believed that his ideas were compatible with a proper understanding of Scripture. Many of his opponents who read their Bibles differently disagreed.

As we have seen, a good number of sixteenth-century thinkers forged their cosmologies with the words of Scripture in mind. In his *Castle of Knowledge* (1556), the Englishman Robert Recorde complained about this:

Manie scrupulous divines by misse-understanding of Scripture, have abhorred the studie of Astronomie and also of Philosophie and often times doe more sharply then discreetly raile at these both, & yet understand they not anything in either of them both.[76]

In the 1640s John Wilkins complained that the Copernican hypothesis was encountering opposition because Englishmen from various social classes thought it contradicted the Bible. He indicated that this was the reason "why the common people in general doe cry it downe, as being absurd and ridiculous" (A Discourse Concerning a New Planet [London: John Maynard, 1640], p. 27). Rogers and McKim's proposal that it was seventeenth-century "scholastics" who initiated the practice of looking to the Bible's words for information about the natural world is a broken reed.[77]

For Rogers and McKim, then, the beliefs of Calvin and Luther constitute a standard of Reformation orthodoxy regarding biblical authority. But we have seen that their interpretation of these two Reformers is less than convincing. And, although the authors do speak about Protestant creeds in the sixteenth century, their coverage of "Reformation" figures is too circumscribed even for a survey. The leaders of the Reformation in Zurich, Zwingli and Bullinger, an English Reformer like William Whitaker, the very important Martin Bucer, Anabaptist spokespersons, and a host of less well-known exegetes and theologians (let alone "the people") have more or less disappeared from their historical horizons.[78] The topic of "biblical authority" in the Reformation demands a more reliable, nuanced, and in-depth treatment than the authors offer, despite several of their valued insights.

Chapter IV

Biblical Authority in the Sixteenth and Early Seventeenth Centuries: Roman Catholic and Protestant Apologetics

To understand Protestant concepts of biblical authority in the sixteenth and early seventeenth centuries, one must place them against the backdrop of surging apologetic debates with Roman Catholics.[1] After the Council of Trent (1545–1563) defined Roman Catholic orthodoxy with some care, sides were drawn up more sharply between the two parties.[2] The tempo of Protestant creed making picked up as theologies became more fixed and the general religious scene less fluid (although a good number of Protestants and Catholics continued to switch camps). Usually the creeds of Protestants distinguished them from Roman Catholics. At the same time these doctrinal confessions, which became highly authoritative for many believers, highlighted differences between competing Protestant groups. Nonetheless, the horrific Wars of Religion testify to the fact that the chief battles that wracked Western Christendom ensued between Protestants and Roman Catholics (except for battles with the Turks).[3] These wars conjoined political and dynastic intrigues to religious fanaticism; they unleashed cruel and unbridled passions.

ROMAN CATHOLICS AND BIBLICAL INFALLIBILITY

In the early sixteenth century, Erasmus, a Catholic humanist who appreciated Lorenzo Valla's philological studies, raised questions about certain texts in the Scriptures.[4] Cajetan, a redoubtable apologist, did the same in a debate with Martin Luther.[5] But many Roman Catholics shared with sixteenth-century Protestants a commitment to complete biblical infallibility. After Trent, however, they were perhaps even more prone to stress the infallibility of the Vulgate rather than that of the "original documents."[6] One of the clearest illustrations of the Roman Catholic attitude in this regard is evidenced in a major dispute that took place in the 1580s between the Jesuit Lenhard Lessius and the Faculties of Theology of Louvain and Douay. In Assertions One and Two of his 1586 Theses, Lessius proposed that the Holy Spirit did not specifically choose each word the biblical writers used in their texts. Rather the Holy Spirit, in an undefined manner, guided the writers so that they made no error even though they chose the words: *". . .ac simul illis specialissimo modo assistat in omnibus verbis ac sententiis, ut ne minimum quidem errorem committere possint."* In 1588 the theologians of Louvain and Douay censured Lessius for departing from Roman Catholic orthodoxy by not insisting that every word of the Scriptures was specifically chosen by the Holy Spirit.[7] It should be noticed that both sides (including the slippery Lessius) acknowledged that the biblical text was infallible (with no limitations of infallibility to matters of faith and practice).

When Roman Catholics debated with Protestants, they recognized that both parties accepted the principle of an infallible Bible. In his *Controversies* of 1595, St. François de Sales (1567–1622) put the matter this way:

> If then the Church can err, O Calvin, O Luther, to whom will I have recourse in my difficulties? To Scripture, they say; but what will I do, poor man that I am? For it is with regard to Scripture itself that I have trouble. I do not doubt whether or not I should adjust faith to Scripture, for who does not know that it is the word of truth? What bothers me is the understanding of this Scripture.[8]

Although St. François readily granted that the Protestants held to an infallible Bible, he doubted that they had the criteria with which to interpret it correctly. How to interpret an infallible text and how to determine the canon of the Bible were two important issues debated by Roman Catholics and Protestants during the Catholic Reformation (Counter Reformation), just as they had been for Luther and Erasmus.

THE NEW PYRRHONISM AND ROMAN CATHOLIC APOLOGETICS

Rogers and McKim create another misleading interpretation when they attempt to describe the apologetic arsenal that Roman Catholics allegedly used against Protestants (and from which Protestants allegedly borrowed). The authors assume gratuitously that Roman Catholic apologists with Thomistic training necessarily used Aristotelian arguments exclusively in their apologetic efforts (p. 147):

> . . . the second generation of Reformers tried to battle Roman Catholicism by using Roman Catholics' own weapons against them. For example, Protestants tried eventually to prove the authority of the Bible, using the same Aristotelian arguments Roman Catholics had used to prove the authority of the church.

In reality, one of the main thrusts of Roman Catholic argumentation against Protestants' claims was not based upon Aristotelian tenets at all.[9] In *The History of Scepticism From Erasmus to Descartes*, Professor Richard Popkin has carefully expounded how Roman Catholic apologists used the arguments of Pyrrhonism (skepticism) in an attempt to force Protestants to accept the tradition and authority of the Church:

> Beginning with the great Jesuit theologian, Juan Maldonat, who came to teach in Paris in the early 1560s..., a type of dialectic was developed, especially by the Jesuit controversialists, for undermining Calvinism on its own grounds by raising a series of sceptical difficulties.[10]

Accepting the traditions of their own communion on fideistic grounds, apologists like Francois Veron attempted to show Reformed spokesmen that their reliance upon the Holy Spirit's guidance or upon the guidance of regenerated reason did not afford them with the capacity to interpret Scriptures correctly.[11] Roman Catholic apologists pointed to differences of interpretations advocated by Protestant exegetes in an attempt to prove their point. From their perspective, Protestants were doomed to fall into skepticism, despite their appeals to the witness of the Holy Spirit. François de Sales challenged Protestants boldly in this regard concerning the canon:

> Now let us see what rule they have for discerning the canonical books from all of the other ecclesiastical ones. "The witness," they say, "and inner persuasion of the Holy Spirit." Oh God, what a hiding place, what a fog, what a night! We are not in this way very enlightened in so important and grave a matter.[12]

According to Roman Catholic apologists, only the traditions of the church accepted on faith permitted Christians to determine what were the canonical books and to interpret the Scriptures with authoritative guides. Popularized by Veron, this Roman Catholic apologetic was used extensively in France and beyond. In France the French pastor Jean Daillé complained that even Catholic bakers employed it against their Huguenot neighbors.[13] The "method" was not grounded in Aristotelian arguments, but in a form of fideism. Rogers and McKim's failure to understand the linkage of the new Pyrrhonism with Roman Catholic apologetics caused them to create a misleading historical backdrop for understanding Protestant thought, particularly that which emphasized regenerated reason's rights.[14]

When Protestant apologists insisted that regenerated reason (and right reason per se) helped them to know that the Bible was authoritative, they often did so apologetically because Roman Catholic disputants had challenged the criterion of the witness of the Holy Spirit to confirm biblical authority. These same Protestants often understood that the witness of the Holy Spirit was the primary means whereby the faithful come to a conviction of the Bible's authority.[15] When the Roman Catholic oratorian Jean Morin highlighted difficult passages to exegete in the Scriptures, he did so with the intention of forcing Protestants to acknowledge that without church traditions, they could never arrive at a proper interpretation of the text. Protestants argued in response that the Bible was a sure, infallible Word and that Scripture interprets Scripture. These apologists did not borrow their arguments essentially from "Aristotelian Roman Catholic opponents" as Rogers and McKim assert. The authors have apparently not had the occasion to assess the dynamics of Roman Catholic/Protestant interchanges in the sixteenth and seventeenth centuries. The "new Pyrrhonism" was evident in Roman Catholic apologetics as late as Richard Simon's day (1638–1712).

THE BIBLE AS AN INFALLIBLE RULE OF FAITH AND PRACTICE IN THE SIXTEENTH AND THE EARLY SEVENTEENTH CENTURIES

For Rogers and McKim, the designation that the Bible is an infallible rule for faith and practice is pivotal for their argument. They find this expression, or ones similar to it, in Reformation and post-Reformation discourse. They cite these expressions as proof that the Reformers and their immediate followers limited the infallibility of the Bible to matters of faith and practice. But once again Rogers and McKim unfortunately misread the context out of which Reformation Christians made these statements. Certainly these Christians did believe the Scriptures communicate infallible truths about "faith and practice." But they did not intend to create by their expressions a limitation on the extent of infallibility of the biblical text. The issue was otherwise. As we indicated earlier, Roman Catholic apologists had argued in the sixteenth and seventeenth centuries that Protestants needed the teachings of the Church (councils, tradition, papal pronouncements) in addition to biblical data, in order to apprehend correct instruction about salvation. For example, in his 1609 Catechism the famous Roman Catholic Guillaume Baile presented this question and answer for lay persons:

> Are all things necessary for our salvation found expressly in Scripture? No. It is for this reason that Scripture sends us back to Traditions some of which being divine have as much authority as if they were written.[16]

To this kind of Roman Catholic claim, Protestants frequently responded that the Bible alone was the sufficient and infallible rule of faith and practice. That is, Christians do not ultimately need other sources of information (councils, tradition, et al.) in order to formulate their soteriology, useful as some of these sources were. It did not cross the minds of these Protestants to use this expression as a phrase circumscribing the extent of biblical infallibility.

Article V of the French Confession of Faith (A.D. 1559) establishes well the context for the expression "rule of faith":

> ... And inasmuch as it [the Bible] is the rule of all truth, containing all that is necessary for the service of God and for our salvation, it is not lawful for men, nor even angels, to add to it, to take away from, or to change it. . . .[17]

The Bible alone is sufficient to inform us about our salvation and how we should serve God; we do not need any other source of information as Roman Catholics constantly stipulated. The Bible is also "the rule of all truth."

Frequently Protestant churches and individual writers proposed in one section of a creed or theological treatise that the Bible is an infallible rule of faith and practice, and elsewhere in the same creed or treatise that all the words of the biblical text are without any error whatsoever. In that Rogers and McKim do not fully acknowledge the context into which many Protestants placed the expression "the only infallible rule of faith and practice," they tend to ignore passages that counter their interpretation. For example, in treating the Belgic Confession of Faith (1561), they cite the seventh article, "The Sufficiency of Holy Scriptures to be the Only Rule of Faith."[18] They point out a reference in it to the Bible as an "infallible rule," but they pass over a clause of Article 5 of the same confession that indicates that "all things contained within them (the Scriptures)" are to be believed:

> We receive all these books, and these only, as holy and canonical, for the regulation, foundation, and confirmation of our faith, believing, without any doubt all things contained in them, not so much because the Church receives them. . . .[19]

Or, in considering the Scots Confession of 1560, Rogers and McKim note Article XX's discussion of councils, but do not make explicit the reason why the Scots were to refuse the authority of councils:

> For plaine it is, as they wer men, so have some of them manifeslie erred, and that in matters of great weight and importance.[20]

The teachings of councils could be accepted to the extent that they reflected the Word of God, which by implication did not err as did the participants at councils.[21]

In his *Sur les Conciles et les Commandments* . . . , Pierre Viret (1511–1571), an associate of Calvin, declared that he accepted the Scripture's authority on the basis of the Holy Spirit's witness.[22] Citing St. Augustine as his mentor, he noted that books of the Bible contained no errors and thus served as "infallible rules" for judging doctrine:

[The Holy Spirit] did not permit any error to be mixed in their books, because He wanted to leave them for us as infallible rules with which to examine doctrines.[23]

Viret contrasted the supreme authority of a completely infallible Bible with that of popes, councils, and other Roman Catholic authorities.

Pierre Du Moulin's *Du juge des controverses traitté auquel est defendu l'authorité & la perfection de la Saincte Escritures* (1630) represents an important Reformed apologetic of the early seventeenth century.[24] In it the author indicates that French Reformed Christians believed the Bible to be a sovereign judge and *"regle infaillible de nostre foy"* and that all Christian churches of the world agreed that it was "divine," "sacred," and "the word of God" (pp. 64–65). He noted that the apostles were infallibly inspired by the Holy Spirit (p. 211). He proposed that the *"originaux"* of the Bible were uncorrupted whereas the Roman Catholic Vulgate was error marked (p. 18):

> But if the truth of the *originaux* of the Bible had been put in doubt then the rule of faith would not have been assured (p. 322).[25]

But the Jews kept the *originaux* "en leur pureté" (p. 322). Even though his philosophical propensities were Aristotelian, as Rogers and McKim rightly observe, Pierre du Moulin in good Reformed fashion argued that Scripture should interpret Scripture (p. 412), that our reason is well founded only when it conforms to the Word of God (p. 261), and that it is by the witness of the Holy Spirit that the *"fideles"* come to accept the authority of the Holy Scriptures (pp. 321–22).[26]

The English apologist, William Whitaker (1548–1595), helps us to understand to what part of the Scripture some Protestants referred in using the expression the "rule of faith." Whitaker was Regius Professor of Divinity at Cambridge University for many years.[27] The famous Catholic disputant Bellarmine recognized him as one of Protestantism's most able defenders.[28] Writing in the last quarter of the seventeenth century, the Roman Catholic biblical critic, Richard Simon, did the same in his *Histoire critique du Vieux Testament* (1678):

> In addition, I have gone into more detail about the sentiments which Whitaker had of Bellarmine and other Jesuits, because that ought to serve as a key for understanding countless books which have been written thereafter by Protestants of France, England, and Germany against the books of Bellarmine.[29]

Not well known to us today, Whitaker was a godly man, held in high esteem by his contemporaries.[30]

Whitaker identified the rule of faith with the Bible in his *Disputation on Holy Scripture* (1588), the most extensive book on Scripture written by an Englishman in Elizabeth's day.[31] In response to a Bellarmine charge, Whitaker makes it clear that the rule of faith included everything written in the Scriptures—histories and the like, not "salvation truths" only:

> Is it not necessary for us to know the commencement of the church, its propagation, and continual conservation and government, and the promises made to the patriarchs concerning the Messiah? Surely he blasphemes who denies this... although it may be conceded that all the histories are not equally useful and necessary, because many may be saved without the knowledge of many histories; yet in reality they are all not only useful, but necessary also. For although they are not all requisite to the being of faith, yet they contribute greatly to its better being... although perhaps more things than can be styled simply necessary are delivered in scripture, yet it does not therefore follow that the scripture is not a rule. For although the scripture contains some things which are not simply and absolutely necessary; nevertheless, it is a rule to which all doctrine ought to be conformed. We say that the Scriptures are a rule, because they contain all things necessary to faith and salvation, and more things may be found in them than absolute necessity requires. We do not attach so strict and precise a notion to the term "rule" as to make it contain nothing but what is necessary ... (pp. 660–61).[32]

Whitaker's description of the Bible's contents resembles closely one proposed by Bishop John Jewel in his *Treatise of the Holy Scriptures* published eighteen years earlier (1570).[33]

In his *Disputation on Holy Scripture*, Whitaker, an Anglican known for his Puritan sympathies, affirmed his belief in complete biblical infallibility:

> But, say they, the church never errs; the pope never errs. We shall shew both assertions to be false in the proper place. We say that scripture never errs, and therefore judge that interpretation to be the truest which agrees with scripture (p. 476).

He cited St. Augustine as an authority who had earlier advocated this same position:

> ...we cannot but wholly disapprove the opinion of those, who think that the sacred writers have, in some places, fallen into mistakes. That some of the ancients were of this opinion appears from the testimony of Augustine, who maintains, in opposition to them, "that the evangelists are free from all falsehood, both from that which proceeds from deliberate deceit, and that which is the result of forgetfulness."[34]

Whitaker suggested that, whereas Erasmus and perhaps even St. Jerome, had allowed for small errors due to "slips of memory," "...it becomes us to be so scrupulous as not to allow that any such slip can be found in Scripture."[35] Continued Whitaker:

For, whatever Erasmus may think, it is a solid answer which Augustine gives to Jerome: "If any, even the smallest, lie be admitted in the scriptures, the whole authority of scripture is presently invalidated and destroyed."[36]

Whitaker denied specifically, for example, that Stephen had made an error in Acts 7:16:

Stephen, therefore, could no more have mistaken than Luke; because the Holy Ghost was the same in Luke and in Stephen. . . . Therefore we must maintain in tact the authority of Scripture in such a sense as not to allow that anything is therein delivered otherwise than the most perfect truth required.[37]

Whitaker's own beliefs and his interpretation of St. Augustine belie Rogers and McKim's interpretation that Englishmen with Augustinian sympathies advocated a biblical infallibility limited to matters of faith and practice.

Was Whitaker himself an early Protestant "rationalist," emphasizing reason's powers to establish biblical authority? No, he saw himself differently. He reviewed Calvin's discussion of the external testimonies to biblical authority but, like Calvin, he stressed the Holy Spirit's role in this regard:

These topics may prove that these books are divine, yet will never be sufficient to bring conviction to our souls so as to make us assent, unless the testimony of the Holy Spirit be added. When this is added, it fills our minds with a wonderful plentitude of assurance, confirms them, and causes us most gladly to embrace the scriptures, giving force to the preceding arguments. Those previous arguments may indeed urge and constrain us; but this (I mean the internal testimony of the Holy Spirit) is the only argument which can persuade us.[38]

Or, he wrote: "But in like manner as no man can certainly assent to the doctrine of faith except by the Spirit, so can none assent to the scriptures but by the same Spirit."[39] Whitaker wrote as a person much indebted to John Calvin.

We could refer to other spokesmen drawn from Puritan and Continental Reformed and Lutheran ranks to demonstrate our contention that Protestants did not intend to limit the extent of infallibility by describing the Bible as an "infallible rule of faith and practice." Such an idea was foreign to their mind-set (but not to that of some later Calvinists). Rogers and McKim do not faithfully represent their perspectives in this regard.

THE POST-REFORMATION PERIOD AND BIBLICAL INFALLIBILITY

Rogers and McKim should be applauded for their conversance with recent scholarship concerning what some have called post-

Reformation orthodoxy, which others have labeled Protestant scholasticism. Studies by Jill Raitt, Brian Armstrong, John P. Donnelly, and others have broken new ground in our understanding of the thought of late sixteenth- and seventeenth-century theologians.[40] Much work remains to be accomplished in this field where several new hypotheses are more exciting than reliable.[41]

Rogers and McKim are less helpful, however, when they attempt to relate these studies to one of their paramount interests: biblical infallibility.[42] They portray many of the continental Protestant theologians of the seventeenth century as uncritical disciples of Aristotle and therefore "scholastics." These theologians were the ones who introduced complete biblical infallibility to Protestant communions and began to treat the Bible's words as conveyors of technically correct information about the world. Whereas the Reformers accented the saving function of the Bible's message, the "scholastics" emphasized its literary form. In brief, they departed significantly from the teachings of Luther and Calvin.

For Rogers and McKim, Melanchthon launches what became the scholastic movement for the Lutherans, while Theodore Beza (1519–1605), influenced by several Italian Aristotelians, did the same for the Reformed communities.[43] In England, Puritans were largely spared from falling under scholasticism's sway. Their philosophical premises, frequently drawn from Ramist sources, acted as effective antidotes.[44] Unfortunately, John Owen (1616–1683) eventually turned some of his fellow Englishmen toward scholasticism later in the seventeenth century.[45]

Rogers and McKim's analysis stumbles at several points. First, despite much discussion about the place of predestination in seventeenth-century Reformed thought, the divines' penchant for metaphysics and other matters, the authors never elucidate persuasively why the usage of "Aristotelian" logic or categories led so-called "scholastics" to formulate a belief in complete biblical infallibility.[46] Perhaps it is for this reason they do not tell us who was the first theologian to make the doctrinal innovation. If no Protestant theologian had previously entertained the idea, it is strange that contemporaries did not signal the name of this influential innovator, so concerned were they about doctrinal innovations. Second, and on a contrary note, Rogers and McKim do not adequately explain why the Ramist philosophical dispositions of certain English Puritans should have kept them from affirming biblical inerrancy. Perhaps their silence on the point stems from the disconcerting reality that there were Ramists who affirmed complete biblical infallibility. Third, the authors' categories for understanding the philosophical options of the seventeenth century are quite restricted. They do not capture the complex philosophical combinations sometimes found in the thought of an individual theologian. We should explain the nature of our reservations in greater detail.

After commenting upon the careers of Melanchthon, Peter Martyr, G. Zanchi, and Theodore Beza, among others whom they describe as "transitional figures," Rogers and McKim wisely observe, "It remains difficult to give a clear and comprehensive definition of Reformed scholasticism" (p. 185).[47] And they note, "We need to speak of shifts of emphasis rather than drastically different doctrines when we contrast Calvin with his scholastic followers" (p. 185). And yet two pages later (p. 187), the authors abandon their former caution:

> In theological method and especially in their view of the authority and interpretation of Scripture, post-Reformation scholastics were more like Thomas Aquinas and his medieval approach than they were like Calvin and his Reformation position.

This latter charge is a remarkable one, given their previous statements. The comments of Professor Olivio Fatio (University of Geneva) about the misleading character of that historiography (works by H. E. Weber, E. Bizer, W. Kickel, and others) that poses "a process of increasing objectivization from the existential beginnings of the Reformation" to a rational doctrinal system should have been considered by the authors.[48]

Absent from Rogers and McKim's study is any sustained interaction with Robert Preus's detailed studies of Lutheran divines in the late sixteenth and seventeenth centuries.[49] Preus, who has examined the primary sources of these Lutheran theologians more than any other present-day scholar, does not find that they engaged in any essential distortion of Luther's thought about biblical authority.[50] Also absent from the authors' discussion are the conclusions of John Robinson, who has studied the primary sources of continental Reformed theologians with remarkable care. His doctoral dissertation, "The Doctrine of Holy Scripture in Seventeenth Century Reformed Theology" (1971), was directed by François Wendel, the renowned Calvin scholar from the Protestant Faculty, the University of Strasbourg.[51] A reading of this thesis would have well served the authors, who beginning with the seventeenth century, focus their attention almost exclusively upon Reformed traditions, despite the title of their volume.

Based upon his reading of the writings of the principal Reformed theologians of France, the United Provinces, and Switzerland, Robinson makes these general observations that have a bearing upon Rogers and McKim's interpretation:

1) The use of scholastic terminology (essence, accidents, materia . . .):

> This scholastic terminology regarding Scripture was used in a standing controversy with the Roman Catholics concerning the chronologi-

cal precedence of the Scripture versus that of the Church.... Perhaps the most significant thing about the use of these scholastic terms in defining the nature of Scripture is that the majority of the seventeenth-century Reformed theologians made relatively little use of them (pp. 28–29, 183).

2) The commitment to biblical infallibility *before* the writings of John Owen and Francis Turretin:

[Johannes Hoornbeeck (1617–1666) offered excerpts from a number of prominent Dutch theologians of the late sixteenth and early seventeenth centuries in support of the following statement.]

All the Scriptures are divinely inspired; nothing at all was written except what the Holy Spirit himself included; thus nothing whatsoever was in fact able to be in error (p. 41).

3) The role of the Holy Spirit in confirming the authority of Scripture:

Regardless of how the Scriptures were related to the work of the Spirit in the heart, it is this interior action of the Holy Spirit which was considered to be decisive (pp. 55, 185).

[Robinson cites a passage from Polanus (1561–1620) in this regard. Polanus was twice rector of the University of Basel, philosophically sympathetic to Ramus, and a believer in complete biblical infallibility]:

So that one may be persuaded by the certainty of faith that Scripture is from God, and that he accepts it not as the word of men but, as it is in truth, as the word of God which acts in you who believe, it needs the internal witness of the Holy Spirit (p. 56).

According to Robinson, the seventeenth-century Reformed divines molded their thought about the Scripture in the context of polemics with Roman Catholics, in contact with Aristotelian philosophy, and under the influence of John Calvin. He concludes, however, with a pivotal remark: "Their efforts to present a theology of the Scriptures consisted above all in an attempt to determine the teaching of the Bible about itself" (p. 195). Against the panoply of Robinson's sturdy analysis of the primary sources, Rogers and McKim's analysis appears less than strong.

The authors reveal one of the weaker interfaces of their interpretation when they link different philosophical preferences with inerrancy or errancy. Their paradigm that "Aristotelians" were generally deductivists, rationalistic, and inerrantists whereas Platonists/Ramists were generally inductivists, fideistically inclined, and believers in limited infallibility is simplistic and reductionistic.[52] And yet they use a form of these paradigms throughout their volume. It is particularly inappropriate for any analysis of seventeenth-century theologians. In that century one can find individuals with sympathies for either Aristotle, or Plato, or Descartes, or Ramus, who affirmed complete biblical infallibility. The philosophical presuppositions of a thinker did not necessarily fashion his attitudes about that subject.

The authors' presentation wavers at another point as well. Paul Dibon, Hautes Études, Paris, has analyzed painstakingly the relationship between philosophical currents and theological discourse in the United Provinces in the seventeenth century. He finds that there were theologians who combined in one person an appreciation for Ramus and Aristotle.[53] In his study, *Scripture in the Westminster Confession*, Rogers himself notes that the Westminster Divines had been influenced by both Aristotle and Ramus.[54] Then again, some Reformed theologians attempted to discover the teachings of the real Aristotle, whom they opposed to the Aristotle of the "scholastic" Roman Catholics.[55] Moreover, in the works of these theologians, praise for Aristotle can fall upon one page and praise for Plato on another.[56] Or, a theologian could appreciate Aristotle's emphasis upon syllogistic logic while being disconcerted about other aspects of the Greek's teachings.[57] Rogers and McKim's interpretative grid does not fit well over the multiformed contours of theological and philosophical discourse in the seventeenth century. Interestingly enough, Rogers presents a more refined interpretation in his *Scripture in the Westminster Confession* (1967) than in the present volume.

In the present study the authors' blanket charges are simply overdrawn. Many of the seventeenth-century divines were pious Christians, sincere in following their Lord.[58] It is quite unfair to infer, that for them, "reason had at least equal standing with faith in religious matters . . ." or to suggest that they had "substituted philosophical speculation for growth in the Christian life as the goal of theological work . . ." (p. 186).[59]

Geoffrey Bromiley, for many years Professor of Church History at Fuller Theological Seminary, warns us about digging a chasm between Luther and Calvin and the continental Protestant theologians of the late sixteenth and early seventeenth centuries:

> In these writers the doctrine of scripture is no doubt entering on a new phase. Tendencies may be discerned in the presentation which give evidence of some movement away from the Reformation emphases. The movement, however, has not yet proceeded very far. The tendencies are only tendencies. What change there has been is more in style, or, materially, in elaboration. The substance of the Reformation doctrine of scripture has not yet been altered, let alone abandoned.[60]

Unfortunately, Rogers and McKim, who cite Professor Bromiley extensively concerning the "tendencies" of post-Reformation theologians, did not take the church historian's warning to heart, as judged by their more extreme statements.[61]

THE "AUTHENTIC ORIGINALS" AND INFALLIBILITY

Another point of dispute between Protestants and Roman Catholics in the sixteenth and early seventeenth centuries centered upon the "authenticity" of their respective Bibles. The quest by Christian humanists to establish the authentic originals set the stage for this debate. Basil Hall writes: "The desire of the biblical humanists had been to arrive at an authentic text of the Hebrew and Greek originals which they believed to have greater authority than the Vulgate since it was taken for granted that this version came later in time than the others."[62] After the Fourth Session of the Council of Trent (April 8, 1546)[63] declared that the Vulgate was the only "authentic" version, the question of the "authentic originals" became even more hotly contested.

In his debate (1588) with Bellarmine, the English apologist Whitaker, whom we encountered earlier, discussed in detail the meaning of the word *authentic* as it relates to the "originals." In consonance with the Council of Trent, Bellarmine and other Roman Catholic apologists had claimed that Jerome's Latin Vulgate was authentic. Whitaker, and other Protestants with him, responded by saying that only the Hebrew and Greek originals were the authentic ones:

> We, on the contrary side, say that the authentic and divinely-inspired scripture is not this Latin, but the Hebrew edition of the Old Testament, and the Greek of the New.[64]

Translations were not authentic (pp. 144–45):

> . . . we do not say that one should stand by these translations as of themselves authentic, but appeal to the originals alone as truly authentic.

Like the Westminster Confession after him, Whitaker indicated that the Holy Spirit was the source of truly authentic Scripture:

> For authentic scripture must proceed immediately from the Holy Ghost himself . . . (2 Tim. 3:16); now Jerome's translation is not divinely inspired; therefore it is not authentic scripture (p. 148).

But what specifically did the Englishman mean by the "originals"? Was he referring to the original autographs or to the Greek and Hebrew texts he had in hand? He apparently used the expression *originals* for both. Whitaker wrote about the original autographs:

> That Scripture only, which the prophets, apostles, and evangelists wrote by inspiration of God, is *in every way* [italics mine] credible in its own account and authentic (p. 138).

But he assumed that the Hebrew and Greek texts of his own day (except for the Septuagint) so closely reflected the autographs that they too, in one sense, could be justly classified as "originals."[65] God had protected His Word as it passed from copyist to copyist through the ages (Protestants generally believed that the Jews had been very solicitous to preserve the integrity of the Hebrew text).[66]

When Bellarmine claimed that there were errors in the "originals" as represented by the extant Hebrew and Greek texts, Whitaker responded sharply:

> These then are the passages which Bellarmine was able to find fault with in the originals; and yet in these there is really nothing to require either blame or correction. But, even though we should allow (which we are so far from doing, that we have proved the contrary), that these were faulty in the original, what could our adversaries conclude from such an admission? Would it follow that the Hebrew fountain was more corrupt than the Latin streamlets, or that the Latin edition was authentic? Not, surely, unless it were previously assumed, either that canonical books of scripture cannot be erroneously copied sometimes by transcribers . . . (p. 160).

Whitaker, then, blamed any conceivable error on transcribers' mistakes.[67] No error existed in the autographs. On the contrary, the Vulgate possessed real errors in the autograph itself that were not due to the negligence of copyists:

> The Latin Vulgate edition is most certainly and most plainly corrupt. And the corruptions I speak of are not casual, or slight, or common errors, such as the carelessness of copyists often produces in books; but errors deeply rooted in the text itself, important and intolerable. Hence is drawn the weightiest argument against the authority of this edition (p. 162).

By appealing to the "originals" as the authentic text of Scripture, Whitaker believed he had admirably countermanded the Roman Catholic claim regarding the authority of the Vulgate.

The concept of "originals" was not restricted to Reformed communities. Hugo Grotius, the influential "political scientist," who was associated with the Remonstrant, or Arminian, cause in the early seventeenth century, argued that the originals of the New Testament had remained extant until Tertullian's day, after which they were lost.[68]

So closely did some Protestants tie biblical authority to the "originals" hypothesis that the Roman Catholic apologist, Jean Morin, specifically determined to overthrow that premise in his important *Exercitationes* on the Bible.[69] He argued that the originals could possess little authority because they had been lost. Richard Simon, the biblical critic, felt constrained to censure Morin for his faulty scholarship and for the ultimately skeptical implications of his proposal:

> He [Morin] declared at the beginning [of his *Exercitationes*], that his purpose is to combat Protestants, who boast that they have no other rule in their Religion than the originals of the Bible; as if it is not evident that the first originals have been lost. . . . This is why the opinion of P. Morin

must be modified, who under the pretext of defending the authority of ancient translations received by a long usage in the Church, tried to destroy the authority of the Hebrew text, as it was given to us by the Jews.[70]

Simon preferred to follow the tack of St. Augustine whom he described as one who wanted to approach the lost originals as closely as possible through the exercise of criticism.

> But because men were the depositories of the Sacred Books, as well as all other books, and because the first originals have been lost, it was in some regards impossible to avoid several changes, due more to the passage of time, than to the negligence of copyists. It is for this reason that St. Augustine above all recommends to those who wish to study the Scripture, to apply themselves to the Criticism of the Bible, and to correct the mistakes in their copies.[71]

In espousing this position, Simon gingerly walked a fine line just as Erasmus, Cardinal Cajetan, Santi Pagnini, and others had tried to do before Trent. To placate Catholic authorities, he acknowledged that the Vulgate was the "authentic" version; to be true to his own scholarship, he informed his readers that more accurate versions of the Scriptures lay behind Jerome's version.[72] Simon's perplexing dilemma had been experienced by other informed biblical critics after Trent. Jacques Le Brun's recent essay, *"Sens et portée du retour aux origines dans l'oeuvre de Richard Simon,"* provides a superb summary of Simon's discussion of the "lost originals" hypothesis.[73] The "authentic originals" concept played an important role in the controversies of some but not all Roman Catholics and Protestants in the sixteenth and seventeenth centuries. Those scholars who suggest that the idea of a completely infallible Bible in the original autographs is a late nineteenth-century construction would do well to reconsider these controversies. Moreover they should recall Erasmus's line of argument in his 1515 letter to Martin Dorp.

The attitudes of Protestants toward Holy Writ come into much better focus by placing them in the context of their multifaceted debates with Roman Catholics regarding biblical authority (its provenance and its actualization). These attitudes become even more clearly delineated when one examines diverse challenges to biblical infallibility in the sixteenth and seventeenth centuries. These challenges were mounted by both Christians and non-Christians alike. We now turn to that subject.

Chapter V

Challenges to Biblical Infallibility in the Sixteenth and Seventeenth Centuries

If Luther, Calvin, and other Reformers held that biblical infallibility extended to all the words of the canonical Scriptures, and if, as Professor Bromiley indicates, the post-Reformation "orthodox" did no more than elaborate or emphasize too heavily certain aspects of Reformation doctrine about Scripture, an important question comes to mind: What was the nature of the first significant attacks against complete biblical infallibility during and after the Reformation? Rogers and McKim do not treat this subject as such. Nowhere do we find in their essay sustained discussions dedicated to continental thinkers like Hugo Grotius[1] who influenced Jean Le Clerc, La Peyrère (who influenced Spinoza and Richard Simon),[2] William Holden (who influenced Simon),[3] Spinoza[4] (who particularly set the stage for biblical criticism in the Enlightenment), Richard Simon (another important biblical critic for Enlightenment authors), or to Jewish writers whose works on occasion caused consternation among Christians. Because the story the authors tell lacks several pivotal elements, it calls for a careful exposition of the attacks against complete biblical infallibility in the late sixteenth and seventeenth centuries.

A forthcoming study will treat the origins of modern biblical criticism in some detail.[5] Here we will briefly sketch the general configurations of some of the diverse challenges to complete biblical infallibility. To this day scholars debate how these challenges tore at the fabric of traditional world views in "Christian" Europe.[6] Much work remains to be accomplished regarding these challenges and their impact on developments in science, changing appreciations of non-Christian cultures, and new concepts of the state.

Already, in the first half of the sixteenth century, Christian humanists struggled with textual problems in the Bible. They encountered them as they applied a historical-grammatical hermeneutic to the available biblical manuscripts. Following the example of Lorenzo Valla and Erasmus, they generally refused to escape these problems by retreating to an allegorical approach, which was so frequently summoned during the Middle Ages.[7] A few exegetes demonstrated a noticeable tolerance for admitting potential "errors" in Holy Writ (including perhaps Erasmus himself).[8] Nevertheless, they often felt uneasy. How could they reconcile their findings with traditional beliefs about biblical infallibility? Other Christian humanists with like philological and critical skills exercised dexterity and discipline in attempts at harmonizing any potential contradiction in the Bible. The brilliant John Calvin was a well known participant in this latter group. Thus, for some, the very pursuit of the historical-grammatical meaning of biblical texts (rather than their allegorical significance) aroused concern about the Bible's infallibility.

Another challenge emerged from a loosely knit group of thinkers variously called *libertines* (both theological and moral).[9] Calvin himself wrote against them. Their common beliefs have been well surveyed by René Pintard in his massive study, *Le libertinage érudit dans la première moitié du XVIIe siècle* (Paris: Boivin, 1943). Numbering in their midst Pierre Charron, La Mothe le Vayer, Gabriel Naudé, Gui-Patin, and others, these individuals borrowed many of their arguments from the Pyrrhonistic arsenal in their veiled swipes at Christian authorities (the Bible, church traditions and leaders, et al.).[10] Perhaps a few were atheists; others were bare-boned deists who had shucked off Christian revelation and ecclesiastical authority. The sophisticated Roman Catholic priest, Mersenne, claimed in 1625 that there were 50,000 atheists in Paris.[11] Undoubtedly Mersene's figures are bloated, but they do point to a current of outright skepticism about the Christian religion in early modern France. Descartes hoped to provide a counter stroke to this form of skepticism in his own work.[12] As intellectual heirs of the Italian school of Padua (Pomponazzi, Vanini, Cremonini, and Bonamica), the *libertines* according to Henri Busson's studies did much damage in their concerted attacks on Christian miracles and rational apologetics.[13]

Roman Catholic writers such as Father Jean Morin so pushed the Pyrrhonistic argumentation against the clarity of Scripture that they also contributed to the undermining of biblical authority. Richard Simon complained about this unexpected result coming from Morin's writing.[14] Morin, a fellow Oratorian, had tried to force Protestants into the Roman Catholic camp by citing the difficulty of exegeting certain biblical passages without the help of Roman Catholic traditions. In this regard he followed the lead of Bellarmine and Stapleton whose arguments were more nuanced.

Another source of unease for defenders of biblical infallibility stemmed from Jewish sources. Anti-Semitic though some of them were, Christians on occasion sensed that Jews probably understood the Old Testament better than they.[15] In the late fifteenth century several Christians and Jews of Northern Italy cooperated in their study of the Hebrew texts and rabbinical commentaries.[16] In 1506 the Christian Hebraist Reuchlin published his *De Rudimentis Linguae Hebraicae*, which included a Hebrew dictionary designed to help Christians to learn Hebrew. He observed that "before me among the Latins no one appears to have done this."[17] Sebastian Münster of Basel created the first Aramaic grammar to be produced by a Christian. Moreover he drafted in Latin translation several works by Elias Levita (1468–1549). The writings of Levita, in particular, gave some Christians pause.

Levita raised questions about the Massoretic pointing of the Hebrew text. He suggested that the vowel points and accents were appended to the Hebrew text by Tiberian Jews centuries after Christ's life.[18] The Jesuits Genebrard and Guillaume Baile used this observation in an attempt to shake Protestants' confidence in the certainty of their Hebrew texts.[19] Could not unpointed Hebrew words be interpreted in many different ways? How could Protestants know that they interpreted the Old Testament correctly without the church's help? This question became all the more sensitive when the Reformed theologian, Louis Cappel, reiterated Levita's arguments in his *Arcanum punctuationes* (1624). In this work the theologian argued strongly against the inspiration of the Massoretic pointing. Protestant scholars throughout Europe were thrown into consternation by this development.[20] They had appealed to the originals in their apologetic skirmishes with Roman Catholics, and had done so with some success. Now Roman Catholics could cite Cappel's study (based on Levita and other Jewish writers) to undermine the certitude of those originals.[21]

Also of great import for Christian theologians were the writings of Aben Ezra (1089–1164).[22] This rabbi "wondered" how a complete Mosaic authorship of the Pentateuch could be defended, given various texts that militated against it (such as the account of Moses' death).[23] In his influential *Tractatus-theologico-politicus* (1670), Baruch Spinoza (himself having been expelled from a synagogue) specifically exploited Aben Ezra's list of problem texts and pointed out other ones from other books in the Old Testament in his attempt to destroy complete biblical infallibility. Spinoza wrote about the beliefs of his opponents:

> I grant that they [contemporary theologians] are never tired of professing their wonder at the profound mysteries of Holy Writ; still I cannot discover that they teach anything but speculations of Platonists and Aristotelians to which . . . they have made Holy Writ conform; . . . The very vehemence of their admiration for the mysteries plainly attests, that their

> belief in the Bible is a formal assent rather than a living faith; and the fact
> is made still more apparent by their laying down beforehand, as a foun-
> dation for the study and true interpretation of Scripture, the principle
> that it is in every passage true and divine.[24]

It should be noted that Spinoza assumed that Christians, whether
Platonists or Aristotelians, viewed all the contents of the Bible as infallible. He thought that if he could find only minor contradictions in the
Pentateuch and elsewhere, he could claim that he had accomplished
his task. Richard Simon, who developed his famous "public-scribes
hypothesis" in part to fend off the brunt of Spinoza's argumentation,
interacted vigorously with Aben Ezra's list of problem passages as
well.[25] Thus Jewish authors provided some of the data that both
Roman Catholics and skeptics employed in their duels with Protestants.[26]

Several prominent Protestant divines argued that the Massoretic
pointing was inspired by the Holy Spirit. The Buxdorfs of Basel, John
Owen, Francis Turretin, and others in the United Provinces and
elsewhere, did so. Eventually this retrograde stance was given creedal
status for several cantons of Switzerland in the Helvetic Consensus
Formula (1675). By arguing in this fashion, the divines wanted to
guarantee the certainty of the biblical text.[27] The records of the Company of Pastors at Geneva for September 21, 1677, reveal that its members were aware that Calvin and Luther had not held to the inspiration
of the pointing. Nonetheless the company approved the consensus
because

> the intention of those who drew up the formula had not been to decide
> about the antiquity or novelty of the points so as to combat one or the
> other or to condemn Zwingli or Pellican. It was only to establish the
> certitude of a Hebrew text as being alone authentic [and] by which ver-
> sions ought to be examined and interpreted and not the text by the
> versions. Without this there would be no certitude of the faith.[28]

The Company of Pastors (including Francis Turretin) was less doc-
trinaire and more theologically sophisticated than we often suppose.[29]

Rogers and McKim observe correctly that those Protestant theologians who accepted the divine inspiration of the Massoretic pointing
stepped beyond the teachings of the Reformers. But, as we saw earlier,
they assume incorrectly that these theologians' commitment to the
principle of complete biblical infallibility was itself novel. This belief
was well in line with the best Reformed and Lutheran traditions.

In his article, "Scepticism, Theology, and the Scientific Revolution
in the Seventeenth Century," Richard Popkin has convincingly argued
that the Christian world faced one of its most severe scientific challenges concerning biblical authority, not from Galileo and other

Copernicans, who in the face of opposition maintained that their scientific hypotheses accorded with a proper interpretation of an infallible Bible, but from the attempts by Christian thinkers to reconcile biblical history with the "new science":

> The flood, and the descendance of all mankind from Noah and his family provided serious difficulties when examined in the light of new geographical, anthropological, meteorological data, and mechanistic physics. Mersenne and Pascal, among others, had tried to explain how 40 days and 40 nights of rain could provide enough water to inundate the entire Earth so that even the highest mountain could be covered.... Archbishop Ussher (who calculated the date of Creation as 4004 B.C.) made valiant efforts to reconcile with the Bible the data obtained by the explorers.[30]

The problems of reconciling Scripture with new findings began to reach a crisis point particularly in Catholic Europe. Enter Isaac La Peyrère. Writes Popkin:

> ... the whole enterprise of reconciling Scripture and the new science was blown apart by a mad genius, Isaac La Peyrère (Pereira), who, I believe, really set off the warfare between theology and science.[31]

In his far-fetched study, *Men before Adam, or A discourse upon the twelfth, thirteenth, and fourteenth verses of the Fifth Chapter of the Apostle Paul to the Romans, By which are prov'd that the first Men were created before Adam* (Latin ed., 1655; English, 1658), La Peyrère developed his remarkable pre-Adamite theory.[32] He argued that recent data from America, China, and Greenland revealed that human beings existed as far back as 50,000 B.C., thus throwing into jeopardy the 4,004 B.C. date for creation supposedly derived from the historical materials in the Bible.[33] Popkin notes that La Peyrère proposed a "theory of the independent origin of different cultures, the local occurrence of the Flood, the derivation only of Judeo-Christians from Noah, etc."[34] He challenged a commitment to biblical infallibility by spinning hypotheses that directly countered biblical teachings. What's more, he did so as a Roman Catholic.

Reaction was swift. La Peyrère was hauled into prison in Brussels. He eventually recanted his novel ideas before the pope in Rome, blaming his "errors" on his Protestant upbringing.[35]

La Peyrère's influence was selective but immense. The principal founders of modern biblical criticism, Baruch Spinoza (1632–1677) and Richard Simon (1638–1712), were both intellectual debtors to his studies. Simon, for example, had long discussions with La Peyrère when the latter was an aged man in the late 1660s.[36]

The way Christian scholars exegeted the biblical accounts about Noah illustrates how seriously they took narratives that purportedly related historical data and why La Peyrère's ruminations were so unsettling. Commentators ranging from Augustine, Chrysostom, and Alcuin to Christian exegetes in the early seventeenth century exercised great ingenuity in their attempts to defend the historical accuracy of the Noah account.[37] They were obliged to answer questions concerning whether the size and the shape of the ark would have permitted adequate housing for the animals and what was the source that could provide sufficient water to create a universal Flood. Their diligent apologetic efforts did not satisfy all of their questioners.[38] Don C. Allen proposes that by the last quarter of the seventeenth century (and in the wake of La Peyrère and Georg Kirchmaier) a growing number of intellectuals disputed the historical reliability of the Noah story; in consequence, the Bible's own infallibility appeared more and more problematical. Allen writes:

> If the Flood was not universal, and it could not be proved so by either science ... or by reason, then for rational men another legend of the Scriptures was shown to be fallible. But the important aspect of the whole matter is that theologians now required the Bible to conform to the reason of men.[39]

Built upon misleading premises, Rogers and McKim's analysis does not adequately explain the efforts of early modern scientists to reconcile their investigations with biblical teachings. Many of these thinkers believed that all the words of Scripture were infallible.[40] Edward Brerewood, the first astronomer at Gresham College in the 1590s, wrote a lengthy piece, *Enquiries touching the Diversity of Languages and Religions through the chiefe parts of the world* (London, 1614), in which he tried to adjust new data coming from travel literature, the reports of mariners, the writings of antiquity, and his own observations, with what the Bible taught about the origins of languages and peoples.[41] Brerewood and other early modern scientists demonstrated admirable suppleness in attempting to come to grips with all the words of Scripture, not just those that bear on salvation truths. In introducing his uncle's posthumous "scientific" book (1614), Robert Brerewood affirmed that all European Protestants believed in the "infallible verity and full sufficiency of the Scriptures" (despite disagreement about other matters).

Although the writings of the famous Galileo did not precipitate per se a war between science and religion, they did disturb some Christians greatly.[42] As we recall, many believers in the sixteenth and early seventeenth centuries thought that their infallible Bible pictured the earth as the center of the universe. Galileo challenged various Aristotelian theories about motion; he also contended that the Bible, if rightly interpreted, allowed for a heliocentric theory of the universe.[43]

In a hastily written *Letter to Castelli* (December, 1613) and in a more carefully crafted *Letter to the Grand Duchess Christina* (June, 1615) Galileo set forth his highly controverted perspectives on the relationships between Scriptural teachings and science. In his *Letter to Castelli* Galileo addressed the question of biblical infallibility:

> [it was properly propounded to you by Madam Christina] and conceded and established by you, that Holy Scripture could never lie or err, but that its decrees are of absolute and inviolable truth. I should only have added that although Scripture can indeed not err, nevertheless some of its interpreters and expositors may sometimes err in various ways, one of which may be very serious and quite frequent [that is] when they would base themselves always on the literal meanings of the words.[44]

In the same letter he proffered a doctrine of accommodation (different from Calvin's) that implied that the findings of science should serve as a standard for judging the proper exegesis of Scriptural passages:

> ... [it is] moreover manifest that two truths can never contradict each other, [thus] it is the office of wise expositors to work to find the true senses of passages in the Bible that accord with those physical conclusions of which we have first become sure and certain by manifest sense or necessary demonstrations.[45]

Moreover, he tended to think that Scripture had priority over science only regarding articles of salvation.[46]

Learning that his *Letter to Castelli* might be used against him by Roman Catholic authorities, Galileo penned an amended and extended form of it, his *Letter to the Grand Duchess Christina* (June, 1615). In this epistle he appeared to moderate his former judgments:

> Yet even in those propositions which are not matters of faith, this authority [of the Bible] ought to be preferred over that of all human writings which are supported only by bare assertions or probable arguments, and not set forth in a demonstrative way. This I hold to be necessary and proper to the same extent that divine wisdom surpasses all human judgment and conjecture.[47]

A few pages later he noted:

> From the above words [referring to Augustine's *On Genesis* i. 21] I conceive that I may deduce this doctrine; that in the books of the sages of this world there are contained some physical truths which are soundly demonstrated, and others that are merely stated; as to the former, it is the office of wise divines to show that they do not contradict the Holy Scriptures. And as to the propositions which are stated but not rigorously demonstrated, anything contrary to the Bible involved by them must be held undoubtably false and should be proved so by every possible means.[48]

How to relate the contents of Galileo's first letter to those of his second has become a bone of contention for intellectual historians. Jerome Langford concludes that Galileo ultimately capitulated in the second letter to the widely accepted premise that teachings of the Bible are authoritative beyond matters of faith and practice: "Galileo, in this series of passages at least, makes the same mistake as Bellarmine did in conceding the highest authority to Scripture even in matters which are not of faith and morals. He gives strict scientific authority over physical arguments which are only probable."[49] In any case the proposals of Galileo's first letter were exploited by his detractors.

The year 1616 was an important one for the Roman Catholic Church and for Galileo's cherished hopes. Copernicus's *De revolutionibus* was put on the Index ("suspended until corrected") and the Carmelite Paoli Antonio Foscarini's *Lettera*, which defended the Copernican theory, was altogether prohibited. Then again, an epochal decree of 1616 condemned these principles: 1. The sun is the center of the universe and immobile. 2. The earth is neither the center of the universe nor immobile. Persuading certain members of the Roman Catholic hierarchy to accept the heliocentric theory of the universe was a more difficult task than Galileo had imagined. In 1633 he went on trial for his teachings.[50]

Although Galileo may have ultimately espoused complete biblical infallibility, some of his contemporaries used his line of thought to promote the idea that the incidental teachings of Scripture about the natural world do not have a priority over the "established truths of science." Interpreters of Francis Bacon have often portrayed him as one prominent intellectual who compartmentalized religion into its respective sphere and science into its own. Their interpretation is now being challenged.[51]

Galileo, Bacon, and others, therefore, presented Christian scientists with a perplexing question: Does the Bible speak about the external world in an accommodated language that does not capture the "reality" that the astronomer explores with his telescope?[52] If it does, how should biblical commentators interpret this language and relate it to the Bible's infallibility? Defining the meaning of biblical accommodation and establishing the priority of "scientific" claims versus those of the Bible became increasingly urgent tasks, just as they had been for Galileo's predecessor, Johannes Kepler.[53] In Protestant Europe where printers continued to publish the works of Galileo and Copernicus after 1616, these issues loomed especially large.[54] In our discussion of the Puritans we shall evaluate the ways English theologians and scientists interacted with them and other "scientific" questions.

The writings of René Descartes also had a bearing on not a few scholars' thinking about biblical authority. In 1628–1629 Descartes became convinced that a stronger answer was needed to stem the tide of the "new" Pyrrhonism. Richard Popkin describes his resolve:

> It was in the light of this awakening to the sceptical menace, that when he was in Paris Descartes set in motion his philosophical revolution by discovering something "so certain and so assured that all the most extravagant suppositions brought forward by the sceptics were incapable of shaking it."[55]

Although Descartes' program of methodological doubt expressed in his *Discours de la Méthode* (1637) was intended to thwart skepticism, several of his earliest critics, including the Jesuit Father Bourdin of Paris and Gisbert Voetius, the Rector of the University of Utrecht, argued that his negative method "cuts itself off from all hope of attaining to the light of truth" (Bourdin) and plunged its creator into a hopeless skepticism.[56]

Scholars have hotly debated Descartes's intentions in proposing his method.[57] It is very probable that he did not want to subvert the articles of the Christian faith that he had learned as a youth. Nevertheless, his premise that reason is the principal criterion of truth was employed by Baruch Spinoza and others to sift what was "truthful" out of the Bible.[58] And we recall, Spinoza, who was also steeped in rabbinical learning, concluded that the Bible was fallible.

In the early decades of the seventeenth century, Hugo Grotius proposed another approach to the Bible that was pregnant with implications for infallibility. Grotius was prepared to examine the biblical documents in their historical contexts and to conjecture about their emmendation.[59] He did so apparently with little concern for the confessional standards that some of his contemporaries used to guide their exegesis of the text. As long as the Bible was historically reliable, it could afford us with pertinent information about Christ and our salvation. The Remonstrant Jean Le Clerc relied upon Grotius's basic reasoning in his more radical criticism of biblical texts later in the century.

Despite these significant and worrisome attacks upon the Bible's infallibility, it is doubtless safe to say that the vast majority of Europe's theologians, pastors, and reading churchpersons still gave formal assent to that belief as the last quarter of the seventeenth century commenced. The clamor of the orthodox about "enthusiasts" who glorified the authority of an inner light, or "rationalists" who advocated the supreme authority of autonomous reason, should not lead us to assume that the latter individuals constituted more than distinct minorities. Whereas in the second half of the century some Anglican bishops like Edward Stillingfleet (1635–1699) proposed that infallibility must be posited only for "the doctrine we are to believe," English Puritans in the first half of the century generally maintained a commitment to complete biblical infallibility.[60] Celebrated for his cool and reasonable Christianity expressed in his *Reasonableness of Christianity* (1695), John Locke, the noted philosopher, had earlier crafted a defense of biblical infallibility in 1661.[61] On the Continent orthodox Lutherans and Reformed theologians kept the faithful alert to the wiles of *libertines*, Socinians, deists, and mystics by berating them in frenetic bursts of rhetoric. The full impact of Descartes's writings was not felt until after 1650. Protestants and Roman Catholics alike could and did underestimate La Peyrère as an eccentric. Spinoza's *Tractatus* was written in Latin, not in French, the language that had replaced Latin as the common literary coin of the Republic of Letters. Spinoza's devastating piece penetrated France but slowly under the guise of "false" title pages.[62] The Parisian circle of the erudite Henri Justel knew but bits and pieces of its contents as late as 1673. Christians from all communions shied away from Spinoza whom they mercilessly treated as a pariah. With the help of government censorship and ecclesiastical watchdogs like Bossuet, they still thought that they could check the spread of heterodox writings on Scripture. But by the 1680s, believers in England, France, the United Provinces, and elsewhere, whether Roman Catholic or Protestant, were no longer quite so confident. In particular the flow of illegal and heterodox books from the United Provinces, that haven of the French Refuge, could not be effectively dammed.[63] A respected printer like Reinier Leers of Rotterdam was prepared to publish a new edition (1685) of Richard Simon's *Histoire critique du Vieux Testament* (1678) even though the lieutenant of police in Paris had committed it to the flames a few months after its publication; Leers also served as the first publisher of Pierre Bayle's most significant *Dictionnaire historique et critique* (1697).[64] Participants in the Republic of Letters were now more prone to read the writings of a Simon, of a Bayle who exercised an arbitral role as editor of *News of the Republic of Letters* (1684–1687), or a Leibniz whose ideas were not squarely orthodox.[65] Deists in England received a more favorable hearing especially after the appearance of John Locke's *The Reasonableness of Christianity, as Delivered in the Scriptures* (1695). Attitudes toward biblical authority were apparently in full flux for some Europeans in the last two decades of the seventeenth century.

In many regards the vitriolic four-volume debate (1685–87) between Richard Simon and Jean Le Clerc was one of the culminating points in a complex movement away from complete biblical infallibility.[66] Taking place in what Paul Hazard has called, "The Crisis of the European Mind (1680–1715)," this debate shook the confidence of leading members of the Republic of Letters (ranging from John Locke to Pierre Bayle) in the complete infallibility of Holy Writ. Because it recapitulates several aspects of our discussion, we will consider the debate in some detail.

Not graced by physical attributes to commend him, Richard Simon (1638–1712) nonetheless wielded a pen at the end of the seventeenth century and at the beginning of the eighteenth that made many a European scholar take notice of him, if not bemoan his existence. Although he always portrayed himself as a good Catholic cleric, he designed a methodology for the criticism of the Scriptures that earned him the unwanted reputations of a "free thinker," a Socinian in Catholic garb, or even worse designations.[67] Simon's exposition of this methodology in his famous opus, *Histoire critique du Vieux Testament* and numerous other pieces, troubled both Protestants and Catholics, as had Spinoza's call for a rational and morally based critique of the Scriptures as spelled out in the *Tractatus Theologico-Politicus* (1670).[68] Simon argued that the biblical documents should be generally interpreted according to their historical-grammatical sense.[69] Contrariwise, they must not be read through the lenses of preconceived allegorical patterns or established dogma, save the "tradition"[70] of the Roman Catholic Church. Stoking himself with chocolate to stay awake, Simon wrote and researched through the day and deep into many a night as he sought to relieve his self-imposed burden of informing Christian Europe about its naïveté in biblical matters.[71]

Probably Simon, himself a little naïve, never expected the raging storm his publications stirred. Not only did Bossuet force the suppression of the 1678 edition of the *Histoire critique du Vieux Testament* (as he would later bring about the interdiction of Simon's 1702 Trévoux version of the *New Testament*),[72] but Simon's own order, the Oratorians, expelled him in 1678, Jansenists excoriated him, and a bevy of theologians reamed him roundly through rebuttal after rebuttal.[73]

Why did the theological heavens crash down on this French priest in 1678? Why did Simon face rank hatred from certain quarters for the rest of his days despite the righteousness of his campaign as he saw it? Quite simply, Simon wrote in French and too many scholars understood him; he offended too many of them on too many fronts. For conservative Protestants, Simon's attack on the perspicuity of the Scriptures, and any reliance upon the Holy Spirit's guidance in biblical interpretation, his skepticism about ever fully recovering the original autographs,[74] and his insistence upon the use of Catholic tradition in understanding the Scriptures, did not set well. For Bossuet and the Jansenists, Simon's anti-Augustinianism, his severe criticism of the church fathers (which in their eyes rendered the concept of tradition almost meaningless), his seeming disrespect for the Latin Vulgate, were nigh diabolical.[75] However, on one criticism of Simon conservative Protestants and Catholics could agree: Simon had denied that Moses wrote all of the Pentateuch. He must be a fellow traveler of that impious Spinoza—the specter of infidelity hovering over Europe.[76] Simon would have to be silenced.

Paradoxically enough, it was Spinoza about whom Simon was particularly worried. Recent scholarship questions whether Simon actually had in hand Spinoza's critique of the Mosaic authorship of the Pentateuch when he wrote sections of his *Histoire critique du Vieux Testament*.[77] We have argued elsewhere that he in fact did.[78] In any case, Simon boasted in the preface of his work that his own theories about the Pentateuch could handle any objections proposed by the "impious" Spinoza.[79] He argued that a group of "Public-Scribes" in Israel, using the Hebrew commonwealth's historical records, composed sections of the Pentateuch that manifestly Moses did not write—for example, the account of his death. These scribes had been authorized by Moses to do their work of abridging the commonwealth's records, and they were, like he, inspired of God.[80] By referring to this theory of "Public-Scribes," Simon could easily maintain a broad Mosaic authorship of the Pentateuch (Moses gave the scribes the authorization for their enterprise as New Testament writers would later allow their amanuenses to copy down their words), and at the same time explain differences in style, repetition of phrases and the like found in the Pentateuch.[81] To many Christians, Simon had exposed raw nerve endings of Old Testament exegesis rather than presenting an ingenious hypothesis to bolster the claims for the Mosaic authorship of the Pentateuch.

If anything, Jean Le Clerc (1657–1736), a Remonstrant theologian from Amsterdam, created even greater havoc in theological circles concerning that authorship. Even Simon seems to have been genuinely offended by Le Clerc's proposals.[82] Little wonder that in the eighteenth century, Jean Astruc (1684–1766) looked back at the Simon/Le Clerc controversy (1685–1687) as one of the decisive encounters in the history of ideas about the Bible.[83] Little wonder that in his *La Bible enfin expliquée ...* (1776), Voltaire cited the "savant Le Clerc" as one who had furnished proofs that Moses could not have written the book of Genesis.[84]

In 1685, Le Clerc published the *Sentimens de quelques Théologiens de Hollande ...*, which constituted his first wide-ranging critique of Richard Simon's *Histoire critique du Vieux Testament*. The timing of Le Clerc's piece could not have been better in that the famous 1685 edition of Simon's work came off the press in Rotterdam the same year.[85] Le Clerc's publication made him a celebrity in the Republic of Letters. His correspondence for the years 1685–1687, a good portion of which is found in the archives of the Remonstrant Seminary (housed presently at the University of Amsterdam library), indicates that some of his friends found his "advanced" ideas to their liking, while others tried to keep a distance from him.[86] Pierre Bayle, in the *News of the Republic of Letters*, indicated that Le Clerc's theses were too provocative.[87] As to more conservative commentators, they considered his ideas repugnant. Writing in the eighteenth century, Jean Senebier, a historian of Geneva's literature, described some of the reactions to Le Clerc's volume:

> Witsius attacked Le Clerc on the ideas which he had published relative to the inspiration of the Sacred Books in the *Sentimens de quelques Théologiens:* these objections are found in his *Exercitationes academicae.* Buddeus, in his *Institutiones theologicae*, pulverises the system of Le Clerc on inspiration. Fabricius complains that Le Clerc does not have enough respect for the sacred writers ... Simon tears him apart with indecency because he did not think like he did....[88]

Arnauld and Bossuet, both well known for their hostility to Simon, found the former oratorian less offensive than the outlandish Le Clerc.[89]

What was there about Le Clerc's volume that so excited passions? In the *Sentimens*, Le Clerc cleverly construed an account of what several unnamed theologians of Holland thought about Simon's classic work. According to the ruse, Le Clerc was merely reporting the reflections he had gathered while sitting in on their conversations. Thus he was not ostensibly the author of the volume.[90] As a matter of fact, he had penned it, although many contemporaries (including Simon) were partially taken in by his diversionary strategem.

The "theologians of Holland" (Le Clerc) leveled a major blast at Richard Simon's controversial "Public-Scribes" hypothesis. After having allegedly disposed of Simon's argument, they made their own proposal about who authored the Pentateuch:

> All of these traits come together in the person of the Israelite *sacrificateur* who was sent from Babylon in order to instruct the new inhabitants of Palestine concerning how they should serve God, as the author of the books of Kings recounts it in Chapter 17 of the second book.[91]

This hypothesis was by far a more radical one than Simon had propounded, for Moses played no role in its configuration.

Moreover, a Monsieur N. (one of the supposed theologians of Holland) made other daring proposals in Letters 11 & 12, devoted to the matters of biblical inspiration.[92] Relying more on Grotius than Spinoza, Monsieur N. (Le Clerc) conjectured that sections of the Scriptures (apart from the prophetical writings and Christ's own teachings) were merely historical accounts or lessons about a good system of morality, but they were not divinely inspired by the Holy Spirit.[93]

Nonetheless, Monsieur N. believed that orthodox doctrines about the divinity of Christ could be upheld even if the Gospels had not been directly inspired. The Gospels only needed to be reliable historical documents, which according to Monsieur N. they were.[94]

In brief, Le Clerc's volume encompassed a brazen attack upon orthodox views concerning not only the Mosaic authorship of the Pentateuch, but also the inspiration of the Gospels, and in consequence, the infallibility of the Bible. That the book caused a commotion is no surprise.

And yet the times were changing. Paul Hazard's description of the period (1680–1715) as the "Crisis of the European Mind" is perhaps too dramatic. But it does alert us that intellectual ferment was widespread. Among other considerations, individuals were reevaluating their ideas about the Bible's authority and what Christian doctrines could be affirmed with certitude. In 1690 the anonymous translator of an abridged edition of Le Clerc's *Sentimens* into English (*Five Letters Concerning the Inspiration of the Holy Scriptures Translated out of French*)[95] noted this spirit of inquiry as he tried to prepare his readers for the contents of Le Clerc's controversial letters:

> We live in an Age (as at all times) unbecoming the Dignity of such Sacred Truths, as the Christian Religion teaches us, to build them upon unsound Principles, or defend them by Sophistical Arguments; but it is also vain to attempt it, because impossible to execute. The Doctrine of Implicit Faith has lost its vogue. Every man will judge for himself, in matters that concern himself so nearly as these do. And nothing is now admitted for Truth, that is not built upon the Foundations of Solid Reason. Let not therefore any simple hearted pious Persons be scandalized at these Disquisitions. They are not calculated for their Use. But they are absolutely needful for many others, who are more Curious, and less Religious. And that they may be in some measure useful to the Propagation and Advancement of True Religion amongst such is the strong Hope, and hearty desire of the Translator.[96]

Along with other factors and events, the Simon/Le Clerc debate had undoubtedly played some role in creating this instability about biblical authority.[97] But let us recall that the arguments of the two disputants often reflected the thinking of Jewish, Christian, and even pagan predecessors. Moreover, the Roman Catholic Simon and the Protestant Le Clerc still used arms forged in the hot furnaces of earlier Roman Catholic and Protestant polemics. In fact, Simon and others blamed Protestantism's alleged commitment to private judgment and reason for undermining the authority of the Bible.[98] The crisis of the "European Mind," then, was long in the making. We have looked at only a few of the disparate challenges to complete biblical infallibility that contributed to it.

Let us also note that the reactions of intellectuals who encountered these challenges varied significantly. It has not been our purpose in this chapter to survey the various kinds of responses Christian defenders of biblical infallibility penned to counter the arguments of a Grotius, a Spinoza, a Simon, or a Jean Le Clerc. By the very number of apologetic replies that tumbled off of German presses, for example, we know that the orthodox were by no means pleased.[99] These replies probably strengthened the resolve of the faithful; many theologians and laypersons did uphold a belief in biblical infallibility in the next century. But these rejoinders did not effectively check the spread of anti-infallibility sentiments among certain quarters of the Republic of Letters. In one sense a Rubicon was traversed during the prelude to the European Enlightenment (1680–1715). Savants such as John Locke, Isaac Newton, and Pierre Bayle participated in that last generation in which notable European shapers of culture, who were not churchmen, seriously entertained the premise of complete biblical infallibility, at least for a time. The Voltaires, the Humes, the Rousseaus, the Diderots, the Lessings, and the Kants who followed them and who tended the Enlightenment of the eighteenth century no longer found that doctrine credible.

Even with its helpful comments about Bacon, Descartes, Cappel, the "deists," and the "Socinians," Rogers and McKim's study does not afford us with the makings of an ample backdrop for understanding the forces that drove some Europeans to consider abandoning their commitment to complete biblical infallibility.[100] In the late sixteenth and seventeenth centuries, the doctrine was not being created; a large number of Europeans experienced the trauma of trying to uphold it in the face of criticism sweeping in from many different directions.

Chapter VI

Reformed Traditions in the Seventeenth Century: A Reappraisal

Against the surging advances of the Counter Reformation, or Catholic Reformation, Protestants often proffered a united front. At least, that is the impression their apologists tried to promote as they faced off with Roman Catholic disputants. We recall that the Englishman Robert Brerewood unflinchingly proclaimed that all European Protestants believed in the "infallible verity and full sufficiency of the Scriptures" (1614).

Not only did "Protestants" sometimes declare that their beliefs were one regarding the crucial doctrines of the Christian faith, but Reformed Christians claimed on occasion that the Reformed churches scattered across Europe shared common doctrinal concerns. To ignore the existence of a movement of international Calvinism does not do justice to the perception of contemporaries. The Reformed Christians from various lands who gathered at the Synod of Dort (1618–1619) thought it important to resolve outstanding problems troubling the Reformed churches.[1] Their continuing concern about the Eucharistic controversy also gives evidence of their loyalties to each other. Roman Catholics and Protestants had engaged in a longstanding debate over the history of the Roman Catholic concept of transubstantiation.[2] Protestants consistently argued that the belief was innovative (a concept based on Aristotelian categories) and not biblically derived. In the late 1660s and early 1670s the Jansenists Pierre Nicole and the "Great Arnauld" defended the "perpetuity" of the belief in the Eucharist in several massive volumes. They provided alleged attestations from the eastern churches to the effect that the easterners had always advocated transubstantiation as well. If easterners had always held the belief, then it must be valid, or so went the polemical logic. Protestant spokespersons in England, the United Provinces, Switzerland, and France began to despair that an apologetic defeat of

Jean Claude, a French Reformed pastor of Charenton and the chief Protestant apologist in this round of the debate (1670s), might inflict a dangerous wound not only to the French Reformed churches but to European Protestantism. When one Reformed apologist suffered, Protestants suffered with him (if the dispute were with Roman Catholics). Anglican governmental officials attempted to furnish Jean Claude with eastern attestations of his own gathered by chaplain John Covel, a member of their diplomatic corps in Constantinople. A wild "attestation" chase ensued, involving not only the English diplomatic corps but the French and Dutch corps as well. European Protestants tried to stave off a Jean Claude defeat. His defeat would be their defeat. Their sense of solidarity cannot be denied.

Contrariwise, to minimize genuine differences of theological opinion and strategies among Reformed pastors and theologians, let alone between Reformed, Lutheran, and Anglican communions, does little justice to the varied theological, philosophical, and political contexts in which Protestant churches flourished. Then again, those "Christians without churches" whom Professor Leszek Kolakowski discusses with admirable encyclopedic erudition, upheld Christian beliefs and practices, a few of which were borrowed from Protestant stock ideas.[3] The unity and diversity of European Protestantism (and for that matter Roman Catholicism) render facile church histories of the seventeenth century less than helpful.

Rogers and McKim tend to play down the international character of Calvinism in the late sixteenth and early seventeenth centuries. They pit English Puritans who espoused a biblical infallibility that was limited to faith and practice against "scholastic" Reformed and Lutheran theologians on the Continent who became proponents of biblical inerrancy (pp. 200–203). Moreover they seek to isolate those factors that permitted the English Puritans to escape the unwelcomed fate that was supposedly befalling their colleagues across the channel. They conclude that the philosophical Ramism of the Puritans and the Aristotelianism of the continental Reformed and Lutherans go a long way to explain respective attitudes toward Holy Writ. We should consider this segment of Rogers and McKim's interpretation more fully.

I. THE WESTMINSTER CONFESSION OF FAITH AND BIBLICAL INFALLIBILITY

One of the most prominent pillars Rogers and McKim hoist into place to support their book's central proposal concerns the attitudes of English Puritans (particularly the divines of the Westminster Assembly, 1643–1649) toward Holy Writ.[4] Much of their discussion (pp. 200–218) is based on Rogers's study, *Scripture in the Westminster Confession: A Problem of Historical Interpretation for American Presby-*

terianism.[5] That work, therefore, should come under our purview in an evaluation of Rogers and McKim's joint study. On several counts it is a very impressive piece; on others, it confuses rather than illuminates.

According to our authors, the English Puritans affirmed limited biblical infallibility but did not adhere to a belief in biblical inerrancy. Rogers writes:

> For the authors of the Confession of Faith, the Scripture is infallible as a rule of interpreting its own central message of salvation in Jesus Christ. This certainly implies a different kind of infallibility than that contained in Papal authority.[6]

Remarkably enough in his brief discussion of inerrancy, Rogers does not offer a single illustration of a Westminster Divine who indicated that the Bible did err in any way (Rogers, *Scripture*, 305–6). This silence can be explained in several ways. Rogers would have us believe that "the question of the errancy or inerrancy of Scriptures is one which is strange to the Westminster Divines," because they drew up their Confession in an age (prescientific) when the problem had not yet emerged (Rogers, *Scripture*, 305–6). Thus the silence. On the contrary, Professor John Gerstner, against whom Rogers and McKim frequently spar in their joint book, argues that Rogers cannot find Westminster Divines who affirmed that the Bible did err in matters of history, science, geography, and the like.[7] Thus the silence. For Gerstner, the Westminster Divines' concept of infallibility should be equated with inerrancy. The Rogers/Gerstner discussion bears several striking resemblances to the Briggs/Warfield debate, which took place nearly one hundred years ago.[8] Moreover, Rogers does appreciate Briggs's scholarship, whereas Gerstner prefers Warfield's historical research on the matter.

It would be fruitless for us to enter into a thorough analysis of this debate, which has exercised these scholars and others for many years. Nonetheless, it might prove helpful to propose several general remarks based on additional mining of primary sources.

The burden of Rogers and McKim's demonstration tends to rest upon historical disjunctions; because the Westminster Divines believed that the primary purpose of the Bible is to teach salvation truths, and because they indicated that the internal witness of the Holy Spirit confirms the authority of the Scripture to the faithful, it follows that they did not believe in complete biblical infallibility (or inerrancy).[9] And once again, we suggest that adherence to those particular beliefs does not preclude a belief in the latter doctrine.

If we are to understand what the word *infallible* meant for the Divines, it might be valuable to consider the connotations their Puritan forebears gave to that term. Rogers and McKim argue that they were preserved from "scholasticism" because their philosophical premises were generally Ramist in orientation. In setting the stage for the Westminster Confession of Faith, Rogers in his thesis speaks about the theological influence of the Ramists, William Temple (1555–1627), William Perkins (1558–1602), and William Ames (1576–1633).[10] In that Ames is the last Ramist before Westminster whom Rogers approvingly discusses, the theologian's use of the word *infallible*, given Rogers's perspective, should be of particular import. Rogers observes: "Ames represents the Puritanism of which Miller [Perry] speaks when he says that 'the dialectic of Ramus was blended perfectly with the theology of Augustine and Calvin'" (p. 94).

Ames presents his views on Scripture in a popular text, *The Marrow of Sacred Divinity* (1623, 1627, 1629), a work used for many years at Harvard College and later at Yale College in North America, and elsewhere on the Continent.[11] We cite his statement on Scripture in full because of its significance (Book I, Chapter 34):

2. Only those could set down the rule of faith and conduct in writing who in that matter were free from all error because of the direct and infallible direction they had from God.

4. They also wrote by the inspiration and guidance of the Holy Spirit so that the men themselves were at that point, so to speak, instruments of the Spirit. . . .

5. But divine inspiration was present among those writers in different ways. Some things were altogether unknown to the writer in advance, as appears in the history of past creation, or in the foretelling of things to come. But some things were previously known to the writer, as appears in the history of Christ written by the apostles. Some things were known by a natural knowledge and some by a supernatural. In those things that were hidden and unknown, divine inspiration was at work by itself. In those things which were known, or where the knowledge was obtained by ordinary means, there was added the writers' devout zeal so that (God assisting them) they might not err in writing.

6. In all those things made known by supernatural inspiration whether matters of right or fact, God inspired not only the subjects to be written about but dictated and suggested the very words in which they should be set forth. But this was done with a subtle tempering so that every writer might use the manner of speaking which most suited his person and condition.[12]

Like other Protestants, Ames declares that the Bible is an infallible rule of faith and practice. But he goes on to claim that Scripture is inerrant. He notes that the authors of the rule of faith and conduct were "free from all error" because God infallibly directed them (2). The authors could not err in writing about creation, history, and so forth (5). In matters of right and *fact* (my italics) God inspired not only the subject matter but suggested the words, while he yet preserved the authors' integrity (6). In brief, Ames apparently equates biblical infallibility with inerrancy.[13] Moreover, in articles 27–31, he implies that biblical infallibility should be associated with the original autographs and not with translations made by men (nonprophets) who err:

27. The Scriptures are not so tied to these first languages that they cannot and ought not to be translated into other languages for common use in the church.

28. But, among interpreters, neither the seventy who turned them into Greek, nor Jerome, nor any other such held the office of a prophet; they were not free from errors in interpretation.

29. Hence no versions are fully authentic except as they express the sources, by which they are also to be weighed.

31. God's providence in preserving the sources is notable and glorious, for neither have they wholly perished nor have they been injured by the loss of any book or blemished by a serious defect—though today not one of the earlier versions remains intact.[14]

It is clear from the Ames example that Ramism did not deter Puritans from embracing with other Protestants (whom Rogers and McKim label "scholastics") the idea that the Bible is "completely" infallible. Rogers, who cites exclusively secondary sources about Ames, evidently did not become acquainted with the actual writings of the theologian.

Another Puritan whom Rogers sees standing in the "line of Ramist influence on Puritanism and in the background of the Westminster Divines" (p. 90) is William Perkins (1558–1602). Perkins was a towering personality whose influence continued in the first half of the seventeenth century and whose disciples included William Ames. His doctrine of Scripture resembles in many ways that of Ames. Like other Protestants of his day, Perkins argued that the Scriptures inform us sufficiently about our salvation; we have no need to seek further information from Roman Catholic traditions:

PAPISTS TEACH THAT BESIDE THE WRITTEN WORD there be certain unwritten traditions, which must be believed as profitable and necessary to salvation. And these they say are two-fold: apostolical—namely such as were delivered by the apostles and not written; and ecclesiastical; which the church decreeth as occasion is offered. We hold that the scriptures are most perfect, containing in them all doctrines needful to salvation, whether they concern faith and manners and therefore we acknowledge no such traditions beside the written word which shall be necessary to salvation, so as he which believeth them not cannot be saved.[15]

Perkins declared that we should not believe the writings of the church fathers as the Word of God because they err:

And we may not believe their sayings as the word of God, because they often err, being subject to error: and for this cause their authority when they speak of traditions may be suspected and we may not always believe them upon their word.[16]

He indicated that the Bible does not err:

It is a privilege of God's word, and so of the true religion gathered forth of it, to be consonant to itself in all points: which properly no doctrines nor writings beside can have.[17]

He described the purity of the Word of God in this fashion:

The purity thereof is whereby it remaineth entire in itself, void of deceit and error.[18]

Although Ian Breward, a modern editor of Perkins's works, does not appreciate the Puritan's doctrine of inspiration and biblical infallibility, he nonetheless acknowledges it:

The divine origin of the scriptures was guaranteed by the testimony of the Spirit and the mode of inspiration which obviated error in matter or words. The vital consideration was that nothing human or potentially sinful marred the transmission of the revelation.[19]

Once again, Rogers, who cites exclusively secondary sources about Perkins, evidently did not become acquainted with the actual writings of the theologian he discusses.

That William Perkins and William Ames should affirm complete biblical infallibility is not surprising. We saw earlier that their fellow countryman, William Whitaker, advocated the same position in his *Disputation on Scripture* (1588). And, as Professor Philip Hughes has demonstrated, other English Reformers before Whitaker did the same.[20] If Ames and Perkins did set the theological stage for the Westminster Assembly, as Rogers maintains, then his interpretation that the divines limited biblical infallibility to matters of faith and practice becomes all the more problematical.

Rogers's interpretation of the Westminster Divines' attitudes toward biblical infallibility is based on a pivotal presupposition: the divines created their confession in an unspecified "prescientific" period. Thus, they could not have entertained the idea of biblical inerrancy:

... the problem [of inerrancy] is formed in the beginnings of the scientific era following the Westminster Assembly, and particularly in relationship to eighteenth-century deism.... To contend that the Westminster Confession teaches the inerrancy of the Scripture because it does not assert that there are errors in the Scripture is to impose a modern problem on a pre-scientific statement.[21]

More recently (summer, 1981), Rogers has written: "In the late seventeenth century, the concept of the Bible's infallibility in religious matters was transmuted into a notion of Scripture's inerrancy in matters of science and history."[22] According to Rogers's logic, no Christian could have been an inerrantist until the "scientific era" began.

Unfortunately, Rogers uses "private language" in his discussion of this pivotal presupposition. He does not inform us regarding the circumstances of this new era's birth, nor when the birth took place, nor what the decisive characteristics of the new era might have been. Because his language is "private," we find it incapable of sustaining the argument.

In their joint study Rogers and McKim do provide us with some helps with which to decipher Rogers's private language. They affirm that in the "scientific period" theologians adopted uncritically a "mechanistic, mathematical model by which the Bible was judged" (p. 235). These theologians began to use Newtonian notions of perfection and to seek some accord between the Bible's message and Lockean reason (p. 235). In this discussion our authors give little indication of understanding the twisting routes, the time lags, and the multiple formats that characterized the penetration of the thought of Newton and Locke into the Republic of Letters.[23] Moreover, by arguing that biblical inerrancy emerged in the "scientific" period, which for them evidently commenced in the late 1680s (after Newton's *Mathematica Principia* [1687] and after Locke's principal writings of the late 1680s and early 1690s), the authors inadvertently make a shambles of their other thesis that inerrancy had been created by Roman Catholic and Protestant "scholastics" of earlier decades and centuries. Francis Turretin, "an inerrantist" according to our authors, had written his chief theological work in the 1670s and died in 1688 (that is, before the works of Newton and Locke were well known). The authors need to reconsider the logical underpinnings of their proposal with more care.

Rogers and McKim suggest that the Westminster Divines were open to the teachings of "natural science" and did not use the Scriptures "as a source of information in the sciences to refute what scholars were discovering" (p. 206). Our authors build this conclusion in part upon the idea that the response of English scientists and theologians "stood in sharp contrast to the reactions of the Protestant scholastics on the Continent" regarding the "Copernican system" (p. 224). It is true that the Copernican hypothesis made disciples in England at a fairly rapid rate as it did in other Protestant countries (compared to the acceptance rate in Roman Catholic countries).[24] But it is also true that not a few sixteenth-century Christians offered stiff resistance to it. The complaints made by Robert Recorde (1556) and others that English theologians were using their interpretations of the Bible to counter philosophy and science underscore this point.[25] In 1640 John Wilkins complained, we recall, that the "common people" cried down the Copernican hypothesis because it contradicted their interpretation of the Bible. The English and continental Protestants did not react to Copernicus in ways that were as radically opposed as Rogers and McKim propound.

John Wilkins (1614–1672) represents for our authors a *virtuosi* (an individual interested in the natural sciences and experimental philosophy) who allegedly followed the "Augustinian approach" to harmonizing science and religion (p. 225). Wilkins entered into a heated debate with Alexander Ross (1590–1654), a headmaster of a school in Southampton, concerning the significance of the Copernican hypothesis for biblical teachings.[26] Although English theologians and laypersons had earlier critiqued the thesis on biblical grounds, Ross became worried that a small but influential group of savants (including Nathaniel Carpenter and Philip Landsberg) were promoting the teachings of Tommaso Campanella's *Apologia pro Galileo* (1622) that the Bible does not speak to scientific matters.[27] Ross attacked the new astronomy and the ideas of Landsberg in a piece entitled *Commentum de terrae motu* (1634). John Wilkins then turned his sights upon Ross and a Nicholas Fuller, especially in a volume written in English, *A Discourse Concerning a New Planet* (1640). It is upon this latter work that Rogers and McKim found their interpretation of Wilkins's "Augustinian" approach to the Bible and science.

Our authors declare that in his *Discourse Concerning a New Planet* Wilkins said that the Bible did not speak about scientific matters (pp. 225–26). They present two of Wilkins's propositions taken from secondary sources and recounted out of sequence to back up their analysis:

> There is not any particular by which philosophy has been more endangered, than the ignorant superstition of some men, who in stating the controversies of it, do so closely adhere to the mere words of Scripture.... It were happy for us, if we could exempt Scripture from philosophical controversies: If we could be content to let it be perfect for that end unto which it was intended, for a Rule of our Faith and Obedience, and not stretch it also to be a Judge of such Natural Truths, as are to be found out by our own Industry and Experience. [The Holy Spirit could have easily given us information on the latter yet] He has left this travel to the sons of men to be exercised with.[28]

Because our authors apparently did not have recourse to Wilkins's actual writings, they fail to note his continuing discussion in Proposition III (their first citation) in which he affirms that a link exists between the natural world and some of the Bible's teachings. Wilkins cites a comment by Vallesius:

> I for my part am persuaded, that these divine treatises were not written by the holy and inspired penmen, for the interpretation of philosophy, because God left such things to be found out by men's labour and indus-

try. But yet whatsoever is in them concerning nature is most true: as proceeding from the God of nature, from whom nothing could be hid.

Then Wilkins adds his own observation:

And questionless, all those things which the scripture does deliver concerning any natural point, cannot be but certain and infallible, being understood in the sense, wherein they were first intended.[29]

Rogers and McKim's presentation of Wilkins's viewpoint is simply misleading.

The relationship Wilkins attempts to establish between the Bible's teachings and "natural points" is quite nuanced. In Proposition II he suggests that the Holy Spirit accommodated His teachings to the ways things appear to us:

That the Holy Ghost in many other places of scripture, does accommodate his expressions into the error of our conceits: and does not speak of divers things as they are in themselves, but as they appear unto us. Therefore it is not unlikely, that these phrases also may be liable unto the same interpretation.[30]

The Englishman wanted to warn Christians not to read certain passages in the Scriptures in such a literalistic way that their interpretations became hindrances to the acceptance of the Copernican hypothesis. Wilkins apparently believed that the Bible's phenomenological statements when properly interpreted (that is, not literally) encompassed no "errors." Nonetheless he struck out at those who assumed that the divine penmen (themselves uninstructed on certain points) revealed all there is to know about science or who took the Bible's words concerning the natural world in too literalistic a fashion.[31]

Sincerely offended by Wilkins's ideas, Ross wrote a harsh reply, *The New Planet no Planet* (1646). He scolded Wilkins for having impugned the integrity of the infallible biblical texts: "Wee must beleeve the Scripture, not our own phansies.... The Scripture never patronizeth a lye or an error, nor doth it apply it self to our capacity in naturall things, though it doth in supernaturall mysteries ... Wee must stick to the literall sense, when the Scripture speaks of naturall things."[32] From Ross's point of view, Wilkins's arguments for the heliocentric hypothesis contradicted the Bible, our perceptions, and reason:

The Scripture tells us in plaine tearmes, the Earth is immoveable.... and yet you spurning at Scripture, sense, and reason, as if your phansie were *instar omnium*, would have our judgments, senses, Scripture, Church, and all regulated by your absurd dictates; therefore it is an unreasonable thing in you to desire that the Holy Ghost should not be Judge of his owne assertions in naturall truths; and that there should be more credit given to your conceits, (which you call industry and experience) than to God's own words.[33]

Ross believed that Wilkins was emptying the Bible of its authority by not interpreting its words literally. But Ross's own failure to understand the accommodated character of the Bible's language led him into unfortunate interpretative culs-de-sac.

We have lingered on the Wilkins/Ross debate because it casts needed light on several issues. First, it emphasizes the prickly and complex hermeneutical difficulties which Englishmen of good faith encountered as they began to sense that Christian theologians and scientists had been mistaken in espousing the geocentric theory of the universe. Second, it underscores the contention that many Englishmen (including Ross and Fuller) read their infallible Bibles for "scientific" information before the Westminster Assembly convened. And third, it reveals the tenuous character of Rogers's assumption that the Westminster Divines, the contemporaries of Wilkins and Ross, lived in some kind of prescientific era.

Did the Westminster Divines interact with the positions advocated by Wilkins and Ross in their debate? To our knowledge, scholarly studies do not presently exist that permit us to answer this question with certitude. Rogers and McKim would have us believe that the Westminster Divines did not view the Bible as a "source of information in the sciences to refute what the scholars were discovering" (p. 206). They cite the dictum of Westminster Divine Samuel Rutherford that the Scripture is not a rule in "things of Art and Science, as to speak Latine, to demonstrate conclusions of Astronomie" as the only evidence to support their understanding.[34] But once again, Rogers and McKim have probably misread their sources and extrapolated too gratuitously.

What did it mean for a person to propose that the Bible was not such a rule? For Wilkins, who speaks a language similar to Rutherford's, it evidently meant that the Bible does not afford us with every possible secret concerning the arts and sciences. In Proposition IV he complained about the opinion

> that the law of *Moses* did containe in it, not only those things which concernes our Religion and Obedience, but every secret also that may possibly be known in any Art or Science; so that there is not a demonstration in Geometrie, or rule in Arithmeticke; not a mysterie in any trade, but it may be found out in the Pentateuch....[35]

But we recall, he had earlier argued in Proposition II that the Bible is infallible when it does touch upon "natural things."[36] Wilkins seems to be saying that the Bible as a rule tells us all we need to know about faith and practice; we do not need the additional teachings of the Roman Catholic Church in this regard.[37] Although the Bible does give us incidental infallible information regarding the arts and sciences, it does not provide us with sufficient data (secrets) to qualify as a rule in these areas.[38] It does not teach us every rule of arithmetic or every trick of the trades. Thus we must proceed with our own investigations in the arts and sciences. It is not unlikely that Rutherford's discussion of the respective spheres in which the Bible is and is not a rule resembles Wilkins's to a certain degree.[39]

As we saw, Rutherford indicates that the Bible is not a rule in art such as to teach Latin, or a rule in astronomy such as to present demonstrations in that domain. He was apparently indicating that the Bible does not teach us everything we can know in the arts and astronomy. It is not a divine encyclopedia as some medieval scholars had proposed. But there is no hint in Rutherford that he thought that the Bible was fallible when it touched incidentally upon the things of art and astronomy. He was affirming what other Christians from St. Augustine to Charles Hodge propounded: the Bible is not a scientific textbook per se.

If our interpretation of Rutherford is correct (and further research is required to corroborate it), then Rogers and McKim have not properly assessed the import of his comments. It is by no means clear that Rutherford intended to argue that Scriptural teachings have *no* bearing upon science. The tenor of his other comments about Scripture does not complement that stance. Rutherford goes so far as to advocate a dictation theory of inspiration:

> . . . in writing every jot, tittle or word of Scripture, they [the biblical writers] were immediately inspired, as touching the matter, word phrases, expression, order, method, majesty, stile and all: So I think they were but Organs, the mouth, pen and *Amanuenses;* God as it were immediately dyting, and leading their hand at the pen.[40]

Rogers and McKim rightfully note Rutherford's statement but attempt to dismiss it as one drawn up in the heat of religious controversy (p. 250, note 23). Rutherford's views on biblical inspiration and the relationship between science and the Bible's teachings deserve more careful study. The writings of John Lightfoot, James Ussher, and other Westminster luminaries on the same subjects warrant further scrutiny as well.[41]

Rogers and McKim do not contend that there were Westminster Divines who actually acknowledged errors in Holy Writ. Nonetheless, for reasons we have already indicated, they do not believe that the Confession's statement about the Bible's infallibility is related to the concept of biblical inerrancy. We recall the definition of infallibility

Rogers proposes in his thesis: "For the authors of the Confession of faith, the Scripture is infallible as a rule of interpreting its own central message of salvation in Jesus Christ."[42] He suggests that his study of the works of several prominent participants at the Westminster Assembly substantiates this definition.[43] Nevertheless, he provides no illustrations of Westminster Divines proposing that there were errors in Holy Writ.

Perhaps we can provide additional data concerning this issue of definition by referring to the works of the Westminster Divine William Gouge (1578–1653). Gouge is a significant personage because he was elected to the Assembly by the parliamentary ordinance of 12 June 1643; he sat on the committee for the examination of ministers (1644) and on the committee for drafting a confession of faith (12 May 1644); he also held other prominent posts at the Assembly.[44] As one who attended the meetings of the Assembly assiduously and who apparently helped draw up the Assembly's statements about the Bible, Gouge's discussion of biblical infallibility merits our consideration. Moreover Rogers speaks favorably of Gouge in his discussion of Ramism's relationship to Puritanism.[45]

In commenting on Hebrews 11, Gouge answers the question concerning how the author of the book could have had knowledge of the persons he discusses in the chapter when not all of their names are mentioned in the Old Testament:

> Ans. He might have them either out of human records, or from traditions conveyed from fathers to children, age after age....
>
> Ques. Doth not this make human records as authentic as sacred Scripture? and traditions equal to the written Word?
>
> Ans. In no wise. For though in human records there may be and are many truths, yet we cannot absolutely rest upon them, because there may be falsehood in them, but sacred Scripture is the word of truth, James I.18. Yea, truth itself, John XVII. 17, and that in these respects:
>
> 1. In regard of the author, who is the God of truth, Ps. XXXI. 5, from whom nothing but truth can come. He "cannot lie," Tit. I. 2.
> 2. In regard of the matter. There is nothing but truth in it, no falsehood, no errors, no uncertainty, Ps. XIX. 8.
> 3. In regard of the effect. It persuades a man of the truth revealed in it, so as what God's word revealeth may safely, and ought to be confidently believed. It is not so with human writings.
>
> Ques. Why then doth the apostle produce matters to be believed out of human writings?
>
> Ans. The Holy Ghost so assisted the apostles as they were able to discern betwixt truth and falsehood, so as what they took out of human writers was without question most true, and by their quoting the same they have made them authentic.[46]

Elsewhere, in responding to objections to proofs taken from the testimonies of Scripture, Gouge is even more specific about the meaning of infallibility:

> Obj. A testimony is but an artificial argument which is counted the last and lightest of all arguments.
>
> Ans. A testimony receiveth its force from the witnessbearer. An human testimony is not counted infallible, because men are subject to ignorance, error, and manifold corruptions. But a divine testimony is infallible, in that it resteth on the highest and soundest ground of truth, which is the word of God; for it is impossible for God to lie. Heb. VI. 18.... Thus this proof is more sure and sound than any logical or mathematical demonstration can be.[47]

Or he declares:

> It [the Bible] is a most true, right, certain, infallible, undeniable word, alwaies constant, ever one and the same: so absolutely perfect, as nothing can be added to it, or may be taken from it. Whosoever teacheth any otherwise than it teacheth, is accursed.[48]

Gouge does not fit Rogers's characterization of the Westminster Divines' beliefs: "Scripture is the Word of God because man finds the saving gospel of Jesus Christ there." Rather, for Gouge, the Bible is the Word of God because God is its author. Rogers indicates that the Bible is infallible for its effect; Gouge says that the Word is true in regard to its author, matter, and effect. A sifting through the writings of other Westminster Divines makes it clear that Gouge was not alone in these sentiments.[49] If Gouge is representative of the Ramist Westminster Divine whom Rogers appreciates, then Rogers's definition of what biblical infallibility meant for the Westminster Assembly stands in need of serious revision.

The interpretation of Chapter I, Section viii of the Westminster Confession has long perplexed Reformed theologians:

> The Old Testament in Hebrew (which was the native language of the people of God of old), and the New Testament in Greek (which at the time of the writing of it, was most generally known to the nations), being immediately inspired by God, and by His singular care and providence, kept pure in all ages, are therefore authentical; so as, in all controversies of religion, the Church is finally to appeal unto them.

Rogers and McKim give this commentary about the authenticity of the originals: "The authors of the Westminster Confession apparently meant by the word *authentical* that the text of Scripture in the original language was to be considered the final source of reference for understanding" (p. 212). In *Scripture in the Westminster Confession*, Rogers is more specific: "Orr is right in denying that the authors of the Confession of Faith separated the autographs from the working copies of the Hebrew and Greek Scripture" (p. 398). In making this observation, Rogers challenges the interpretation of B. B. Warfield and John Gerstner that the Westminster Divines were alluding to the "original autographs" as authentical.[50]

The twists and turns of this debate are tortuous; we dare not seek to map them in this brief essay. We should remember, however, that William Whitaker and William Ames had earlier inferred that a distinction exists between the original autographs and the Greek and Hebrew manuscripts in hand. Roman Catholic and Protestant polemics over the authenticity of the Vulgate hovered in the background of their discussions. At the time the Westminster Assembly met, English theologians were exercised by a dispute regarding the inspiration of the Massoretic pointing of the Hebrew text.[51] We recall that Louis Cappel's *Arcanum punctuationes* (1624; later amplified in his *Critica sacra* [1650]) had helped precipitate this theological fire storm which rained on Protestant circles even in the second half of the seventeenth century. John Lightfoot, a distinguished Christian Hebraist at Westminster, was well known for his cogent defense of the divine inspiration of the vowel points.[52] In a word, when the Westminster Assembly convened, English theologians were concerned about biblical critical problems and a few of these problems focused upon the distinction between the original autographs and the extant Hebrew and Greek texts.

The renowned Presbyterian Richard Baxter (who did not personally attend Westminster) gives us an apt summary of the various options open to his English compatriots who considered these matters. In *The Saints Everlasting Rest* (1652), Baxter reviews the options from the least advisable to the one he especially appreciated. He believed that the authority of Bishop James Ussher, the distinguished biblical scholar, sustained this latter position. Because Baxter's comments provide a valuable aperture through which to view these issues, we shall present them at some length:

> Though all Scripture be of divine authority, yet he that believeth but some one book, which containeth the substance of the doctrine of salvation, may be saved; much more they that have doubted but of some particular books.... They that take the Scripture to be but the writings of godly, honest men, and so to be only a means of making known Christ, having a gradual precedency to the writings of other godly men, and do believe in Christ upon those strong grounds which are drawn from his doctrine, miracles, &c. rather than upon the testimony of the writing, as being purely infallible and divine, may yet have a divine and saving faith.... Much more, those that believe the whole writing to be of divine inspiration where it handleth the substance, but doubt whether God infallibly

guided them in every circumstance.... And yet more, those that believe that the Spirit did guide the writers to truth, both in substance and circumstance, but doubt whether he guided them in orthography; or whether their pens were as perfectly guided as their minds.... And yet more, may those have saving faith, who only doubt whether Providence infallibly guided any transcribers, or printers, as to retain any copy that perfectly agreeth with the autograph: yea, whether the perfectest copy now extant may not have some inconsiderable literal or verbal errors, through the transcribers' or printers' oversight, is of no great moment, as long as it is certain, that the Scriptures are not *de industria* corrupted, nor any material doctrine, history, or prophecy thereby obscured or depraved. God hath not engaged himself to direct every printer to the world's end, to do his work without any error. Yet it is unlikely that this should deprave all copies, or leave us uncertain wholly of the right reading, especially since copies were multiplied, because it is unlikely that all transcribers, or printers, will commit the very same error. We know the true copies of our statute books, though the printer be not guided by an unerring spirit. See Usher's Epistle to Lud. Capell.[53]

Baxter's dependence upon Ussher is intriguing, for Ussher's writings influenced the composition of the Westminster Confession.[54] Rogers's confident statement (following Orr) that the Westminster Divines did not separate the autographs from the working copies of the Hebrew and Greek Scriptures should not be considered a definitive judgment on the question. Nor should scholars continue to assert with assurance that B. B. Warfield and A. A. Hodge innovated in the Reformed tradition when they spoke of the biblical infallibility of the original autographs (1881).[55] Baxter assumed that, although the infallible autographs had been lost, scholars might approach them by doing textual critical work on the extant manuscripts available in his day. The infallible autographs were scattered through those manuscripts.[56]

Obviously, we have not established a final resolution to the complicated interpretive questions related to the Westminster Confession and Holy Scripture. Much technical research needs to be accomplished before we understand more adequately the connotative freight the Divines placed upon their carefully crafted formula.[57] Nevertheless, it appears that when the Divines described the Bible as infallible, they primarily meant that it was "without error." They would also note in their writings that the Scriptures had a persuasive "effect" (Gouge) bringing us to believe confidently in the truth of Holy Writ.

It should be clear from our excursus that Rogers and McKim's presentation of the thinking of the Westminster Divines and the intellectual climate in which they did their theological reflection is not ultimately satisfying. On several key points it seems to confuse more than illuminate.

II. THE FULL FLOWERING OF "REFORMED SCHOLASTICISM": FRANCIS TURRETIN

Rogers and McKim propose that John Owen (1616–1683) is a transitional English figure in the development of "Reformed Scholasticism" whereas the Swiss Francis Turretin (1632–1687) represents its full flowering. We shall leave to others to make a systematic assessment of our authors' treatment of Owen and Turretin.[58] It is interesting to note, however, that both theologians (inerrantists from Rogers and McKim's perspective) died before the impact of Newton's works and those of Locke was manifest. And we should comment upon our authors' discussion of Francis Turretin; it is one of the most disappointing segments in their entire work.

In this section our authors simply reword segments of a Th.M. thesis (1958) by Leon M. Allison, "The Doctrine of Scripture in the Theology of John Calvin and Francis Turretin."[59] In all fairness to our authors, they do cite Allison's work (they refer to him almost exclusively in footnotes 170–239, pp. 196–97). They also acknowledge that they relied heavily upon the thesis for quotations from Turretin (p. 196, note 170), but they do not make clear that their debt to Allison is far more extensive than that.

The borrowing issue becomes even more troubling because our authors turn the basic thrust of Allison's thesis on its head. Citing Allison as their source, our authors describe Francis Turretin's relationship to John Calvin in these terms (pp. 174–75):

> Turretin apparently realized that Calvin's approach to Scripture was antithetical to his own. In Turretin's theology, post-Reformation scholasticism had matured to the point that it could dispense with any attempt to reconcile its teaching with that of the original Genevan reformer.[60]

In point of fact Allison did not think Turretin's views of Scripture and those of Calvin were antithetical. In his "Summary and Conclusion" Allison writes (p. 97):

> Before these differences are summarized, it is proper to point out the striking similarities in the thought of Calvin and Turretin in their treatment of the doctrine under discussion. It would be grossly unfair to Turretin and "classical" Calvinism to leave the impression that the only result of the study has been to substantiate the premise of the thesis— viz. that there are real differences between the theology of John Calvin and that of his "classical" supporters. The study has not revealed the existence of two separate and distinct systems of theology. Concerning the doctrine of Scripture, at least, there are remarkable similarities.

What are these similarities? Allison enumerates many of them including the following (p. 98):

> The objective authority of the Bible depends upon its divine authorship. God inspired the human writers of Scripture to such an extent that there is a verbally inerrant Scripture. There is an inseparable relationship between the Spirit and Scripture.

From Allison's point of view, both John Calvin and Francis Turretin espoused complete biblical infallibility and shared many other beliefs about Holy Scripture. Rogers and McKim's principal judgment that a radical disjunction existed between Turretin's thinking on the Bible and that of Calvin stems from a misreading of their essential secondary source. Their overall exploitation of Allison's thesis is not a model of historical scholarship.

The theological world stands in need of a competent study of Turretin's thinking about biblical authority. W. Robert Godfrey, who has offered telling criticisms of Rogers and McKim's understanding of Turretin, believes that Allison's thesis, though helpful, is understandably not the last word on this topic.[61] Quite simply, Francis Turretin has not been captured in the historical rush of his life and in his fascinating relationships with Louis Tronchin, Jean Claude, and a host of other figures. Hagiographically inclined, earlier biographers of Turretin used the Turretin family archives only selectively.[62] Unfortunately, it is difficult to gain access to these private archives, which are located in a small Swiss town. Moreover Turretin's correspondence is scattered through archives in Europe and does not figure in most studies. It is remarkable that many American scholars have been emboldened to write much about Francis Turretin's views of Scripture without having consulted his papers. The real Francis Turretin was quite a different person than the rigid ideologue usually depicted by historians.[63] We surmise that a technical study of his career and thought will paint his portrait with different strokes. It will probably establish his greater dependence upon Musculus, William Whitaker, Jean Daillé, and other divines of the sixteenth and seventeenth centuries and tone down perceptions of his dependence upon Thomas Aquinas.[64]

Many other subjects come to mind as we consider the "Reformed traditions" of the seventeenth century: the importance of "rationality" and "certitude" in those traditions,[65] the distinctive attitudes of Francis Turretin toward reason versus those of his son Jean-Alphonse Turretin,[66] the relationship between the "Platonism" of the Cambridge Platonists and the "Platonism" of the Dutch Remonstrants,[67] the apologetic efforts of Reformed theologians to fend off "enthusiasm" and personal special revelations,[68] and the rapport between Cartesian thought and the shaping of Dutch Reformed theologies.[69] The list of topics could be continued almost without end. In this light the evocative character of our study becomes even more patent. Nonetheless we must press on down the path that Rogers and McKim have largely staked out for us. But we now know that their seventeenth-century signposts regarding the Westminster Confession and Francis Turretin, though at times quite instructive, do not always provide us with reliable guidance on these points that particularly interest us in our journey.

Chapter VII

Biblical Infallibility in the Nineteenth Century: The Princetonians

Curiously enough, Rogers and McKim do not discuss in detail the struggles over biblical authority during the Enlightenment (the *Siècle des lumières*, the *Aufklärung* . . .).[1] They limit themselves to comments about Robert Boyle,[2] Isaac Newton,[3] John Locke,[4] Thomas Reid, David Hume, and several other Scottish and English thinkers. But even in these segments they show little awareness of the personal struggles several of these thinkers experienced as they reflected upon questions related to biblical infallibility. Members of the Church of the Desert in southern France (Reformed Christians, incidentally), the progressive Reformed theologians Jacob Vernes and Jacob Vernet in Geneva, Reformed theologians and men of letters in the United Provinces, John Wesley and Methodist Evangelicals in England, Pietists and the Lutheran Orthodox in Germany, Protestants in Scandinavia, the Eastern Orthodox and Roman Catholics in general, are missing persons in their story.[5] Rogers and McKim do not inform us about their perceptions of biblical authority.

By generally ignoring the Enlightenment in continental Europe and the American Enlightenment in the Thirteen Colonies, our authors inadvertently create a distorted context for discussing their principal subject. The multiple evidential apologetics designed by theologians and pastors to defend prophecies, miracles, and the inspiration and infallibility of the Bible against the hard hitting rhetoric and arguments of deists, Socinians, libertines, infidels, and atheists, are largely forgotten.[6] The developments in hermeneutics that Professor Hans Frei discusses in his important but difficult *The Eclipse of Biblical Narrative A Study in Eighteenth and Nineteenth Century Hermeneutics* (1974) are bypassed.[7] The relationship between Jean-Jacques Rousseau's subjective defense of natural religion based on "sentiments interieurs" and Reformed apologetics for the truthfulness of the Christian faith is not explored.[8] The readers of our author's volume do not feel the sting of those satirical jibes that witty essayists like Voltaire (*La Bible enfin expliquée*, 1776) poked at biblical authority; nor do they learn the reasons Voltaire believed his ridicule and sarcasm were intellectually justifiable.[9] As a period in which many *philosophes*, politicians ("patriots") and others self-consciously cut themselves loose from biblical authority (or standard interpretations of Holy Writ) in establishing ethics, political theory, and explanations of "nature," the "Enlightenment" deserves far more analysis than our authors give it.[10]

For that matter Rogers and McKim generally make but scattered remarks about the attitudes of nineteenth-century European Christians toward Scripture. They do, however, consider Scottish and English theologians, and there are certain nineteenth-century American Christians who especially interest them.

THE OLD PRINCETONIANS AND BIBLICAL INFALLIBILITY

Rogers and McKim fix concerted attention on what they call "Reformed scholasticism" in the United States. They identify its flowering with the instruction dispensed at Princeton Seminary (founded in 1812).[11] They propose that the influence of Francis Turretin's "scholastic" beliefs about Scripture determined to a large extent those of the Old Princetonians, particularly concerning biblical inerrancy. For example, they explain Professor Archibald Alexander's commitment to that stance with these words (p. 273):

> Because of his roots in Turretin, however, Alexander held fast to the postulate of the Bible's inerrancy in all things. He wrote: "And could it be shown that the evangelists had fallen into palpable mistakes in facts of minor importance, it would be impossible to demonstrate that they wrote anything by inspiration."

This explanation has a marked reductionistic quality, when we recall that Christians from various communions had held complete biblical infallibility throughout the centuries and had assumed that this belief accorded with the Bible's teaching about itself.[12]

The authors bring to their study insights drawn from the burgeoning literature about Old-School Presbyterians in the United States (including the Princetonians). The studies of Sydney Ahlstrom, Theodore Bozeman, and others have informed scholars about the impact of Common Sense Realism/"Baconianism" on Presbyterians as well as on American culture in general during the nineteenth century.[13] Rogers and McKim suggest that the Princetonians joined "Baconianism" to their "Protestant scholasticism." Earlier in their analysis they note the impact of Scottish Common Sense Realism on John Witherspoon (1723-1794). Witherspoon was destined to play a major role in Princeton's history (p. 246):

Thus Witherspoon brought from Scotland to America the apologetic approach to Scripture that had led to conflicts between Scripture and emerging science in Switzerland and England. He prepared the groundwork on which the nineteenth-century Princeton theology would be built.

"Reformed scholasticism," Princeton style, married Common Sense Realism. According to the authors, this union spelled trouble ahead for American Protestants: ". . . the later fundamentalist/modernist controversy over the inerrancy of Scripture in the twentieth century was, in principle, already set in motion [by Witherspoon]" (p. 246). The Princetonians were the culprits in preparing its denouement. Once again we encounter a strangely reductionistic hypothesis for so knowledgeable scholars as are Rogers and McKim.

Rogers and McKim's general analysis of the Old Princetonians contains some valuable insights, particularly regarding the career of Charles Hodge. Yet it is ultimately disappointing. Several considerations lead us to make this unwelcome judgment.

I. BIBLICAL INFALLIBILITY IN THE THIRTEEN COLONIES

The authors do not set the historical stage well for understanding the nineteenth-century Princetonians. They make a few glancing remarks (pp. 242–47) about the importance of Witherspoon's moral philosophy and Baconianism in the last decades of the eighteenth century, but then turn full bore to the first prominent theologian at Princeton Seminary, Archibald Alexander (1772–1851). By taking this tack, our authors essentially skirt more than one hundred and fifty years of Reformed thinking in the Thirteen Colonies. If they had discussed Reformed traditions in the colonies, they might have noted William Ames's *Marrow of Christian Divinity* (1623, 1627, 1629), which served as an important textbook at Harvard, We recall that Ames advocated complete biblical infallibility in that volume.[14] They might have discovered that Jonathan Edwards (1703–1758), one of the most brilliant intellects of the eighteenth century, maintained a similar belief.[15] They might have observed that some Americans had questions concerning the concept of biblical infallibility in the early eighteenth century, that is, more than one hundred years before the idea of founding Princeton Seminary was more than a twinkle in the eyes of Archibald Alexander or Ashbel Green.[16] They might have encountered the discussions of Timothy Dwight and Samuel Hopkins who in the early national period defended complete biblical infallibility.[17] Although there were important Enlightenment personalities such as Thomas Jefferson, Benjamin Franklin, Elihu Palmer, Thomas Paine, and others who very firmly denied biblical infallibility as well as several cardinal doctrines of the Christian faith, many colonists apparently affirmed complete biblical infallibility years before Witherspoon arrived in this land and before Princeton Seminary was planted in Princeton, New Jersey.[18] Rogers and McKim do not tell the story of these colonists; if recounted, it would not accord well with their recurring theme that the Old Princetonians developed something new (and yet "scholastic") by speaking about the Bible's absolute infallibility.

II. THE CONCEPT OF BIBLICAL INFALLIBILITY IN THE ORIGINAL AUTOGRAPHS IN THE NINETEENTH CENTURY

Rogers and McKim do their best to paint the Princetonians into a corner as if they were the doughty defenders of an outmoded and yet paradoxically innovative doctrine. In point of fact many contemporary Europeans and Americans from non-Presbyterian communions affirmed the same belief. Samuel Taylor Coleridge caused an uproar in the British Isles by challenging the concept of complete biblical infallibility in his posthumous *Confessions of an Inquiring Spirit* (1841).[19] Coleridge acknowledged that he was attacking a belief that many English Christians from diverse ecclesiastical backgrounds cherished. He cited the remarks of a well-disposed skeptic about the point:

> I have frequently attended meetings of the British and Foreign Bible Society, where I have heard speakers of every denomination, Calvinist and Arminian, Quaker and Methodist, Dissenting Ministers and Clergymen, nay, dignitaries of the Established Church,—and still have I heard the same doctrine,—that the Bible was not to be regarded or reasoned about in the way that other good books are or may be; ... What is more, their principal arguments were grounded on the position, that the Bible throughout was dictated by Omniscience, and therefore in all its parts infallibly true and obligatory, and that the men, whose names are prefixed to the several books or chapters, were in fact but as different pens in the hand of one and the same Writer, and the words the words of God himself; ...[20]

Coleridge responded:

> What could I reply to this?—I could neither deny the fact, nor evade the conclusion,—namely, that such is at present the popular belief.[21]

According to Coleridge (writing at the same time as the early Princetonians), many of his fellow Englishmen believed in complete biblical infallibility.[22]

In a letter dated January 24, 1835, to Justice Coleridge (Samuel's nephew), Dr. Thomas Arnold of Rugby commented about the explosive character of Coleridge's writings on Scripture:

> Have you seen your uncle's "Letters on Inspiration," which I believe are to be published? They are well fitted to break ground in the approaches to that momentous question which involves in it so great a shock to existing

notions; the greatest, probably, that has ever been given since the discovery of the falsehood of the doctrine of the Pope's infallibility.[23]

In this letter Arnold was referring to Coleridge's criticisms of complete biblical infallibility and a dictation theory of inspiration.

Thomas Arnold did much to propagate Coleridge's thinking about Scripture. Evangelicals found it difficult to berate him because his own Christian piety could not be doubted.[24] Matthew Arnold, the distinguished essayist, commented on his father's role in making Coleridge more palatable to Englishmen:

> In papa's time the exploding of the old notions of literal inspiration in Scripture, and the introducing of a truer method of interpretation, were the changes for which, here in England, the moment had come. Stiff people could not receive this change, and my dear old Methodist friend, Mr. Scott, used to say to the day of his death that papa and Coleridge might be excellent men, but that they had found and shown the rat-hole in the temple.[25]

In his posthumous study *The Human Element in the Inspiration of the Sacred Scriptures* (1867), the American theologian T. F. Curtis portrayed Coleridge and Thomas Arnold as those among others who had prompted much debate about biblical infallibility. He noted Coleridge's prominent role in precipitating the debate:

> Coleridge may be said to have broken ground on this subject in England, and his *Confessions of an Inquiring Spirit,* published after his death, have produced a greater effect morally among thinking Christians, than all he had published during his life.[26]

Curtis observed that Arnold of Rugby, "the Apostle of Christian culture of Young England in its best form,"

> ... openly exhibited a freedom from, and dislike to the current belief in the infallibility of the Inspiration of the Bible; while he foresaw in this, as he said, as great a shock to the feelings of Protestant Christendom as Roman Catholic Christianity had received three hundred years ago, from the downfall of the belief in the infallibility of the Church.[27]

In his influential *Inspiration of Holy Scriptures: Its Nature and Proof* (1854) William Lee of Trinity College, Dublin, complained that Coleridge's *Letters of an Inquiring Spirit* "has done more than any modern work to unsettle the public mind, in these countries, with respect to the authority of the Bible *considered as a whole.*"[28] The writings of Coleridge and Arnold (who were themselves the tributaries of Schleiermacher and other German theologians) did much to generate unrest about the concept of biblical infallibility in England; the effects of their arguments were also felt in the United States as Professor Noah Porter (1811–1892) recounted in a lengthy article entitled, "Coleridge and his American Disciples" (1847).[29]

The American T. F. Curtis whom we mentioned earlier gives us some idea of what early nineteenth-century divines meant by the word *infallible*. Favorably disposed to Coleridge, Curtis called for a "Reformation" in which this concept of infallibility would be overthrown:

> But the Protestant world must now open its eyes upon another Reformation, and learn not only that the Church is fallible, but that the Scriptures, especially of the Old Testament, though truly and properly to be venerated as holy, inspired and sacred documents of the Christian faith, are not therefore to be esteemed, especially in matters of current opinion, as science and history, absolutely infallible, but as having partly received their color from the ages in which they were produced, and from the sincere yet fallible opinions of holy men, moved by the Holy Ghost, who wrote them.[30]

We should notice that Curtis defines the "Protestant world's" concept of biblical infallibility in terms that parallel Rogers and McKim's definition of inerrancy: the Bible is absolutely infallible in every domain including history and science. The Princetonians suddenly become less lonesome figures when they are viewed in the broader Protestant context Curtis spreads before us.

Curtis's perception is astute. Evangelicals did debate the mode of inspiration as they attempted to sidestep the inconveniences of the mechanical dictation theory, which Coleridge, Morell, and others had successfully exploited.[31] But in the first half of the nineteenth century most Evangelicals in England and the United States did agree upon one of the effects of inspiration: the Bible is completely infallible when properly interpreted.[32] In the United States Christians other than Old-School Presbyterians held that position.[33] The important New Hampshire Confession (1833), which summarized Baptist credal beliefs, reads:

> We believe that the Holy Bible was written by men divinely inspired, and is a perfect treasure of heavenly instruction; that it has God for its author, salvation for its end, and truth, without any mixture of error, for its matter....[34]

In his well-crafted essay, "Baptists and Changing Views of the Bible, 1865–1918," Norman H. Maring observes: "In the 1860's Baptists shared a predominant belief in the inerrancy of the Bible."[35] L. Russ Bush and Tim Nettles provide extensive documentation about the careers of nineteenth-century Baptists (John L. Dagg; J. P. Boyce; Basil Manly, Jr.; and Alvah Hovey among others) who affirmed complete biblical infallibility.[36] The famous evangelist Charles Finney (1792–1875) criticized an author who denied the inerrancy of historical sections of the Bible:

The ground taken by the writer is that the *historical* parts, especially, of the New Testament are not inspired, not even with the inspiration of such a degree of divine superintendence as to exclude error and contradiction from them. He takes the ground that there are palpable inconsistencies and flat contradictions between the writers of the Gospels, and points out several instances, it appears to me, very much with the art and spirit of infidelity, which he affirms to be irreconcilable contradictions. The ground taken by him is that the *doctrinal* parts of the New Testament are inspired, but that the *historical* parts, or the mere narrative, are uninspired.

Who will not see at first blush, that, if the writers were mistaken in recording the acts of Christ, there is equal reason to believe they are mistaken in recording the doctrines of Christ?[37]

Certainly no friend of Old-School Presbyterians, Finney affirmed complete biblical infallibility:

... there is a real substantial agreement among all the writers, and that when rightly understood, they do not in any thing contradict each other. It implies, that the several writers always wrote under such a degree of divine illumination and guidance, whether of suggestion, elevation, or superintendence as to be infallibly secured from all error. That they not only wrote nothing false, but that they communicated authoritatively the mind and will of God.[38]

Like John Wesley, Methodist theologians such as Samuel Wakefield (1799–1895), espoused the same doctrine. In his influential *A Complete System of Christian Thought* (1869), Wakefield wrote:

But if it is once granted that they, the Scriptures, are in the least degree alloyed with error, an opening is made for every imaginable corruption. And to admit that the sacred writers were only occasionally inspired, would involve us in the greatest perplexity; because, not knowing when they were or were not inspired, we could not determine what parts of their writings should be regarded as the infallible word of God.[39]

C. F. Walther, an early leader among nineteenth-century Lutherans, understood that if one finds errors in Scriptures he establishes his reason above God's Word. Walther declared in 1858:

He who imagines that he finds in the Holy Scripture even only one error, believes not in Scripture, but in himself; for even if he accepted everything else as truth, he would believe it not because Scripture says so, but because it agrees with his reason or with his heart. "Dear fellow," writes Luther, "God's Word is God's Word, and won't tolerate much doctoring."[40]

The attempts of Rogers and McKim and others to isolate Princetonians as reactionary and lonely defenders of complete biblical infallibility becomes less than convincing when placed against the broad sweep of European and American Christianity in the nineteenth century.

Not only did many Protestants advocate complete biblical infallibility, but some were careful to qualify their affirmation by circumscribing that infallibility to the original autographs. Moreover they defended this doctrinal stance without any references to the Old Princetonians. Randall Balmer's important study on the original autographs hypothesis in the nineteenth century reviews the writings of these Evangelicals.[41] One of the earliest nineteenth-century presentations of the view in question is found in *An Essay on the Inspiration of the Holy Scriptures of the Old and New Testament*, published in 1800 by Scottish divine John Dick:

> While we admire the care of divine providence in the preservation of the Scriptures, we do not affirm that all the transcribers of them were miraculously guarded against error. Various motives, among which a veneration for the sacred books may be considered as having exerted the chief influence, contributed to render them scrupulously careful; but that they were under no infallible guidance, is evident from the different readings, which are discovered by a collation of manuscripts, and the mistake in matters of greater or less importance, observable in them all. A contradiction, which would not be imputed to the blunder of a transcriber, but was fairly chargeable on the sacred writers themselves, would completely disprove their inspiration.[42]

In a subsequent two-volume set, published posthumously in 1836, Dick warns that "no single manuscript can be supposed to exhibit the original text, without the slightest variation; it is to be presumed that in all manuscripts, errors more or fewer in number are to be found."[43]

In *Lectures on the Evidence of the Revealed Religion* (multiple editions, 1838), the clergy of the Church of Scotland in Glasgow gave a detailed analysis of their commitment to complete biblical infallibility in the original documents.[44] Reverend Andrew King argued that should contradictions be proved in Holy Writ, "... they would indeed form a conclusive argument not only against the *inspiration* of Scripture, but against its character generally as a revelation from God" (p. 125). Then King, representing the other pastors, proposed that any alleged contradictions are due to copyists' errors:

> Some contradictions are owing to incorrect readings in the manuscripts from which our present text has been formed. You may remember that, in the argument which was so ably stated in the preceding lecture, proving the genuineness of the books of the Old and New Testaments, the thing maintained was not that we have the books *absolutely* but that we have them *substantially* as they were written (p. 127).

On the Continent theologians like the learned Beck, whose essay, "Monogrammata Hermeneutices N.T." Charles Hodge published as the first essay in the first volume of *The Biblical Repertory* (1825), pointed out the distinction between original autographs and translations, and the role of copyists' errors:

> The scrupulous care taken of the sacred Writings, and the custom of using them constantly in the church, is sufficient to convince us that they have been preserved from serious alterations, yet they could not be entirely defended from the fate of all other ancient writings. The autographs appear to have perished early, and the copies which were taken, became more or less subject to those errors, which arise from the mistakes of transcribers, the false corrections of commentators and critics, from marginal notes, and from other sources. These errors may have been extensively propagated, and in some instances they may have had an origin anterior to any manuscript or means of correcting the text now extant (p. 27).[45]

It is not startling that European scholars made these distinctions in the nineteenth century; since the days of Erasmus and before, some of their predecessors who were biblical critics had made them and wanted to establish a text of the Scriptures that resembled as closely as possible the original autographs of Holy Writ. Moreover Protestants in their debates with Roman Catholics over the authenticity of the Vulgate were aware of the same distinction as the works of William Whitaker, William Ames, and others attest.

The distinction between original autographs and extant copies was also a well known piece of theological furniture in the United States before 1879, the year Rogers and McKim indicate that A. A. Hodge formulated the doctrine of the "inerrancy of the original autographs." In December 1803, the *Connecticut Evangelical Magazine* published an article entitled "On Inspiration." Its author declared that because

> the scriptures were designed to be translated into different languages, this made it more necessary that they should be written, at first, with peculiar accuracy and precision. Men always write with exactness when they expect their writings will be translated into various languages. And upon this ground, we may reasonably suppose, that the Divine Spirit dictated every thought and word to the sacred penmen, to prevent, as much as possible, errors and mistakes from finally creeping into their writings by the translation of them into other languages (p. 234).

He assumed that the original must have been completely infallible.[46]

A short-lived periodical entitled *Spirit of the Pilgrims* published in Boston from 1828–1833 carried an extended serialization on "The Inspiration of the Scriptures." The author, identified simply as "Pastor," was unequivocal in his belief that inspiration extends only to the original autographs of Scripture:

> Instances of incorrectness in the present copies of the Scriptures, cannot be objected to the inspiration of the writers.

How can the fact, that God has not infallibly guided all who have transcribed his word, prove that he did not infallibly guide those who originally wrote it? ... And if, in some instances, we find it necessary to admit, that in the present copy of the Scriptures there are real contradictions, even this cannot be relied on as a proof, that the original writers were not divinely inspired; because these contradictions may be owing to the mistakes of transcribers.[47]

Similarly, an article in the *Christian Review* (1844) avers that the

objections to the plenary inspiration of the Scriptures, from the inaccuracy of the translations, and the various readings of the ancient manuscript copies, is totally irrelevant. For what we assert is, the inspiration of the original Scriptures, not of the translations, or the ancient copies. The fact, that the Scriptures were divinely inspired, cannot be expunged or altered by any subsequent event. ... The integrity of the copies has nothing to do with the inspiration of the original.[48]

A reviewer in the *Baptist Quarterly* (1868) states:

Of course inspiration can be predicated only of the original Scriptures, because they only are the writings of inspired men. There is no evidence that these books have been miraculously preserved from errors of transmission. ... Nor can translators and interpreters, of their work, claim exemption from human infirmity.[49]

The Baptist Alvah Hovey claims infallibility for the original autographs in his *Manual of Systematic Theology and Christian Ethics* published in 1877.[50] Concerning the present copies of Scripture, A. H. Kremer writing in the *Reformed Quarterly Review* (1879), asks:

Admitting some defects in the translations from the original, or some omissions, and even interpolations in the transcribing, is it not of infinite moment to have had a true and perfect original text?[51]

A treatise in the *Methodist Quarterly Review* (1858) defines the role of biblical criticism as "ascertaining the precise words of Holy Scripture as they stood in the original autographs of the sacred writers."[52] These kinds of statements from the pens of evangelical authors in the nineteenth century can be reduplicated many times.

Rogers and McKim's hypothesis (pp. 302–9) that A. A. Hodge in particular created a "new doctrine of inspiration" (1879) by referring to the infallibility of the autographs reflects in fact their own unfamiliarity with nineteenth-century discussions of the matter. Our authors, joined by many other recent scholars, have rested too confidently on Ernest Sandeen's interpretation that A. A. Hodge and B. B. Warfield created the innovating doctrine of "inerrancy in the original autographs." The confidence of Rogers and McKim was misplaced.

III. ERNEST SANDEEN'S INTERPRETATION
OF THE OLD PRINCETONIANS AND THE BIBLE

Rogers and McKim rely too heavily upon Ernest Sandeen's analysis of the Princetonians as it relates to the question of biblical infallibility.[53] Elsewhere we have made a critical evaluation of Ernest Sandeen's interpretation.[54] In a word, Sandeen argues that Archibald Alexander (1772–1851), one of Princeton Seminary's first theologians, was not dogmatic about verbal inspiration and complete infallibility. His student, Charles Hodge (1797–1878), began to stress verbal inspiration, but remained reticent to affirm biblical inerrancy dogmatically. Buffeted by the findings of higher criticism and developmental science, A. A. Hodge (1823–1886) and B. B. Warfield (1851–1921) advocated the doctrine of inerrancy in the original autographs (1881) as a dodge to escape mounting attacks on Scripture. Sandeen boldly affirms that this doctrine "did not exist in either Europe or America prior to its formulation in the last half of the nineteenth century."[55]

Happily, Rogers and McKim dismiss Sandeen's judgment that Archibald Alexander was not dogmatic about his commitment that the words of Scripture were inspired. In an article that Rogers and McKim cite, Sandeen declares: "First, the Princeton theologians agreed that the 'inspiration of the Scriptures extends to the words.' Archibald Alexander did not feel obliged to be dogmatic about the point, but after Charles Hodge adopted the position, no change occurred at Princeton regarding verbal inspiration."[56] On the contrary, Alexander was dogmatic on the point. He defined inspiration as

> SUCH A DIVINE INFLUENCE UPON THE MINDS OF THE SACRED WRITERS AS RENDERED THEM EXEMPT FROM ERROR, BOTH IN REGARD TO THE IDEAS AND WORDS.
>
> This is properly called PLENARY inspiration. Nothing can be conceived more satisfactory. Certainty, infallible certainty, is the utmost that can be desired in any narrative; and if we have this in the sacred Scriptures, there is nothing more to be wished in regard to this matter.[57]

As we saw, Rogers and McKim acknowledge that Archibald Alexander held to complete biblical infallibility, attributing this commitment to the influence of Francis Turretin upon his thought.

But the authors follow Sandeen too closely in his interpretation of Charles Hodge's famous "flecks in the Parthenon" comment. In his *Systematic Theology* (I, 170), Hodge speaks about "errors" in the Bible:

> The errors in matters of fact which skeptics search out bear no proportion to the whole. No sane man would deny that the Parthenon was built of marble, even if here and there a speck of sandstone should be detected in its structure. Not less unreasonable is it to deny the inspiration of such a book as the Bible, because one sacred writer says that on a given

occasion twenty-four thousand, and another says twenty-three thousand, men were slain. Surely a Christian may be allowed to tread such objections under his feet.

Sandeen uses this statement as his principal evidence to demonstrate a new shift at Princeton between Charles Hodge and his son A. A. Hodge. According to Sandeen, A. A. Hodge and B. B. Warfield were obliged to create the doctrine of inerrancy in the original autographs due to mounting pressures of higher biblical criticism and science.[58] A. A. Hodge and B. B. Warfield articulated this new doctrine in their joint article of 1881, "Inspiration." Writes Sandeen: "One could no longer dismiss them [errors] as had Charles Hodge—as flecks of sandstone in the Parthenon marble. Hodge and Warfield retreated."[59]

Sandeen, unfortunately, fails to cite Charles Hodge's next lines following the Parthenon illustration:

> Admitting that the Scriptures do contain, in a few instances, discrepancies which without our present means of knowledge, we are unable satisfactorily to explain, they furnish no rational ground for denying their infallibility (I, 170).

Elsewhere in his theology text, Charles Hodge declares:

> The whole Bible was written under such an influence as preserved its human authors from all error, and makes it for the Church the infallible rule of faith and practice (I, 182).

In other words, Charles Hodge did not accept the possibility that the "errors" were genuine ones.[60] It should be observed that in an earlier review of William Lee's significant volume, *The Inspiration of the Holy Scripture* (see *The Biblical Repertory* 29 (1857): 660–98), Charles Hodge had indicated his belief in the complete infallibility of the Bible: "It was only when acting as the organs of the Holy Ghost, that they [the biblical writers] were preserved from all mistakes.... The Scriptures may be absolutely free from error, although the knowledge of the men who wrote them was limited to the things which are therein recorded (p. 670)." He had attributed "serious difficulties" in the text to errors of transcription and "our ignorance." With regard to alleged contradictions that cannot be satisfactorily explained, he declared: "... it is rational to confess our ignorance, but irrational to assume that what we cannot explain is inexplicable (p. 687)."

Already in the 1880s several critics had claimed that Charles Hodge had not believed in inerrancy, citing the Parthenon illustration as proof. To this charge, B. B. Warfield replied:

> Dr. Charles Hodge justly characterizes those [alleged errors] that have been adduced by disbelievers in the plenary inspiration of the Scriptures, as "for the most part trivial," "only apparent," and marvelously few "of

any real importance." They bear, he adds, about the same relation to the whole that a speck of sandstone detected here and there in the marble of the Parthenon would bear to the building. [Footnote 60 reads]: We have purposely adduced this passage here to enable us to protest against the misuse of it, which in the exigencies of the present controversy, has been made, as if Dr. Hodge was in this passage admitting the reality of the alleged errors.... How far Dr. Hodge was from admitting the reality of error in the original Biblical text may be estimated from the frequency with which he asserts its freedom from error in the immediately preceding context—pp. 152, 155, 163 ... 165, 166, 169....[61]

Much like Richard Baxter, Hodge was apparently arguing that even if one should suppose that there were minor errors (which Hodge himself did not allow), that should not keep an inquirer from contemplating "the sacred Scriptures filled with the highest truth" (I, p. 170; from the preceding line to the Parthenon illustration). Hodge was observing that a person could learn about the truths of the Christian religion without believing in biblical infallibility. Hodge was not here building a case for a fallible Bible.

Rogers and McKim do not misread Charles Hodge's Parthenon illustration quite as badly as Sandeen does. They write (p. 286):

> Hodge the teacher was able to dismiss such problems as minor. Hodge the theorist, however, was unable to admit that the problem might reside in his understanding of the issue.

They misleadingly intimate that the teacher in Hodge did not take the possibility of real errors in the text seriously. And, although they propose that Hodge upheld an "errorless" Scripture (p. 288), they leave the distinct impression that he believed the "errors" were genuine ones (p. 285). "Hodge was even willing to admit that there could be some errors in minor matters in Scripture...." Or, they note (p. 308): "The 'specks of sandstone' Charles Hodge had admitted could be detected in the 'marble of the Parthenon' were becoming more numerous." Warfield's rejoinder still stands. Our authors did not assess Charles Hodge's published writings with sufficient care.[62]

Rogers and McKim draw even closer to Professor Sandeen's analysis when they discuss what they believe were innovating traits in the theology of Archibald Alexander Hodge, Charles Hodge's son. They propose that A. A. Hodge's *Confession of Faith: A Handbook of Christian Doctrine Expounding the Westminster Confession* (1869) represented marked departures from the teachings of the Westminster Confession. Concerning the role of the Holy Spirit in confirming biblical authority, for example, the authors declare (p. 300):

> Hodge could not accept the authority of the Scripture as the Westminster Divines had because of the internal testimony of the Holy Spirit.

They evidently overlooked Hodge's emphatic discussion about the Holy Spirit's role in his *Confession of Faith* ... :

> Yet that the highest and most influential faith in the truth and authority of the Scriptures is the direct work of the Holy Spirit in our hearts.
>
> The Scriptures to the unregenerate man are like light to the blind. They may be felt as the rays of the sun are felt by the blind, but they cannot be fully seen. The Holy Spirit opens the blinded eyes and gives due sensibility to the diseased heart; and thus assurance comes with the evidence of spiritual experience.[63]

Why our authors neglected this important passage is difficult to ascertain.

Rogers and McKim also aver that A. A. Hodge changed the content "of the Princeton defense of Scripture."[64] Like Sandeen, they suggest that the Princetonian introduced the hypothesis of inerrancy in the original autographs in the 1879 revised edition of his *Outlines of Theology*, whereas he made no allusion to it in the 1860 edition of the same work.[65] The "new" stress on inerrancy in the original autographs was necessary due to the increased number of "scientific" and "higher critical" problems opponents of complete biblical infallibility were raising.

Rogers and McKim do not indicate that this belief was a common one, widely shared by contemporaries. It also underlay the thinking of many of A. A. Hodge's Princeton predecessors. In his 1831 review of Woods's *Lectures on the Inspiration of the Scriptures*, Archibald Alexander indicated his keen awareness of copyist errors entering into extant versions of the biblical texts:

> There are in the Bible apparent discrepancies which can easily be reconciled by a little explanation; and there may be real contradictions in our copies, which may be owing to the mistakes of transcribers. Now, when such things are observed, there should not be a hasty conclusion that the book was not written by inspiration, but a careful and candid examination of the passages, and even when we cannot reconcile them, we should consider the circumstances under which these books have been transmitted to us, and the almost absolute certainty, that in so many ages, and in the process of such numerous transcriptions, mistakes must necessarily have occurred, and may have passed into all the copies extant.[66]

Apropos to the "originals," Alexander could declare "... that we have the best evidence that the Scriptures which were in use when Christ was upon the earth, were entire and uncorrupted, and were an infallible rule."[67] Inaccuracies within copies or versions did not have a bearing on the infallibility of the original texts of Scripture.

Randall Balmer's study of Charles Hodge's manuscripts informs us that the Princetonian was well aware of the same distinction between infallible originals and error-pocked, extant texts as early as the

1820s. In an introductory lecture of a course devoted to "Biblical Criticism" (November, 1822), Hodge observed:

> When we remember the period which has elapsed since the Sacred writings were originally penned, the number of transcriptions to which they must have been subjected, the impossibility of transcribers avoiding many mistakes, and the probability that interested persons would intentionally alter the sacred text, it really becomes a matter of considerable concern to enquire how the Bible has sustained these dangers and in what state it has survived to the present day. It is vain to fold our arms in security and take it for granted that it has not been materially affected by these and similar causes, that a kind of Providence has carefully preserved it. This assumption will neither satisfy the enemies of the truth nor its enlightened friends.[68]

We recall that Hodge published an essay by Beck (*The Biblical Repertory*, 1825) in which the European scholar, citing the authority of earlier German savants, distinguished carefully between the original autographs and copies.[69] In the 1820s Hodge was fully cognizant of the proposition that errors existed in the extant copies of the Scriptures and that the original autographs had been lost. He had read European scholars on the subject.[70] Rogers and McKim's description of Hodge as one who moved "late in life" (1870s) toward a theory of the inerrancy of the original autographs has a misleading character about it.[71]

Another Princetonian who shared Charles Hodge's line of thought was Francis L. Patton. In 1869, four years after his graduation from the seminary and fully ten years before (according to Professor Sandeen) A. A. Hodge first articulated the original autographs theory, Patton published *The Inspiration of the Scriptures*. The chapter entitled "Explication of the Doctrine of Inspiration" opens with the following italicized statement: *"When it is claimed that the Scriptures are inspired, it must be understood that we refer to the original manuscripts."*[72] Patton observes:

> This remark is necessary in view of the objections which are based on the various readings of the MSS. and on differences in translation. The books of the Bible as they came from the hands of their writers were infallible. The autographs were penned under divine guidance. It is not claimed that a perpetual miracle has preserved the sacred text from the errors of copyists. The inspired character of our Bible depends, of course, upon its correspondence with the original inspired manuscripts. These autographs are not in existence, and we must determine the correct text of Scripture in the same way that we determine the text of any of the ancient classics.[73]

Patton, who later became a professor and president at Princeton, plainly argued that the infallibility of the Bible extends only to the original autographs.[74]

We shall leave to others to analyze Rogers and McKim's controversial interpretation of B. B. Warfield's apologetic for biblical authority. We should, however, comment about their reference to Warfield and A. A. Hodge's "Inspiration" article (1881) and the original autographs hypothesis. Rogers and McKim write (p. 347):

> Warfield, with Hodge, thereby shifted the arena of discussion away from what the actual Bible said and was. They based their entire apologetic case on the inability of anyone to bring forth evidence from the nonexistent autographs. With such an unassailable, though artificial, position Warfield felt secure. Individual facts that arose from critical study could never topple the Princeton theory of inerrancy.

Rogers and McKim follow Sandeen's suggestion that Warfield and Hodge joined together to create an unassailable apologetic for Holy Writ's inerrancy. The critic of the doctrine could only prove the errancy of Scripture by locating errors in the original autographs. Since the autographs were lost, the critic could never gain access to them in order to prove his or her case.

In reality, Warfield and Hodge were emphasizing a position long honored by many Christians throughout the ages. The Bible gives no indication that copyists of Scripture were inspired; only the biblical authors were.[75] As Augustine, Erasmus, Richard Baxter, the English apologist Whitaker, and the Roman Catholic critic Richard Simon pointed out, copies in fact do have errors. Then again William Ames observed that God providentially protected the biblical writings as they passed through time such that no gross distortions ruined them. For many Protestants, versions were "authentical" to the extent that they reflected the "originals." The autographs could be approached through the use of what we today would call textual criticism.

When this background is taken into consideration, we can understand better why A. A. Hodge and B. B. Warfield did not view themselves as innovators when they crafted their 1881 "Inspiration" article. They could look back at their predecessors at Princeton as holding the doctrine of biblical infallibility in the original autographs as well as at Christians from other communions and other centuries.[76] Moreover, despite a modern day assumption to the contrary, A. A. Hodge and B. B. Warfield did not use the word *inerrancy* in that article, but employed the traditional word *infallibility* and expressions like "without error."[77] And—irony of ironies, given Sandeen's perspective—they were accused by some conservative critics of having probably "let down the claims of inspiration too low."[78] Professor Sandeen's suggestion that "the first reference to the original autographs in the Princeton Theology occurs in 1879" and his suggestion that the

1881 inspiration article represented the "formulation of a new doctrine" stands in need of serious revision.

Ongoing research in the correspondence of A. A. Hodge and B. B. Warfield for the late 1870s and early 1880s gives no hint of a conspiratorial mentality shared by these two men.[79] What they said privately to each other, neither Sandeen nor any other scholar knows. As a result, the conspiratorial thesis can only be based on a psychological reconstruction, which is methodologically illegitimate in historical studies. In his bibliography for the *Roots of Fundamentalism*, Sandeen acknowledges that he did not consult the B. B. Warfield papers because at the time of his study they were not available to scholars.[80]

Rogers and McKim have relied too heavily upon Ernest Sandeen's analysis of the Princetonians as it relates to the question of biblical infallibility. Although Sandeen's essay on the origins of Fundamentalism contains many worthwhile elements, its discussion of the Princetonians and Scripture is seriously flawed. A growing number of scholars are beginning to understand this.[81]

IV. THE IMPACT OF FRANCIS TURRETIN'S THOUGHT AND BACONIANISM/COMMON SENSE REALISM UPON THE PRINCETONIANS

The authors limit the major formative factors concerning the Old Princetonians' view of Scripture to the impact of Francis Turretin's thought and Baconianism. Undeniably, those two sources of influence were important ones. But those acquainted with the Old Princetonians' cosmopolitan reading fare know that they poured over many works on Scripture other than those of Francis Turretin.[82] They read the studies of Germans, Englishmen, and fellow Americans on biblical inspiration. They were very familiar with the standard books on biblical inspiration by Louis Gaussen (1841) and William Lee (1854).[83] Warfield was quite familiar with William Whitaker. For that matter, as Rogers and McKim observe, the Princetonians specifically rejected Turretin's belief concerning the inspiration of the Massoretic pointing, whereas Charles Hodge indicated that he disliked the "tincture of scholasticism which pervades his work" (p. 280). Turretin's teachings were greatly appreciated, but within limits.[84] Rogers and McKim's premise that the Princetonians' commitment to complete biblical infallibility was due to the influence of Francis Turretin upon their minds promotes a false impression. We recall that our authors declare (p. 273): "Because of his roots in Turretin, however, Alexander held fast to the postulate of the Bible's inerrancy in all things." Archibald Alexander, in fact, believed in the Bible's complete infallibility for many reasons other than his conversancy with Turretin's writings.

Moreover scholars have not yet fully clarified what the

significance of Common Sense Philosophy/Baconianism might have been for the Old Princetonians. Did the Princetonians view "truth" differently than the Reformers? We propose that in the main they did not. Did not Calvin and Luther, despite their great concern to understand the meaning of God's mighty acts in history, treat the Bible atomistically on occasion in their sustained efforts to harmonize the words of Scripture? Did not Luther and Calvin give heed to what philosophers today call a "correspondence theory of truth" in their harmonization studies while at the same time they grasped the "saving truth" that Jesus Christ is the way, the truth, and the life? The Princetonians' Baconianism did not quarantine them in another cultural paradigm such that they could not share with the Reformers several common grounds for understanding religious and epistemological issues.[85] As we have seen, the Princetonians' stress on complete biblical infallibility was not an innovation among those who considered themselves to be children of the Reformation.

It is true, however, that the Old Princetonians (influenced by Common Sense Realism) may have overestimated mankind's ability to understand an apologetic case for Christianity based on external evidences, and this despite their Reformed anthropology. They may have underemphasized the role of the Holy Spirit in persuading the faithful of the authority of Scripture. In addition, Common Sense Realism did engender several problems for evangelical Protestants, including the Princetonians. Professor Mark Noll writes aptly that Common Sense Realism

> was unwilling to rest with traditional tensions in Christian thought: for example, how divine sovereignty and human responsibility could exist together, or how the sacraments could be valuable for salvation without denying justification by faith. Most theologians in the nineteenth century were not content until they had "settled" these difficulties.[86]

Noll wants to determine if "Baconianism" brought a nonbiblical concept of causation into the thought of evangelical theologians.[87]

But on some of these points we should speak with great caution. Charles Hodge was not the uncritical proponent to Common Sense Realism that Rogers and McKim and more recently George Marsden have made him out to be.[88] After praising William Hamilton, a major Common Sense Realist, for his defense of the "Philosophy of Common Sense," Hodge in his *Systematic Theology* (I, p. 363) declares that "The theory, therefore, of Hamilton and Mansel as to the knowledge of God is suicidal."[89] Then the Princetonian gives his own nuanced analysis of human nature. It does not mesh perfectly with Common Sense Realism's appraisal of reason and conscience. Hodge indicates that reason and conscience are no longer adequate guides regarding "the things of God" because we are in a state of "darkness and confusion" (I, pp. 363–64):

> God has not so constituted our nature as to make it of necessity deceptive. The senses, reason, and conscience, within their appropriate spheres, and in their normal exercise, are trustworthy guides. They teach us real, and not merely apparent or regulative truth. Their combined spheres comprehend all the relations in which we, as rational creatures, stand to the external world, to our fellowmen, and to God. Were it not for the disturbing element of sin, we know not that man, in full communion with his Maker, whose favour is light and life, would have needed any other guides. But man is not in his original and normal state. In apostatizing from God, man fell into a state of darkness and confusion. Reason and conscience are no longer adequate guides as to "the things of God." Of all men, the Apostle says: "That when they knew God, they glorified him not as God, neither were thankful, but became vain in their imaginations, and their foolish heart was darkened. Professing themselves to be wise, they became fools; and changed the glory of the uncorruptible God into an image made like to corruptible man, and to birds, and four-footed beasts, and creeping things" (Rom. 1. 21–23); or, worse yet, into an absolute and infinite being, without consciousness, intelligence, or moral character; a being which is potentially all things, and actually nothing. It is true, therefore, as the same Apostle tells us, that the world by wisdom knows not God.

In this passage Charles Hodge places a serious qualification on his commitment to the postulate of Common Sense Realism that conscience and reason are reliable guides.[90] Not only did Charles Hodge have critical words for William Hamilton, but he reserved dissenting comments for the anthropology of Thomas Reid, one of the most prominent advocates of Common Sense Realism.[91] Charles Hodge's debt to Common Sense Realism is a complex one. The scholarly world awaits a careful study of his commentaries, theology texts, and correspondence; it might help explain what appear to be the unresolved tensions between his professed Reformed anthropology and his appreciation for aspects of Common Sense Realism.[92]

The Princetonians did not neglect the role of the Holy Spirit in confirming biblical authority as much as Rogers and McKim and some recent interpreters would have us believe.[93] We have already noted A. A. Hodge's statement concerning the decisive role of the Holy Spirit in this regard.[94] Professor Theodore Bozeman warns us that

> Ernest R. Sandeen's comment that "it is with the external not the internal" that Princetonian Old Schoolers dealt is a substantial exaggeration, as applied to the ante-bellum development.[95]

B. B. Warfield, who probably did overemphasize the apologetic value of evidences for the truth of Scripture (in comparison with John Calvin's approach), nonetheless could write:

It lies more fundamentally still in the postulate that these Scriptures are accredited to us as the revelation of God solely by the testimony of the Holy Spirit—that without this testimony they lie before us inert and without effect on our hearts and minds, while with it they become not merely the power of God unto salvation, but also the vitalizing source of our knowledge of God.[96]

The Princetonians knew far more about Christian piety and the work of the Holy Spirit than we often suppose.[97]

Rogers and McKim's interpretation of the Princetonians and biblical infallibility is not ultimately satisfying. It ignores the broader evangelical context for the Princetonians' advocacy of biblical infallibility in the original autographs. It also tends to neglect the Princetonians' discussions of the "internal evidences" for the Bible's authority, their references to God's accommodation in human language, and their affirmations that the Bible is not a scientific textbook per se.[98] Our authors' analysis bears the marked inprint of Sandeen's intriguing but misleading hypotheses.[99]

Much more could be said about Rogers and McKim's attempt to isolate the Old Princetonians from "the central tradition on biblical authority," and to place them in what our authors call a "stagnant tributary."[100] However, we should conclude this segment of our essay by making more general remarks about the broad subject of biblical infallibility in the nineteenth century.

Despite several excellent studies, our knowledge of the religious world in which Christians from the various evangelical denominations lived in the nineteenth century remains somewhat restricted.[101] Our own discussion highlights how pertinent this observation is for questions of Evangelicals and biblical authority. We are just beginning to understand better the various ways Methodists, Baptists, and Lutherans wrote and talked about biblical inspiration, biblical infallibility in the original autographs, and other related topics.[102] Moreover, several of the "assured results" about Evangelicals and the Bible should be modified, if not altogether abandoned. Ernest Sandeen's influential interpretation of the Princetonians is less than helpful; its scaffolding for an understanding of the nineteenth century should be dismantled. It is unfortunate that scholars ranging from Rogers and McKim to James Barr have based much of their own interpretation upon Sandeen's work.[103]

We need fresh looks at that marvelously complex world of "Democratic Evangelicalism" before the Civil War in which many Christians fought and had fellowship with each other. We need to read the dusty denominational journals to discover what letters to the editors, book reviews, and articles can tell us about theories of inspiration, doctrines of biblical infallibility, and concerns about Roman

Catholics, "infidels," "mystics," "German biblical critics," and others.[104] We need to read dictionary articles for definitions of biblical inspiration. In the *Union Bible Dictionary* (1839) prepared for a popular audience by the American Sunday School Union the article "Inspiration (2 Tim. iii 16)" reads:

> Nor is it necessary that the particular style and method of the writer should be abandoned. God may have wise purposes to answer in preserving this, while he secures, through his agency, an infallible declaration of his will. So that style, manner, etc., may be of the author's own choice, provided the facts stated and the doctrines taught as of divine authority, are stated and taught under an immediate divine influence, without the possibility of error. And even if it should appear that the copies of such a book now in the world have suffered from the injuries of time, and the carelessness of transcribers and printers, so that inaccuracies and discrepancies of unessential importance might be detected, still if the substance of the book, if the grand system of truth or duty revealed, is evidently, as a whole, the result of such divine inspiration, it is to be received, and may be entirely credited as an inspired book.[105]

Scholars with expertise in the history of the book trade should study the dissemination and book production of volumes like Louis Gaussen's *Theopneusty, or the Plenary Inspiration of the Holy Scriptures* translated from the French as early as 1841.[106] The *Methodist Quarterly Review's* description (1863) of Gaussen as "the ablest writer of our age on the subject" indicates the high esteem in which this work and its author were held by some, but not all Evangelicals.[107] In his definition of inspiration, Gaussen says that the sacred books "contain no errors; all their writings are inspired of God" and the Holy Spirit guided the authors "even in the employment of the words they were to use, and to preserve them from all error, as well as from every omission."[108] How influential were Gaussen's teachings among Methodists and other Evangelicals at the middle of the century? We do not know. Scholars of the book trade should also chart the dissemination of William Lee's *Inspiration of Holy Scriptures, Its Nature and Proof* (1854). This volume was apparently popular and taught a similar doctrine of Scripture.[109] Strange as it may seem for us who have been influenced by the recent heavy press given to the Princetonians, the writings of Archibald Alexander, Charles Hodge, and others were frequently not noted in the works of Baptists, Methodists, Lutherans, and others who spoke about the Bible's absolute infallibility. These Christians had their own denominational spokesmen to quote on the subject; they did not need to seek specific Princetonian guidance.[110] Or they could refer to the works of Gaussen, Lee, Robert Haldane, David Dyer, Eleazar Lord, and a host of other writers.[111] The well known Baptist A. J. Gordon advocated a doctrine of biblical inerrancy, citing

Gaussen and Lee, and doing so with the "almost complete lack of reference to the Princeton men."[112]

When we begin to realize how widespread the doctrine of the Bible's absolute infallibility was among the American public, then we will understand how odd it is that scholars have portrayed the Princetonians (sometimes with dispensationalists) as those who more or less singlehandedly created "Fundamentalism's" stance in this regard.[113] We will be wary of those recent interpretations that suggest that Methodists, Baptists, and Lutherans only became committed to the Bible's inerrancy after they had become affected by strains of Fundamentalism or the "Princetonian mutation," whereas before they had held biblical infallibility limited to matters of faith and practice.[114] And finally, we will grasp more fully why the well-known advocate of the Social Gospel, Washington Gladden, certainly no friend of biblical inerrancy, acknowledged in 1891 that most American Protestants believed that the Bible was "free from all error, whether of doctrine, of fact or of precept" (Charles Hodge's expression). He continued:

> Such is the doctrine now held by the great majority of Christians. Intelligent pastors do not hold it, but the body of laity have no other conception.[115]

It becomes readily apparent from our own comments, cursory though they may be, that much research remains before us concerning Evangelicals and biblical infallibility in the nineteenth century despite Rogers and McKim's concerted efforts to enlighten us on that subject.

Chapter VIII

The Shaping of the Rogers/McKim Proposal

Rogers and McKim do not hesitate to tout their volume as one that puts in bold relief the central church tradition concerning biblical authority. To define that tradition and to chronicle its history are worthy goals. But we have seen that their description of the tenets of the central tradition does not always match the beliefs of those theologians whom they selected as its spokespersons. For example, Augustine, Calvin, and Luther did not restrict the concept of potential errors in the Bible to purposeful deceits; they did not define biblical infallibility in terms of the Bible's capacity to lead us infallibly to salvation; they did not make a disjunction between the imperfect words of Scripture and its perfect message, basing this distinction upon a form/function dichotomy; they did not discuss the concept of accommodation as a means to explain why there were "technical errors" or other errors in the Scripture; they did not propose that Scriptural teachings have *no* bearing on the natural world or "science"; they did not argue that the Bible has "technical errors" or other errors in it due to the humanness and limited understanding of the biblical authors; they did not associate the authority of the Bible primarily with its capacity to lead us to salvation. If Augustine, Calvin, and Luther do represent the central-church tradition regarding biblical authority, then Rogers and McKim have seriously misunderstood benchmark features of that tradition.[1]

In this context the overarching paradox of the Rogers and McKim proposal becomes patent. Whereas its architects announce that the proposal recovers the central church tradition on Scripture, it in fact departs from that tradition at very significant junctures. Despite their claims to the contrary, Rogers and McKim are much more "innovators" than "restorers."

Several questions, then, come to mind: What niche does their proposal fill in the vast literature devoted to biblical authority? What were some of the factors that helped shape its particular configuration? These questions warrant further commentary.

What does the Rogers and McKim proposal signify? In a word it is simply an attempt to find historical precedents for the belief that the Bible's infallibility extends to matters of faith and practice (but not to matters of history and science). The authors apparently believe that if this delineation is allowed, then the Bible's central salvation message cannot be affected by any negative inferences drawn from studies in higher criticism or in the developmental sciences. The reason for this is clear: the Scriptures do not claim to speak infallibly in history and science. Consequently scholars can pursue their studies in these disciplines and other ones without fear that their investigations might subvert either the Bible's authority or its central salvation message.[2] Rogers and McKim's proposal represents a strenuous effort to persuade Christians that the authors' definition of infallibility resides squarely in the church's central tradition and that it is not theologically innovative.

Although several churchmen like the Roman Catholic William Holden and the Anglican William Stillingfleet made similar efforts to restrict the Bible's infallibility to faith and practice in the seventeenth century, and a theologian like Soame Jenyns did the same in the eighteenth century, the general enterprise did not make much headway in the Christian churches at large until the full impact of historical criticism and of the theory of evolutionary development in the natural sciences was felt in the nineteenth century.[3] Thus we should backtrack briefly to that century to gain a more long-range perspective on the Rogers and McKim proposal.

In his *Historical-Critical Method*, Edgar Krentz describes the decisive impact of historical criticism upon biblical interpretation during the nineteenth century:

> It is difficult to overestimate the significance the nineteenth century has for biblical interpretation. It made historical criticism *the* approved method of interpretation. The result was a revolution of viewpoint in evaluating the Bible. The Scriptures were, so to speak, secularized. The biblical books became historical documents to be studied and questioned like any other ancient sources. The Bible was no longer the criterion for the writing of history; rather history had become the criterion for understanding the Bible. The variety in the Bible was highlighted; its unity had to be discovered and could no longer be presumed. The history it reported was no longer assumed to be everywhere correct.[4]

Krentz traces the emergence of nineteenth-century historical criticism from George Niebuhr's *Römische Geschichte* (1811–1812) through Ernest Troeltsch's essay "On Historical and Dogmatic Method in Theology" (1898).[5] He observes that by the end of the century historical criticism "reigned supreme in Protestantism on the Continent" and that it had been "radicalized to a strictly historical discipline, free, independent, and in no way responsible to the church."[6]

Orthodox apologists felt an even greater need to demonstrate that new discoveries regarding Near Eastern cultures confirmed the historical accuracy of the biblical accounts.[7] They were shocked by the appearance of David F. Strauss's *Das Leben Jesu* (1835), which raised serious questions about the historical reliability of the biblical accounts of Christ's life.[8] A growing sense of unease gripped them, whether in Germany where historical criticism's influence spread with remarkable rapidity at Protestant faculties of theology, or in England where rumors about the shifting theological scene in Germany caused alarm. Particularly after 1850, orthodox theologians in England had to come to grips with "German Theology" more than ever before.[9]

In 1859, the same year that Charles Darwin's *Origins of Species* appeared, George Rawlinson delivered the distinguished Bampton Lectures before the community of Oxford University, England. His lectures carried the telling title, *The Historical Evidences of the Truth of the Christian Records Stated Anew, with Special References to the Doubts and Discoveries of Modern Times.* Rawlinson related the purpose of his lectures in this fashion:

> These Lectures are an attempt to meet that latest phase of modern unbelief, which, professing a reverence for the name and person of Christ, and a real regard for the Scriptures as embodiments of what is purest and holiest in religious feeling, lowers Christ to a mere name, and empties the Scriptures of all their force and practical efficacy, by denying the historical character of the Biblical narrative. German Neology (as it is called) has of late years taken chiefly this line of attack, and has pursued it with so much vigor and apparent success, that, according to the complaints of German orthodox writers, "no objective ground or stand-point" is left, on which the believing theological science can be built with any feeling of security. Nor is the evil in question confined to Germany. The works regarded as most effective in destroying the historical faith of Christians abroad, have received an English dress....[10]

He complained about the partial skepticism of Niebuhr.[11] As for himself, he defended the thesis that the Bible was without error save for those errors that were due to copyists' mistakes.[12] Rawlinson's chief concern was to demonstrate the historical reliability of the biblical documents as confirmed by Near Eastern studies.

The next year, 1860–1861, J. W. Burgon delivered the Bampton Lectures at Oxford. A truculent soul, Burgon later garnered a reputation for defending "lost causes." Nonetheless his comments before the Oxford community do furnish us with another sample of the thinking of English churchmen. Burgon, too, was worried:

> It is quite monstrous, in the first University of the most favoured of Christian lands, that a man should be compelled thus to lift up his voice in defense of the very Inspiration of God's Word.[13]

Among others, Burgon criticized those individuals who in attempting to accommodate the Scriptures with science proposed that the Bible did not touch upon science in any way. He specifically refuted a major principle that Rogers and McKim have enshrined in their volume, namely, that the biblical writers were subject to the same "errors" about the natural world as their contemporaries. Burgon wrote:

> That the Bible is not, in any sense, a *scientific treatise* again, is simply a truism: (who ever supposed that it was?). Moses writes "the history of the Human Race as regards Sin and Salvation: not a cosmical survey of all the successive phenomena of the globe." Further, that he employs popular phraseology when speaking of natural phenomena, is a statement altogether undeniable. But such remarks are a gross fallacy, and a mere deceit, if it be meant that the statements in the Bible partake of the imperfection of knowledge incident to a rude and primitive state of society.[14]

Burgon proposed that God, the Ancient of Days, "*cannot* err."[15] Therefore, the biblical authors could not err in anything that He commissioned them to write. In a lecture on the historical reliability of the Evangelists, he made his position very plain: ". . . I believe that God's Word must be absolutely infallible."[16]

The Bampton Lectures by Rawlinson and Burgon provide snapshots on how two Englishmen perceived troubling challenges to the Bible's utter reliability. They also underscore an important point. The doctrine of the Bible's absolute infallibility received at least a hearing at a seat of English culture, Oxford University, at the very same time that Darwin's *Origin of Species* entered the book market and during the first rounds of the controversy over *Essays and Reviews*. Once again it is evident that American Evangelicals who defended the Bible's complete infallibility were not isolated loners.[17]

But the theological sands were shifting. In 1860 the controversial publication *Essays and Reviews* had appeared. The seven essayists of whom six were respected clergymen appreciated the latest scholarship coming out of Germany.[18] A growing coterie of English theologians felt keenly the strong pressures to accommodate their theories of biblical inspiration with the dictates of historical criticism and developmental theories of science.[19] They believed that this enterprise would have to take place if the Christian faith were to remain intellectually viable for many Englishmen.[20] Such an accommodation would also head off potential conflicts between science and revelation. The thinking of one theologian drawn from the ranks of later Bampton

Lecturers will have to suffice as an illustration of this tendency. Interestingly enough, the lecturer's proposal bears noticeable similarities to the one proferred by Rogers and McKim.

In 1877, C. A. Row, Prebendary of St. Paul's Cathedral, delivered the Bampton Lectures before the University of Oxford. Row entitled his lectures, "Christian Evidences Viewed in Relation to Modern Thought."[21] Rather than defend the Bible's complete infallibility, Row opted to defend a position he believed could diffuse the conflicts between science and revelation that he saw surging around him. In Lecture Eight, "Popular Theories of Inspiration: Their Relation to Scientific Thought," he explained how the "warfare" had arisen:

> What then, is the cause, as far as theologians are concerned, of this unhappy and dangerous warfare which is now proving so trying to the religious faith of multitudes? To this question there can be only one answer. Theologians have claimed for theology departments of thought which form no legitimate portion of its domains, but which really belong to the students of science.[22]

He averred that theologians were upholding a priori theories of inspiration that were deficient because they had not been founded upon a "rigid induction of the facts and phenomena of the Bible."[23] Row believed that if theologians would pursue an inductive approach, they would arrive at his own innovative solution to the impasse:

> This is unquestionably the case with many of the difficulties which have been suggested by modern science, of which no small number would disappear if the popular theories on this subject were abandoned for one which is strictly in conformity with the facts and phenomena of the Bible itself. If, for example, we assume that inspiration was not a general but a functional endowment, and consequently limited to subjects in which religion is directly involved, and that in those which stand outside it the writers of the different books in the Bible were left to the free use of their ordinary faculties, a large number of the objections which are popularly urged against Revelation from the standpoint of physical science and modern criticism would become simply nugatory.[24]

In seeking an armistice for the warfare, Row excluded science and history from the purview of the Bible's specific inspiration.

It is important to observe that Row acknowledged that his proposal would strike many of his contemporaries as novel. He recognized that not only members of the working classes believed that Christianity was inextricably linked to a doctrine of verbal inspiration, but Englishmen from other classes did so as well.[25] He commented upon the mindset of many of his contemporaries:

> Nor are these opinions confined to the classes [working] in question, but with various modifications there is also among educated men a wide-

spread belief that Christianity must answer with its life for our inability to reconcile every statement in Scripture with the discoveries of modern science; and not only so, but with the popularly accepted views of what Scripture affirms. The same thing is true with respect to its historical statements, even to the extent of maintaining the accuracy of the commonly accepted system of Chronology....[26]

Nevertheless, Row was so concerned about the current "warfare" that he was willing to run the risk and put forward his proposal. He did, however, seek "shelter" behind the authority of Bishop Butler as a precursor for his own inductive analysis of the Bible's inspiration.[27]

The three sets of Bampton Lectures to which we have briefly alluded provide very small apertures upon the complex world of English thought about the Bible in the nineteenth century.[28] Nonetheless, they do help us to fix more adequately the place of the Rogers and McKim proposal in the literature devoted to biblical authority. As we indicated earlier, their proposal can be viewed as an attempt to justify historically their limiting of the Bible's infallibility to faith and practice. The need for this historical apologetic arose especially in the Anglo-Saxon world during the last half of the nineteenth century when a sizeable number of English Protestant theologians sought to exclude matters of history and science from the scope of the Bible's infallibility or even from its inspiration (Row). Church people would feel more comfortable if the new definitions of infallibility could be portrayed as part and parcel of the central-church tradition. The studies on the history of interpretation by Frederic Farrar, the 1885 Bampton Lecturer, and by the American Charles Briggs represent serious attempts to demonstrate the thesis that the central or best church tradition did not encompass the doctrine of complete biblical infallibility (or inerrancy).[29] Understandably, Rogers and McKim appreciate these studies.[30] Their own proposal is the most recent of the revisionist efforts to accomplish the same objective. Thus the proposal finds its niche within this genre of apologetic literature.[31]

Our second question is this: To what factors may we attribute the particular configuration of the Rogers and McKim proposal? Our authors provide us with a few clues about their debts. The uncommon parallels that exist between their theses and those of other scholars hint at other formative influences upon their thought. Fully cognizant of the dangers of assigning influences in too facile a manner, we turn to a review of some of the major "influence" candidates.

I. THE ROGERS/McKIM PROPOSAL:
ITS DEBT TO KARL BARTH AND THE LATER BERKOUWER

After reviewing what they call "Evangelical Reactions to Reformed Scholasticism" (pp. 380–405), Rogers and McKim proceed to a pivotal study of Karl Barth, G. C. Berkouwer, and the United Presbyterian Church in the U.S.A. They give their discussion the title, "Recent Efforts to Recover the Reformed Tradition" (pp. 406–56). The authors praise Barth and especially Berkouwer for setting the record straight concerning what the Reformers really taught. Concerning Barth, they write (p. 426):

> Barth's "theological exegesis" allowed him to affirm much of Reformed confessional doctrine.... Barth's theology was a theology for preachers. Those who followed him were helped to proclaim God's Word with confidence in a world that wanted certainty. And yet they were allowed to be modern persons, not confined to philosophical obscurantisms or constricting systems of the past.

Apropos to Berkouwer, they declare (p. 437):

> Berkouwer thus offered twentieth-century evangelicals the Reformation stance as an alternative between scholastic rationalism and liberal subjectivism. He proposed a Reformed doctrine of Scripture that was neither rationalistic nor subjectivistic. It was rather a view that correlated the divine message of Scripture with a human faith in it. It was not a philosophical fideism, but a Reformation focus on the Bible's saving function.

Evangelicals acquainted with Karl Barth's neoorthodox views concerning biblical inspiration at first may be surprised that the authors esteem the Swiss theologian's perspectives so highly.[32] Their surprise might be less intense concerning the authors' encomium for Berkouwer if they recall that Professor Rogers translated the Dutch professor's *Heilige Schrift* into English under the title *Holy Scripture* (1975).[33]

Once we understand Rogers and McKim's great appreciation for the writings of Barth and Berkouwer, then a possible answer to a haunting question finally begins to surface. Why does their volume falter as judged by the standards of careful historical craftsmanship? The answer to that question may be this. Rather than trying to interact even-handedly with the data with which they were acquainted (even if it "went against" their favorite ideas), Rogers and McKim attempted to do history relying especially upon the categories of the later Berkouwer as the lenses through which they viewed their material. By this we mean that the later Berkouwer's "historical disjunctions" probably became Rogers and McKim's working premises. Since Berkouwer does not believe in complete biblical infallibility and argues that the Bible's chief function is to reveal salvation truths (pp. 428–29), then those figures of the past who declared that the Bible reveals salvation truths also did not believe in complete biblical infallibility. Since Berkouwer thinks that God's accommodation to us in human language necessitates an errant Bible (pp. 431–33), then those individuals who spoke of accommodation denied complete biblical infallibility. Since Berkouwer argues that according to the Bible "error" relates solely to "sin and deception" (p. 431), then Augustine, Calvin, and Luther only describe error in that way. Since Berkouwer does not believe that the Bible's incidental comments about history and science are always reliable (p. 431), then Augustine, Wycliffe, Calvin, Luther, and others did not believe this either. Evidently, Rogers and McKim took the later Berkouwer's premises and crushed them down on whatever data they encountered.

It is probable, then, that the Berkouwer lenses blurred Rogers and McKim's historical vision.[34] How else can we explain the repeated historical disjunctions, the unfortunate misquotations, and the selective use of evidence. The authors' categories of analysis lent themselves to a patchwork form of documentation in which secondary sources were sometimes surveyed for statements that, taken in isolation, would support the authors' position. In brief, the authors' apologetic concern along with their failure to consider the conceptual problems in doing good history overwhelmed their obviously well-intentioned desire to "set the record straight" regarding biblical infallibility.

Our hypothesis concerning Rogers and McKim's reliance upon the categories of the later Berkouwer, is just that—a hypothesis. Other influences may have been at work to create their systematic use of historical disjunctions and their method of doing history. Nonetheless the very high marks they give the later Berkouwer tend to add weight to our suggestion. Moreover they identify Berkouwer's teachings with *the* "Reformation stance" (p. 437).

II. THE ROGERS/McKIM PROPOSAL AND OSWALD LORETZ'S CONCEPT OF BIBLICAL TRUTH

A striking similarity exists between Rogers and McKim's definition of biblical infallibility and those of several contemporary Roman Catholic scholars. In his study *The Truth of the Bible*, Oswald Loretz declares that "truth" in the Bible should be related to the Hebrew concept of faithfulness.[35] God is faithful to His promises. The infallibility of the Bible has to do with its capacity to lead us to salvation.[36] Like Rogers and McKim, Loretz too wants to define error as purposeful deceits or lying.[37] He believes that his definition of infallibility captures the actual teaching of Scripture. Loretz wants to provide a justification for Roman Catholics to abandon the word *inerrancy*.[38]

At the 1980 meetings of the American Academy of Religion, Donald McKim observed that he believed that his coauthored volume with Jack Rogers could serve to open up dialogue with Roman Catholics about scriptural authority. McKim specifically cited Oswald Loretz's perspectives as those which seemed to move in the same directions as his own.

Loretz's perspectives are not as helpful as Donald McKim supposed. Anthony Thiselton has aptly criticized Loretz's perception of biblical truth:

> Many writers work exclusively with the model of correspondence between propositions and facts. Others over-react against this approach, so that Oswald Loretz, for example, argues that the truth of the Bible is *solely* a matter of existential truth, in accordance with the supposedly Hebraic tradition. But we have seen in the course of our discussion of polymorphous concepts that "truth" is employed in the New Testament in a variety of language-games.[39]

Even fellow Roman Catholic, Bruce Vawter, who is sympathetic to Loretz's thesis that the opposite of truth in the Bible is not error but deliberate lying, questions the underpinnings of Loretz's position (which in fact are similar to those of Rogers and McKim):

> On the other hand, it may be questioned whether all of this can be or should be done as easily as Loretz wants to do it, by the alleged opposition of Semitic/Biblical truth to Greek/Western (or philosophical) truth.[40]

Moreover, after carefully analyzing the idea of "truth" in the Scriptures, Professor Roger Nicole provides a definition of the concept which constitutes a judicious and needed corrective to the views of Loretz and Rogers and McKim:

> The Biblical view of truth ('emet-alētheia) is like a rope with several intertwined strands. It will not do to isolate the strands and deal with them separately, although they may be distinguished as various lines might be distinguished by color in a telephone cable. *The full Bible concept of truth involves factuality, faithfulness and completeness.* Those who have stressed one of these features in order to downgrade either or both of the others are falling short of the Biblical pattern. Notably those who have stressed faithfulness, as if conformity to fact did not matter are failing grievously to give proper attention to what constitutes probably a majority of the passages where truth is used.[41]

Loretz downplays too severely the "conformity with what is" substructure that must underlie any definition of biblical infallibility (or any definition of faithfulness for that matter). Much like Loretz, Rogers and McKim do the same when they restrict the biblical concept of error to purposeful deceit.

There is another inconvenience about Loretz's stance for Rogers and McKim's own interpretation. Whereas our authors claim that their perspectives on biblical truth represent the central church tradition,

Loretz recognizes that the patristic fathers (allegedly caught up in a mantic theory of inspiration), defined biblical infallibility as an equivalent of biblical inerrancy.[42] Bruce Vawter concurs with Loretz's general assessment of the Fathers.[43] Both Loretz and Vawter face the problem of meshing their own definitions of infallibility with the church's age-old commitment (tradition) to biblical inerrancy.[44] But they do not seek refuge in a vain attempt of "proving" that their perspectives on infallibility were always held by their church. They know that such an undertaking would not do justice to the historical personages whom they would study. In this light, Rogers and McKim's interpretation of the history of biblical authority becomes all the more problematic. There are very few scholars who agree with our authors that Augustine, Calvin, and Luther restricted the concept of error to purposeful deceits and defined *infallibility* in relation to that specific perception of error. And yet this idea serves as the linchpin premise holding their interpretation together.

III. THE ROGERS/McKIM PROPOSAL AND THE WRITINGS OF THOMAS KUHN

A formative influence upon Rogers's present thinking is the writings of the historian of science, Thomas Kuhn. In a 1981 essay, "Mixed Metaphors, Misunderstood Models, and Puzzling Paradigms ...," Rogers discusses Kuhn's shifting and controverted theory of paradigms with approval.[45] He borrows the paradigm motif from Kuhn and then proceeds to distinguish between a so-called "inerrancy" model and an "infallibility" model.[46] We recall that Rogers believes that the "inerrancy model" developed in the late seventeenth century when theologians allegedly transmuted the doctrine of the Bible's infallibility in religious matters to its inerrancy in history and science.[47] Rogers sees himself as working out of the infallibility model that does not associate the Bible's truthfulness with science and history. He thinks that the infallibility model recaptures the "pre-scientific era" that predated the late seventeenth century and thereby corresponds to the Reformers' viewpoint.[48] Moreover he affirms that biblical authors were subject to the common conceptions of their own day and thus could make technical mistakes in history and science even when they were writing under the Holy Spirit's inspiration.

At various points in our essay we have indicated the numerous obstacles that derail this line of argument. Here we shall list only a few of them: 1. Many of the individuals whom Rogers and McKim selected as spokespersons for "the central church tradition" did not indicate that the Bible's teachings have *no* bearing on the external world and science; 2. Many Christians before the late seventeenth century did not exclude history from the purview of the Bible's infallibility; 3. The

Kuhnian "paradigm" analysis upon which Rogers constructs his study is quickly becoming passé (Frederick Suppe's judgment for *Weltanschauungen* views in general) among historians of science; for various reasons it cannot sustain the weight Rogers places upon it.[49]

4. The fact that exegetes from Augustine to Charles Hodge were troubled by many of the same textual problems indicates that these problems were not paradigm dependent; moreover Rogers and McKim assume that "the central salvation message" of the Bible is itself not paradigm dependent, although they never explain why that is not the case.[50] Their use of Kuhn is quite problematic as well.

Obviously, other influences played a role in molding a proposal so ambitious as the one that Rogers and McKim have set forth.[51] But it appears that the writings of the later Berkouwer, several recent analyses of what biblical truth might signify, and Thomas Kuhn's perspectives on "paradigms" and science have especially shaped the Rogers and McKim proposal.

Jack Rogers and Donald McKim's study opens up an array of topics evangelical Christians had previously neglected in their discussion of biblical authority. In this regard it has served a worthwhile purpose. Nevertheless, it is not an adequate survey of the history of biblical authority. Rather it constitutes a revisionist piece of literature that apparently attempts to interpret the history of biblical authority with the categories of the later Berkouwer. Because those categories do not find many antecedents in large tracts of the history of the Christian churches, Rogers and McKim's own proposal becomes forced and not very reliable.

Chapter IX

Conclusion

In our study we first set forth Professors Rogers and McKim's central proposal and then noted several methodological problems that hover behind it. We evaluated specific portions of their argumentation. We walked and sometimes sprinted with the authors down various paths of their own choosing through nearly two thousand years of Christian history.[1] We surveyed many of their "roads not taken." We assessed their own trusted maps.[2] Where our own expertise was limited, we did not venture to evaluate those segments of their itinerary; others may want to pursue that.

What conclusions can we draw from our journey, which, though somewhat lengthy, was paradoxically so brief? Although Rogers and McKim's volume bears the title *The Authority and Interpretation of the Bible: An Historical Approach*, we discovered that their real interests were actually quite narrow and apologetic. They wanted to baptize as staunchly evangelical the hypothesis that the Bible is infallible for matters of faith and practice but subject to "technical mistakes" in science, history, and the like.

If Christians are to accept Rogers and McKim's proposal, they should look over the merchandise they are purchasing. They should understand the nature of the scholarship that underlies it, the kind of Bible that results from it, and the problem of discerning what the Bible's real authority might be under the proposal.

We have already presented our estimation of the scholarship that upholds the proposal. Rogers and McKim give their own description of the Bible that results from it. They distinguish between the "central saving message of Scripture and all of the difficult surrounding material that supports that message" (p. 461). It taxes the imagination to think that Augustine, Luther, or Calvin, whose authority Rogers and McKim repeatedly invoke, would ever have characterized Holy Scripture in this particular dichotomized way.[3] Rogers and McKim's claim upon these past Christians is not secure.

The authors' description of the Bible creates for them the same kind of dilemma that neoorthodox scholars before them faced, namely, how to distinguish the infallible "central saving message" from the errant "difficult surrounding material." This is a critical problem because Christianity is grounded in human history. Salvation truths are planted in the soil of the Bible's historical discourse about things that happened. In his 1861 essay on inspiration, the Roman Catholic, John Henry Newman, who wrestled painstakingly with the issue of the Bible's infallibility, clearly exposed the difficulty of sifting out "salvation truths" from the biblical materials:

> The practical difficulty in the latter solution is that of drawing those facts which are in materia fidei et morum, and those which are not so. Where are we to stop, if once we grant that a sacred writer is not protected from error in any one of his statements? . . . Now since Scripture contains a multitude of facts which in their substance belong to human history, but which it viewed in a religious light and in one way or other connects with the miraculous and providential operations of the Almighty God, how is it possible that we can allow the possibility or error in statements concerning them without infringing the inspired teaching, weakening the arguments for its doctrines, its interpretations of human affairs, and its vehicle of divine appointments (operations)?[4]

Rogers and McKim do not give us answers to Newman's questions. Nor do they afford us with much explicit guidance concerning the criteria by which we may sort out "salvation truths" from the Scriptures.[5] They do say, however, that "Ancient principles must be applied using all that we can learn about language and cultures from the human and social sciences of the twentieth century" (p. 461). What this means in practicality is that the infallible "saving message" material can shrink or expand in accordance with the latest givens in higher biblical criticism, cultural anthropology, or findings from other disciplines. As the changing "givens of modernity" set standards for understanding Scripture's authority for Rudolph Bultmann, so they do for Rogers and McKim. Our reason and current perceptions of scholarship help us to determine an infallible canon within the Scripture. Ironically, then, Rogers and McKim's proposal, which they package as one of "faith" before "reason," cracks the door open to the radical criticism of the Bible. Their unbounded fideism concerning the role of the Holy Spirit in confirming the authority of Scripture to believers is matched by a surprising confidence in reason's rights to superintend biblical studies. They offer to Evangelicals a proposal that, like Karl Barth's, is subject to unraveling. The findings of "higher criticism" can reduce the core of "faith and practice" truths to a smaller and smaller epicenter.

What will become of their book? In several regards Rogers and McKim's study is a disappointing piece. The authors obviously labored long hours upon it, carefully forging their proposal. But despite their sincere Christian motivations for composing it, their efforts will probably be less than satisfying to them. Because they desired so strongly to plead a certain case, they generally sacrificed their claims to even-handed scholarship by discounting out-of-hand contrary evidence, by neglecting a world of technical scholarship bearing on their broad subject, by fixing too uncritically upon a neoorthodox historiography, and by relying too heavily upon secondary literature rather than examining primary sources for themselves. As a result, their volume lacks that quality of reliability that gives good historical surveys their endurance. Unless the authors are prepared to revise their work thoroughly (and we hope they do), their volume's future is cloudy, at least from the point of view of its acceptance by competent specialists. And eventually, scholars' reviews will probably percolate down to lay readers who may have been initially impressed by the daring proposals, the simple prose, and the footnotes that appear impressive until they are scrutinized.[6] It would be regrettable, therefore, if many evangelical pastors and lay people take the book's central proposal too seriously because they are unaware of its deeply-rooted deficiencies.

In a way that the authors probably did not envision, their study creates a call for those historians engaged in the current quest to discover the ancient attitudes of Christians toward Holy Writ. These historians should do their research in an even-handed manner, consider well the conceptual problems associated with their undertaking, and write technically competent analyses on delimited subjects before attempting the grand synthesis. Evangelicals who emphasize with Augustine, Calvin, and Luther that one of the Bible's chief functions is to reveal salvation truths about Christ, who acknowledge the Holy Spirit's role in confirming biblical authority to believers, and who rest confidently in the complete infallibility of God's Word, have no reason to resent their quest, let alone fear their findings.[7] The Bible is God's sure Word to humankind. It was His Word for yesterday, it is for today, and it will be for tomorrow.

Notes

CHAPTER I

[1]These scholars include Timothy Smith (John Wesley), Donald Dayton (Bengel and the Pietists), Mark Noll and George Marsden (nineteenth-century Presbyterians), Robert Webber (church fathers). Mark Noll and Nathan Hatch are interested in how people have treated the Bible, not solely with what they said they believed about it. This functional approach is very important for any study of the role of biblical authority in a church or culture. An individual or group may profess a high view of biblical authority without living under the dictates of Holy Writ. They may take their ethics and political theory from sources other than Scripture while describing themselves as "Bible-believers." However, the conceptual problems involved in the functional approach are complex. At what point do the actions of an individual or group either disprove or prove the sincerity of formal belief statements? Is it not possible that an individual or group may hold a certain belief without maintaining it consistently in practice? The vast literature on "secularization" should be considered when a historian uses a functional approach to these questions (see the works of Michel Vovelle, David Martin, and others). Consult also: David Lyon, "Secularization and Sociology: The History of an Idea," *Fides et Historia* XIII, no. 2 (Spring-Summer 1981): 38–52.

[2]Protestant apologists frequently argued that they were reestablishing orthodoxy because Roman Catholics had innovated in doctrine and practice, particularly from the eighth and ninth centuries. The Reformers did not see themselves as genuine innovators but as the restorers of biblical Christianity. Luther, for example, believed that the influence of Aristotle's thought upon St. Thomas Aquinas (1225–1274) led the Roman Catholic Church into even greater theological innovations and further away from biblical Christianity.

[3]How to establish the criteria by which these kinds of judgments could be made became a focal point of controversy between Roman Catholics and Protestants in the sixteenth and seventeenth centuries. Roman Catholics claimed that they followed church tradition as amplified by the Vincentian canon (A.D. 434): "Now in the Catholic Church itself we take the greatest care to hold that which has been believed everywhere, always and by all." Protestants stressed their use of the analogy of faith and their reliance upon the Holy Spirit, regenerated reason, and witness of the church.

[4]See, for example, the debate between the Reformed pastors of France and Roman Catholic apologists concerning the Eucharist (Remi Snoeks, *L'argument de tradition dans la controverse eucharistique entre catholiques et réformés français au XVII siècle*

[Louvain: Editions J. Duculot, 1951]; Georges Tavard, *La tradition au XVII*^e *siècle en France et en Angleterre* [Paris: Cerf, 1969]).

[5]Consult Wayne Grudem's essay on the Bible's claims about its own authority in *Scripture and Truth* (ed. D. A. Carson and John D. Woodbridge; Grand Rapids: Zondervan, 1983). Consult also: Paul Feinberg, "The Meaning of Inerrancy," in *Inerrancy* (ed. Norman Geisler; Grand Rapids: Zondervan, 1979), pp. 267–304. Both of these essays should be studied carefully.

[6]The authors write: "We will be grateful for every further contribution to our understanding of this extensive and essential topic" (p. xii).

[7]Jacques Le Brun, "Das Entstehen der historischen Kritik im Bereich der religiösen Wissenschaften im 17 Jahrhundert," *Trierer theologische Zeitschrift* 89, 2 (April, Mai, Juni 1980): 100–117. Professor Le Brun and the present author have edited a lost manuscript of the biblical critic, Richard Simon (1638–1712): *Additions aux "Recherches curieuses sur la diversité des Langues et Religions" d'Edward Brerewood* (Paris: Presses universitaires de France, 1982).

[8]For example, the French researcher, Francois La Planche, is presently writing a *doctorat d'état* on the attitudes of French Reformed theologians toward Scripture during the first half of the seventeenth century.

[9]Scholars have on occasion taken pivotal passages out of their contexts. These statements lose their integrity when dissociated from the cultural givens of a day and the intellectual mindset of their authors. Some writers have made too facile comparisons in attempting to demonstrate the similarities or dissimilarities of belief between individuals from different centuries and cultures.

[10]H. D. McDonald's *Ideas of Revelation: An Historical Study* A.D. *1700 to* A.D. *1860* (London: Macmillan, 1959) represents a competent analysis by an evangelical scholar.

[11]Rogers and McKim's discussion of this point throws them into an epistemological quandary. If the Hebrew writers of the Old Testament did not function with the laws of logic in some sense, then it is highly doubtful that St. Augustine, the Reformers, or contemporary Christians could have understood their writings with any accuracy. For helpful comments about the common attitudes toward "truth" shared by the Hebrews and the Greeks, see Anthony C. Thiselton, *The Two Horizons: New Testament Hermeneutics and Philosophical Description* (Grand Rapids: Eerdmans, 1980), pp. 411–15. Thiselton writes: "In Greek literature and in the Old and New Testaments there are abundant examples of uses of the word 'truth' in which the point at issue is correspondence with the facts of the matter. In Homer Achilles sets an umpire to tell the truth of a race, i.e. to report the state of affairs as it really was (*Iliad* 23.361). Plato uses 'truth' to mean simply 'the facts of the matter' (*Epistles* 7.330). . . . It is clear that very often in the biblical writings 'truth' draws its meaning from its function within the language-game of factual report" (Ibid., pp. 411–12). Thiselton treats other language games that determine different meanings for "truth." See also Roger Nicole's essay, "The Truth of Scripture," in *Scripture and Truth* (ed. Carson and Woodbridge), and chapter 8, n. 41, of this book.

[12]Introduction, pp. xvii–xxiii.

[13]Since the pioneering studies of Arnold van Gennep, Gabriel Le Bras, and others, historians of religions have tended to speak of orthodoxies rather than orthodoxy. They want to describe accurately a faith's history and beliefs rather than argue about the ontological truthfulness of the belief system itself. Because Rogers and McKim wish to defend a theological stance through historical argumentation, their volume finds its place in the centuries-old heritage of historical apologetics.

[14]To describe a history of a doctrine is a legitimate enterprise. How to do so in a methodologically responsible fashion remains a difficult problem for a church historian. The present writer has also written in a way that some might deem apologetic in intent: John Woodbridge, Mark Noll, Nathan Hatch, *The Gospel in America* (Grand Rapids: Zondervan, 1979), pp. 99–134.

[15]Why does one thinker represent the "church's position" whereas another does

not? Does a majority opinion among Christians signify the central tradition, or do the clerics and university professors who draw up confessions and treatises on Scripture serve as the determining agents for that tradition? The criteria by which a historian designates his or her representatives for any doctrinal development should be carefully explicated. Rogers and McKim fail to establish carefully these criteria and thereby leave themselves open to the charge of selecting arbitrarily their representatives and data. Even when the authors treat Reformed "traditions," they are quite arbitrary in their selection procedure. For example, French Reformed Christians receive relatively little notice compared to the lavish commentary upon the English Puritans, the American Princetonians, and the later Berkouwer.

[16]See F. F. Bruce's chapter, "Tradition in the Early Catholic Church," in his *Tradition Old and New* (Grand Rapids: Zondervan, 1970), pp. 108–28; H. Cunliffe-Jones, "Scripture and Tradition in Orthodox Theology," *Holy Book and Holy Tradition* (ed. F. F. Bruce and E. G. Rupp; Grand Rapids: Eerdmans, 1968), pp. 186–209; Jaroslav Pelikan, *The Emergence of the Catholic Tradition (100–600)* vol. 1, *The Christian Tradition: A History of the Development of Doctrine* (Chicago: University of Chicago Press, 1971), pp. 7–10; Mark Noll, "Augustine on the Church, Its Nature, Authority, and Role in Salvation," *Trinity Journal*, 5 (Spring 1976): 47–66. See especially, J. N. D. Kelly's chapter, "Tradition and Scripture" in his *Early Christian Doctrines* (New York: Harper and Row, 1960), pp. 29–51; and Heiko A. Oberman, "Quo Vadis? Tradition from Irenaeus to Humani Generis," *Scottish Journal of Theology*, 16, 3 (September 1963): 225–55.

[17]Professor Armstrong writes: "... like Puritanism, Protestant scholasticism is more a spirit, an attitude of life, than a list of beliefs. For this reason it practically defies precise definition" (*Calvinism and the Amyraut Heresy: Protestant Scholasticism and Humanism in Seventeenth Century France* [Madison: University of Wisconsin Press, 1969], p. 32). Armstrong does present an important set of characteristics by which he defines scholasticism (p. 32).

[18]See Dominique Bourel's entertaining though acerbic essay on this form of deficient historical writings: "Orthodoxie, piétisme, Aufklärung," *Dix-huitième siècle* 10 (1978): 27–32. Or consult the entire 1978 edition of the *Dix-huitième siècle* dedicated to the question, "Qu'est-ce que les lumières?" where the problem of defining the "Enlightenment" is evoked. The historiography concerning the definition of the Renaissance is equally abundant and complex. Consult the works of Jacob Burckhardt, Paul Oskar Kristeller, Wallace K. Ferguson, Charles Homer Haskins, Robert Lopez, Erwin Panofsky, and George Sarton. For a definition of Renaissance humanism, see especially Kristeller's *Renaissance Thought: The Classic, Scholastic, and Humanistic Strains* (New York: Harper and Row, 1961). Several evangelical writers have failed to distinguish properly between this humanism, which was especially associated with an educational curriculum, and an atheistic humanism based on the premise that God does not exist (see Jean-Paul Sartre's popular essay, "Existentialism is a Humanism").

[19]For example, if a thinker says that the Bible is not a scientific textbook, Rogers and McKim assume that he or she does not believe that the Scriptures' incidental teaching about the external world is inerrant. In point of fact many Christians ranging from St. Augustine to Charles Hodge denied that the Bible was a scientific textbook, but nonetheless affirmed the complete infallibility of Holy Writ.

[20]Individuals, however, may advocate views that are logically incompatible with each other. Human beings do not always sort out their own thoughts with care.

[21]J. W. Montgomery rightfully labels this the "platonic fallacy": "In the Western tradition, the metaphysical insistence that man must err always and everywhere has its source in Platonic rational idealism: the realm of forms or ideas or ideals is transcendent and can be represented only inadequately and fallibly here on earth.... The center and theme of Christian revelation is that the perfect does come to earth: perfect God becomes perfect Man, with no loss of Godhead. But the pagan Platonist—and the naïve Christian who has absorbed Platonic categories without realizing it—will not permit

unqualified perfection to come to earth even when God himself is responsible for it, as He is in the production of inerrant Scripture" ("Biblical Inerrancy: What is at Stake," *God's Inerrant Word: An International Symposium on the Trustworthiness of Scripture* [ed. J. W. Montgomery; Minneapolis: Bethany Fellowship, 1974], p. 34). See also John Frame, "God and Biblical Language: Transcendence and Immanence," *God's Inerrant Word*, pp. 159–77.

[22]For a good illustration of what the social history of ideas might represent, see Robert Darnton, "Reading, Writing, and Publishing in Eighteenth-Century France: A Case Study in the Sociology of Literature," *Historical Studies Today* (ed. Felix Gilbert and Stephen Graubard; New York: W. W. Norton Company, 1972), pp. 238–80. The *Annales School* literature does not figure in their bibliography. Key articles from the *Annales* have been translated into English and appear in a series entitled, *Selections from the Annales* edited by Robert Forster and Orest Ranum and published by the Johns Hopkins University Press. The 1971 Winter and Spring fascicles of *Daedalus* contain excellent articles on how historians are doing their work. Consult also Jacques Le Goff and Pierre Nora, *Faire de l'histoire: Nouvelles Approaches* (Paris: Gallimard, 1974).

[23]See the classic work by Emmanuel Le Roy Ladurie, *Montaillou: The Promised Land of Error* (New York: George Braziller, 1978). Consult also: Timothy Tackett, *Priest & Parish in Eighteenth Century France* (Princeton: Princeton University Press, 1977); John Woodbridge, "L'influence des philosophes français sur les pasteurs réformés du Languedoc pendant la deuxième moitié du dix-huitième siècle" (Doctorat de Troisième Cycle; University of Toulouse, 1969); Jean Delumeau, *Le catholicisme entre Luther et Voltaire* (Paris: Presses universitaires de France, 1971), pp. 9–30 (a bibliography). For the United States, see, for example: Jackson Carroll, Douglas Johnson, Martin Marty, *Religion in America: 1950 to the Present* (San Francisco: Harper and Row, 1979); Donald Mathews, *Religion in the Old South* (Chicago: University of Chicago Press, 1977).

[24]Consult Robert Mandrou, *De la culture populaire aux 17 e et 18 e siècle: La Bibliothèque bleue de Troyes* (Paris: Stock, 1975); Geneviève Bollème, *Les almanachs populaires aux XVII e et XVIII siècles: Essai d'histoire sociale* (Paris: Mouton, 1969); Michel Vovelle, *Pieté, baroque, et déchristianisation en Provence au XVIII e siècle* (Paris: Plon, 1973); Natalie Davis, *Society and Culture in Early Modern France* (Stanford: Stanford University Press, 1975).

[25]See Robert Darnton, *The Business of Enlightenment: A Publishing History of the Encyclopédie* (Cambridge, Mass.: Harvard University Press, 1979); Henri-Jean Martin, *Livre, pouvoirs et société à Paris au XVII e siècle (1598–1701)* (2 vols.; Genève: Droz, 1969); Raymond Birn, "*Livre et société* after ten years; formation of a discipline," *Studies on Voltaire and the Eighteenth Century* CLI-CLV (1976): pp. 287–312; F. Furet, ed., *Livre et société dans la France du XVIII e siècle* (2 vols.; Paris: Mouton, 1970); Paul Korshin, ed., *The Widening Circle . . .* (Philadelphia: University of Pennsylvania Press, 1976); J. Woodbridge, "Censure royale et censure épiscopale: Le conflit de 1702," *Dix-huitième siècle* 8 (1976): 335–55; Woodbridge, "The Parisian Book Trade in the Early Enlightenment: An Update on the Prosper Marchand Project," *Studies on Voltaire and the Eighteenth Century* (Oxford: The Voltaire Foundation, 1980), vol. 193, pp. 1763–72; see also, pp. 1772–1877 of this same work; Horst Meyer and Werner Arnold, eds., "Bibliographie," *Wolfenbütteler Notizen zur Buchgeschichte* 5 (1980): 162–92; Daniel Roche, *Le siècle des lumières en province: Académies et académiciens provinciaux, 1680–1789* (2 vols.; Paris: Mouton, 1978); Elizabeth Eisenstein, *The printing press as an agent of change* (New York: Cambridge University Press, 1980), pp. 709–67 (an excellent "Bibliographical Index"). See also Raymond Birn, "La contreband et la saisie de livres à l'aube du siècle des lumières," *Revue d'histoire moderne et contemporaine* 28 (Janvier-Mars 1981): 158–73.

[26]A summary book concerning methodological pitfalls in doing good history is David Fischer's *Historians' Fallacies: Toward a Logic of Historical Thought* (New York: Harper and Row, 1970). For several of the problems associated with the historiography of the ancients, see J. J. Finkelstein, "Mesopotamian Historiography," *Proceedings of the*

American Philosophical Society 107, 6 (December 1963): 461–72.

[27]When Thomas Kuhn's *The Structure of Scientific Revolutions* (Chicago: University of Chicago Press, 1962) appeared, it created quite a stir. It continues to do so. Kuhn proposed a theory to help scholars understand the dynamics by which scientific development makes progress through "paradigm" shifts. In 1969 he added a postscript to his work in an attempt to answer his many critics. He particularly wanted to fend off the charge that he believes "proponents of incommensurable theories cannot communicate with each other at all" (Chicago: University of Chicago Press, 1970, pp. 198–204). See Alan Musgrave's criticisms of Kuhn's postscript: "Kuhn's Second Thoughts," *British Journal for the Philosophy of Science* 22 (1971): 287–97. Earl MacCormac comments aptly about Kuhn's work: "Thomas Kuhn's views presented in his *Structure of Scientific Revolutions* are most often associated with the view deplored by many as leading directly to subjectivism. His more recent disavowal notwithstanding, Kuhn does come close to looking at the choice of theories in sociological terms involving group practices and prejudices rather than in terms of objective tests" (*Metaphor and myth in science and religion* [Durham, North Carolina: Duke University Press, 1976], p. 3). In his "Afterword" (1977) to *The Structure of Scientific Theories* (Urbana: University of Illinois Press, 1977), Frederick Suppe describes "The Waning of the *Weltanschauungen* Views" (pp. 633–49) which touches upon Kuhn's perspectives. He writes: "The *Weltanschauungen* views, in a word, today are passé, although some of their authors continue to develop them and they continue to be much discussed in the philosophical literature" (pp. 633–34). He notes that factors which have led "increasing numbers of philosophers of science to reject Kuhn's approach as irredeemably flawed, although not as hopeless as Feyerabend's" (p. 648). Rogers and McKim's analysis, which is based on a radical break between alleged "prescientific" and "scientific" periods (or paradigms), encompasses many of the same deficiencies associated with Kuhn's interpretative model even in its modified restatement.

[28]Ian Barbour, "Paradigms in Science and Religion," *Paradigms & Revolutions: Applications and Appraisals of Thomas Kuhn's Philosophy of Science* (ed. Gary Gutting; Notre Dame: University of Notre Dame Press, 1980), p. 236. Gutting's volume in which Barbour's essay is housed deserves the careful attention of those who would want to come to grips with Kuhn's revised proposals as well as those of his critics.

[29]Pierre Duhem (1861–1916) and some of his successors argued that the foundations of modern science had been put down in the fourteenth century. See among other works, Duhem's *Le système du monde: histoire des doctrines cosmologiques de Platon à Copernic* (10 vols.; Paris: Hermann, 1913–1916, 1954–1959). Consult also Lynn Thorndike, *A History of Magic and Experimental Science* (vol. 3; New York: Columbia University Press, 1934); A. C. Crombie, *Medieval and Early Modern Science* (2 vols.; Garden City, N.Y.: Doubleday, 1959). Important dissenters against Duhem's claims include Alexandre Koyré and Edward Rosen. See Edward Rosen, "Renaissance Science as seen by Burckhardt and his Successors," *The Renaissance: A Reconsideration of the Theories and Interpretations of the Age* (ed. Tinsley Helton; Madison: University of Wisconsin Press, 1964), pp. 77–103. For a good summary of the debate regarding the continuity between medieval and "modern" science, see Richard Dales, *The Scientific Achievement of the Middle Ages* (Philadelphia: University of Pennsylvania Press, 1978), pp. 170–76. Dales comments: "But in mechanics and astronomy there can be no doubt on the question of continuity, and in the important matter of method this is even more true. The way from Grosseteste through the Merton School, the Parisian scientists, to eastern Europe, Padua and other northern Italian cities to Galileo has been quite well illuminated" (Ibid., p. 175). On a somewhat different tack Elizabeth Eisenstein discusses at length the relationship between the printing press and the origins of modern science (Eisenstein, *The printing press . . .* , pp. 488–519).

[30]Clagett writes: "It is generally agreed that the learning of antiquity was digested in the Middle Ages and Renaissance to form the chief nourishment for growth of early

modern thought. Thus early modern science grew out of Greek science and philosophy as modified by natural philosophers of Islam and the Latin West. The acceptance of this essential continuity in the development of Western thought does not obviate the novelty of the scientific activity of the seventeenth century, the century of Galileo, Boyle, Hooke, Leibniz, and Newton. It serves rather to clarify that novelty, to show how it arose in great part from the interplay, modification, and rearrangement of older stock ideas as they were fashioned into an essentially new system" (Greek Science in Antiquity [New York: Collier Books, 1963], pp. 13–14).

[31]O. Neugebauer, The Exact Sciences in Antiquity (Providence: Brown University Press, 1970). See also O. Neugebauer and A. Sachs (eds.), Mathematical Cuneiform Texts (New Haven: American Oriental Society, 1945); H. W. F. Saggs, The Greatness that was BABYLON: A sketch of the ancient civilization of the Tigris-Euphrates valley (London: Sidgwick and Jackson, 1962). As these works demonstrate, the Babylonians and other Near Easterners had remarkable mathematical skills. For example, the "Pythagorean" theorem was known more than one thousand years before Pythagoras. To suggest that Near Easterners (including the Hebrews who lived in a land through which many foreigners passed) were either unconcerned to describe the world as they perceived it or were incapable of doing so with adequate precision betrays a certain unfamiliarity with Near Eastern cultures. In some instances the biblical authors did use descriptive expressions that although accurately relating the state of affairs could have been more precise. They did not err if their statements capture the truth at one level of adequate precision or another. In a similar fashion we moderns do not consider ourselves to have erred when we indicate that the day is twenty-four hours long (it is actually something less than that). If pressed, however, we can provide more "precise" information about a day's length. Or, if a person says, "I will arrive tomorrow," he could be telling the truth by using that expression. But he could be more precise if he indicated that he would arrive tomorrow promptly at 11:20 A.M. Nor are today's scientific discussions always precise. Earl MacCormac observes: "Few philosophers of science today believe that scientific language is always precise or always directly verifiable or that all theoretical terms can be reduced to observation terms" (Metaphor and myth in science and religion, p. 2). And yet we assume that many of the claims of science are broadly true. If we argue, then, that the ancients functioned in a different paradigm in which they did not have adequate means of describing the external world (at least with means somewhat commensurable to our own), then we have misunderstood their culture and ours (see The Place of Astronomy in the Ancient World [ed. F. R. Hodson; London: Oxford University Press, 1974]). For example, we do not attempt to give the full mathematical designation of the symbol π; we usually proffer our approximation, 3.14, which is very close to one of the Babylonian designations for π, $3\frac{1}{8}$. Astronomers' measurement of time has remained more or less the same for a long time. R. R. Newton writes: "The time commonly used in daily life is not sidereal time but solar time, based upon the apparent daily rotation of the Sun. Until 1925, astronomers for many centuries and perhaps millennia had defined solar time to be the hour angle of the Sun" (Ibid., p. 11). It is very important to attempt to discern the intent of the biblical authors when they are describing the external world. On occasion they use very precise expressions; on other occasions they use everyday and phenomenological language, which is also "truthful." The ancients were not as deficient in their capabilities of measurement as Rogers and McKim infer. Shlomo Sternberg, Professor of Mathematics at Harvard University, writes: "In the period of scholarship from 1880 until quite recently, most scholars were operating under two severe handicaps. One of these was a consistent and drastic underestimation of the scientific achievements of the Babylonians and the ancients in general. The late nineteenth century represented the high point of scientific determinism and the triumph of Newtonian mechanics. The major effect this point of view had on those who were less scientifically educated was to implant the assumption that pre-Newtonian and pre-Keplerian astronomy was solely represented by Ptolemy who, in their opinion, had a

misguided view of the subject. Their attitude towards Ptolemy was greatly colored by their attitude towards Aristotle and his scholastic followers. This attitude colored, in turn, their view of the lesser achievements of the ancients to a point where they called into question any mildly precise observational result attributed to ancient sources. Modern scholarship has shown quite the reverse: that in certain fields of observational and theoretical astronomy the ancient astronomers were quite sophisticated and employed procedures which closely resemble those of the scientists of today when faced with empirical data" (Solomon Gandz, *Studies in Hebrew Astronomy and Mathematics* [New York: KTAV Publishing House, 1970], pp. VIII–IX). We are not arguing that the ancients necessarily viewed the world "as it is." We are noting that they did have categories at their disposal for assessing it that are in some regards commensurable to our own. See Article XIII of the Chicago statement on Biblical Inerrancy.

[32]We must be careful not to convert phenomenological discussions in the Scriptures into descriptions that bear scientific weight. This mistake has lead to unnecessary clashes between science and religion in the history of the Christian church. On the other hand, we should not argue that the teachings of the Bible have *no* bearing upon science.

[33]Christians in the Augustinian tradition, for example, have argued that the Bible relates the truth when it speaks incidentally about the world of nature, even if the Bible is not a "scientific textbook."

[34]Valuable studies on hermeneutics include J. I. Packer's essay, "Infallible Scripture and the Role of Hermeneutics," in *Scripture and Truth* (ed. Carson and Woodbridge) and Donald Carson, "Hermeneutics: A brief assessment of recent trends," *Themelios*, 5–2 (January 1980): 12–20.

[35]For one segment of this fascinating debate, consult: Remi Snoeks, *L'argument de tradition dans la controverse eucharistique entre catholiques et réformés français au XVIIe siècle* (Louvain: Editions J. Duculot, 1951).

[36]Sherman Kuhn (ed.), *Middle English Dictionary* (Ann Arbor: University of Michigan, 1968), vol. I–K, p. 170 (s.v. "Infallible"). See various dictionary articles on the word *infallible* and associated terms.

[37]The authors are very anxious to prove that the Bible's infallibility has to do with its "saving purpose" and not with its purported inerrancy.

Notes

CHAPTER II

[1]Stephen Neill writes: "Nothing is more notable than the anonymity of these early missionaries ..." (*Christian Missions* [Grand Rapids: Eerdmans, 1965], p. 24).

[2]A reading of J. N. D. Kelley's superb *Early Christian Doctrines*, rev. ed. (New York: Harper and Row, 1978) takes one into the raging swirl of these disputes. See also studies by Bertold Altaner, Johannes Quasten, Jean Danielou, and others. For bibliography on early Christianity and Judaism, see: Marcel Simon and André Benoit, *Le Judaisme et le christianisme antique d'Antiochus Epiphane à Constantin* (Paris: Presses universitaires de France, 1968), pp. 13–46.

[3]On the church fathers' attitudes toward Scripture, see Geoffrey Bromiley's essay, "The Church Fathers and Holy Scripture," in *Scripture and Truth* (ed. D. A. Carson and John D. Woodbridge; Grand Rapids: Zondervan, 1983).

[4]Bruce Vawter, *Biblical Inspiration* (Philadelphia: Westminster, 1972), pp. 22–28; Charles Costello, *St. Augustine's Doctrine on the Inspiration and Canonicity of Scripture* (Washington, D.C.: The Catholic University of America, 1930), pp. 3–6; Johannes Beumer, *L'inspiration de la Saincte Ecriture*, trans. A. Liefooghe, vol. 5 *Histoire des dogmes* (Paris: Cerf, 1972), pp. 21–38. Eusebius declares regarding some heretics: "For either they do not believe that the holy Scriptures were uttered by the Holy Spirit, and they are thus infidels, or they deem themselves wiser than the Holy Spirit, and what alternative is there but to pronounce them daemoniacs?" (*Ecclesiastical History*, 5.28).

[5]Much debate hovers over the issue of the Fathers' attitudes toward a "mantic theory" of inspiration. According to this theory the biblical writers did not use their own mental faculties while under the inspiration of the Holy Spirit; as a result, their humanness does not enter into the biblical writings. See Kelly, *Early Christian Doctrines*, pp. 60–64; Vawter, *Biblical Inspiration*, pp. 25–26. Consult also Robert Hauck, "The Issue of Ecstasy in the Montanist Debate" (M.A. thesis in Church History, Trinity Evangelical Divinity School, 1980). Hauck reviews the essential literature on this subject in conjunction with his study of the assessment of Montanism by early Catholics.

[6]Bromiley, "The Church Fathers and Holy Scripture," *Scripture and Truth*.

[7]Vawter, *Biblical Inspiration*, pp. 132–33. Vawter himself is not a proponent of biblical inerrancy.

[8]I Clement 45 in *Early Christian Fathers* (ed. Cyril Richardson; New York: Macmillan, 1970), p. 64.

[9]*The Ante-Nicene Fathers* ...: *The Apostolic Fathers-Justin Martyr-Irenaeus* (Alex-

ander Roberts, ed.; Grand Rapids: Eerdmans, 1973), I, p. 230. William Shotwell describes Justin Martyr's stance in this fashion: "Because the words were inspired and from God, they were of inestimable value and could not contradict one another" (*The Biblical Exegesis of Justin Martyr* [London: S. P. C. K., 1964], p. 7). On Justin Martyr, see also: L. W. Barnard, *Justin Martyr: His Life and Thought* (Cambridge: Cambridge University Press, 1967).

[10]Irenaeus, *Against Heresies* 3. 14. 3–4. Cited in John Walvoord, ed., *Inspiration and Interpretation* (Grand Rapids: Eerdmans, 1957), p. 20. Irenaeus also declares: "We should leave things of that nature to God who created us, being most properly assured that the Scriptures are indeed perfect, since they were spoken by the Word of God and His Spirit ..." (*Against Heresies*, 2. 28. 2 in *The Ante-Nicene Fathers*, I, p. 399).

[11]Theophilus to Autolycus 3.17 from *The Ante-Nicene Fathers*, II, p. 116.

[12]We have already made reference to Vawter's perspective in n. 7. J. N. D. Kelly writes: "It goes without saying that the fathers envisaged the whole of the Bible as inspired. It was not a collection of disparate segments, some of divine origin and others of merely human fabrication.... Origen, indeed, and Gregory of Nazianzus after him, thought they could perceive the activity of the divine wisdom in the most trifling verbal minutiae, even in solecisms, of the sacred book. The attitude was fairly widespread, and although some of the fathers elaborated it more than others, their general view was that the Scripture was not only exempt from error but contained nothing that was superfluous. 'There is not one jot or tittle,' declared Origen, 'written in the Bible which does not accomplish its special work for those capable of using it.' In a similar vein Jerome stated that 'in the divine Scriptures every word, syllable, accent and point is packed with meaning'...." (Kelly, *Early Christian Doctrines*, pp. 61–62). Geoffrey Bromiley observes: "If the Fathers did not give any particular emphasis to the term 'inerrancy,' they undoubtedly expressed the content denoted by the word" ("The Church Fathers and Holy Scripture" in *Scripture and Truth*, ed. Carson and Woodbridge).

[13]*Westminster Theological Journal* XLIII (Fall 1980): 154.

[14]Rogers and McKim refer to Vawter's study on p. 57, n. 31. They also mention in passing works by Tholuck and Gogler.

[15]See chap. 1, n. 21. It is true, however, that Origen on one occasion apparently indicated that God could deceive men for their own good much like a doctor may do with a patient (R. P. C. Hanson, *Allegory and Event: A Study of the Sources and Significance of Origen's Interpretation of Scripture* [Richmond: John Knox Press, 1959], p. 229). Earlier in his career (toward A.D. 222) Origen had written: "It is not to be thought that God sometimes tells a lie as a matter of accommodation (*pro dispensatione*). But, if it is to benefit his hearers, he will sometimes use ambiguous words and even cover with a veil what might do hurt if it were openly stated" (*Stromateis*, PG 11.101, cited in Hanson, *Allegory and Event*, pp. 228–29). Reconciling these two sentiments is no small task. But as Hanson argues (see this chapter, n. 17), Origen most generally used the principle of accommodation as a means to defend inerrancy. See also Rogers and McKim's discussion of this issue, p. 57, n. 33.

[16]Consult: John Frame, "God and Biblical Language: Transcendence and Immanence," in *God's Inerrant Word: An International Symposium on the Trustworthiness of Scripture* (ed. J. W. Montgomery; Minneapolis: Bethany Fellowship, 1974), pp. 159–77; J. I. Packer, "The Adequacy of Human Language," in *Inerrancy* (ed. Norman Geisler; Grand Rapids: Zondervan, 1979), pp. 197–226.

[17]Hanson, *Allegory and Event*, p. 224. Origen probably derived this principle from Philo. Origen does not generally attribute problems within the biblical texts to the limitations of their human authors. He repeatedly emphasizes the divine character of the Scriptures: "And therefore we shall endeavor, so far as our moderate capacity will permit, to point out to those who believe the holy Scriptures to be of no human compositions, but to be written by inspiration of the Holy Spirit, and to be transmitted and

entrusted to us by the will of God the Father, through his only-begotten Son Jesus Christ ..." (De Principiis, 4, 1. 9, in The Ante-Nicene Fathers, IV, p. 357). For Origen's concept of tradition, consult: R. P. C. Hanson, Origen's Doctrine of Tradition (London: S. P. C. K., 1954).

[18]On p. 57, n. 34 Rogers and McKim refer to a paper by Arthur Lindsley, entitled "The Principle of Accommodation," as one that informs their understanding of that concept. However Lindsley does not propose that the concept of accommodation was used by Origen, Augustine, and Calvin as a means to explain why the Bible contains "technical errors." Rather theologians used it more prominently to explain how God could communicate His Word to us humble human beings.

[19]Hanson, Allegory and Event, p. 260.

[20]Origen wanted to avoid too literalistic an interpretation of the Scriptures. He believed that some Jews had taken certain biblical prophecies in such a literalistic fashion, that they had not recognized the fulfillment of these prophecies in the life of the Messiah. Origen was also concerned that certain Christians were interpreting the Scriptures too literally and thus incorrectly: "... they attack allegorical interpretation and want to teach that divine Scripture is clear and has nothing deeper than the text shows" (Commentary on Matthew, Sermon 15, cited in Hanson, Allegory and Event, p. 149). The "Literalists" would end up with unfortunate "contradictions" because they did not grasp the fact that the Bible was composed of various kinds of language. Origen was famous for his teaching that the interpretation of Scripture should be pursued at three levels: the literal, the moral, and intellectual or spiritual (De Principiis, 4. 1. 11 in The Ante-Nicene Fathers, IV, p. 359). He knew very well that not every verse of Scripture had meanings at all three levels. See Hanson, Allegory and Event, pp. 235–58; G. L. Prestige, Fathers and Heretics (London: S. P. C. K., 1968), pp. 56–59.

[21]"Origen Against Celsus," The Ante-Nicene Fathers, IV, pp. 395–669. Origen was generally more interested in discovering the spiritual meaning of texts in the Scripture than in establishing their historical veracity. On Origen's thought regarding the relationship between the literal meaning of the text and its deeper meanings, see Jean Danielou, Origen, trans. Walter Mitchell (New York: Sheed and Ward, 1955), pp. 139–99. Nevertheless, it must be reiterated that Origen has a genuine concern for the historical truthfulness of many passages in the Scriptures even though he indicated that some impossibilities and incongruities existed in narratives. The latter were designed to force readers to look for deeper meanings in the text (De Principiis, Book IV, I, 15, 18–20 in The Ante-Nicene Fathers, IV, pp. 364–69). As a textual critic, Origen was also interested in solving "the problem of the variants in the different copies of the Old Testament by checking one version against another." Danielou notes that the "principle behind his method was that of return to the original Hebrew Text" (Origen, p. 135). His Hexapla consists of a six-column presentation of the Old Testament in Hebrew, the Greek transliteration of the Hebrew, the Septuagint, Symachus, Aquila, and Theodotian.

[22]Surveying the debate about Origen's commitment to biblical inerrancy, Michael Holmes observes that Origen did believe in that doctrine. However, for Origen the Bible's inerrancy sometimes lay hidden in its allegorical meaning rather than in its strictly literal meaning. Holmes suggests that several modern writers who have claimed Origen as an inerrantist would be well advised to consider the distinctives of Origen's beliefs in this regard. See Michael Holmes, "Origen and the Inerrancy of Scripture," Journal of the Evangelical Theological Society 24, 3 (September 1981): 221–31. Origen's teachings defy an easy systematizing.

[23]On Chrysostom's remarkable career, consult: Chrysostomus Baur, John Chrysostom and His Time, trans. Sr. M. Gonzaga (2 vols.; Westminster, Maryland: Newman Press, 1960); Donald Attwater, St. John Chrysostom Pastor and Preacher (London: Catholic Book Club, 1960). The present author is indebted to Thomas Dwyer for several insights regarding the way Rogers and McKim have analyzed the thought of St. Chrysostom.

[24]Cited in G. S. M. Walker, The Growing Storm: Sketches of Church History from A.D.

600 to 1350; the Advance of Christianity Through the Centuries (ed. F. F. Bruce; Grand Rapids: Eerdmans, 1961), p. 202. Chrysostom and Augustine would exert a far greater influence upon the thinking of Luther and Calvin about Scripture than Origen did.

[25]Cited in Robert Hill, "St. John Chrysostom's Teaching on Inspiration in 'Six Homilies on Isaiah,'" *Vigilae Christianae* 22 (April 1968): 29–30. Or, Chrysostom writes: "With the Scriptures, however, it is not like this. The gold does not lie before us mixed up with earth; instead it is gold and only gold" (Ibid., p. 28). There is little indication of a form/function disjunction in Chrysostom's writings.

[26]St. Chrysostom, *"The Gospel of St. Matthew,"* Homily I. 8 in *Nicene and Post-Nicene Fathers* (Philip Schaff, ed.; New York: The Christian Literature Company, 1888), vol. 10, p. 4. In his homily on the Gospel of St. Matthew, St. Chrysostom gave this purpose for the study: "But that they [the narratives] are not opposed to each other, this we will endeavor to prove throughout the whole work. And thou, in accusing them of disagreement, are doing just the same as if thou wert to insist upon their using the same words and forms of speech." See also St. Chrysostom, *Homilies on St. John*, Homily 40.1 in *Nicene and Post Nicene Fathers*, vol. 14, pp. 143–44.

[27]Robert Hill writes: "The Word conveys the action of the Spirit, and it is an efficacious action; but of itself it is handicapped, as it were—it lacks direction, it requires the controlling hand of the pilot, Christ, to bring all its force to bear in the direction of the goal." ("St. John Chrysostom's Teaching on Inspiration . . . ," p. 37). Nor should scholars interpret Chrysostom's thinking about condescension to mean that he acknowledged the presence of technical errors in Scripture. Bruce Vawter comments: "The omniscience of the divine author, in other words, had to be communicated somehow to the inspired writer. Chrysostom's formula, therefore, was not always in practice quite the modern insight into the psychology of scriptural inspiration that some patristic enthusiasts have made it out to be" (*Biblical Inspiration*, p. 41).

[28]*The Letters of St. Augustine*, 28, 3. This statement is found in Letter 28 to St. Jerome and is dated toward A.D. 394 to 395. Augustine is challenging Jerome's contention that a good man (St. Paul) might deceive out of sense of duty. In this passage St. Augustine notes: "It is one question whether it may be at any time the duty of a good man to deceive; but it is another question whether it can have been the duty of a writer of Holy Scripture to deceive; nay, it is not another question—it is no question at all. For if you once admit into such a high sanctuary of authority one false statement as made in the way of duty. . . ."

[29]*Letters* 28, 5.

[30]*Letters* 82, 3. See this chap., n. 52, for the context of this statement.

[31]*The City of God* 21. 6. 1.

[32]A. D. R. Polman, *Word of God According to St. Augustine* (Grand Rapids: Eerdmans, 1961), p. 66.

[33]Ibid., p. 56.

[34]Oswald Loretz, *The Truth of the Bible* (New York: Herder and Herder, 1968), p. 72. After citing Augustine's Letter 82, Loretz writes: "Now the implication of this would be that biblical inerrancy is to be identified with the ideal of the perfection of a book. Augustine was not alone among the ancients in holding this. It is maintained by other writers of the Church as well, and, moreover, it is subsequently taken up by the theologians of the Middle Ages." Later in this essay (Chapter 8) we will discuss Loretz's concept of biblical truth as it relates to biblical infallibility. This perspective resembles closely the one Rogers and McKim apparently entertain. However, Loretz acknowledges that the early church fathers generally espoused complete biblical infallibility (inerrancy) whereas Rogers and McKim attempt to argue that they did not.

[35]St. Augustine, in fact, did not allow for such inadvertent "errors" as Bruce Vawter (*Biblical Inspiration*, p. 133) points out: "Even his *Gen. ad litt.*, which is often, and rightly, held up as a patristic example of a felt need to adjust scriptural interpretation to some of the facts of human experience, is for the most part an exercise in concordism, premised

on the assumption of a sacred text that must have been infallible in every respect. 'The evangelists could be guilty of no kind of falsehood, whether it was of the type designed intentionally to deceive or was simply the result of forgetfulness'" (*Cons. Evang.* 2.12.29, PL 34: 1091). Or Augustine declares: "At the same time, as I have said already, it is to the canonical Scriptures alone that I am bound to yield such implicit subjection as to follow their teaching without admitting the slightest suspicion that in them any mistake or any statement intended to mislead could find a place" (*Letters* 82.24).

[36]*De Genesi ad litteram* 2. 9. 20 as cited in Costello, *St. Augustine on Inspiration and Canonicity of Scripture*, pp. 59–60.

[37]In Gen. 1:16 Moses indicates that the sun and the moon are the two great lights of the heavens. From the vantage point of the earth, those planets do appear to be such. St. Augustine interprets the passage from this phenomenological standpoint: "Similarly with the great lights mentioned in Genesis 1:16. We must certainly agree that, to our eyes, these two lights shine more brightly on the earth than all the others" (*De Genesi ad litteram* 2. 34, as cited in Polman, *The Word of God*, p. 60). St. Augustine did not perceive the biblical writers as individuals who lived in some kind of different paradigm than his own. For example, he assumed that when the Old Testament writers spoke of days, they generally referred to solar days of twenty-four hours: "It is plain that the day then was what it now is, a space of four and twenty hours. . . ." His days and the days of Noah were the same (*City of God*, Book XV, Chapter XIV). St. Augustine added up years noted in the Bible and concluded: "They are deceived, too, by those highly mendacious documents which profess to give the history of many thousand years, though, reckoning by the sacred writings, we find that not 6000 years have yet passed" (*The City of God*, Book XII, Chapter X).

[38]*Gen. ad. litt.* 2. 18. 38; PL 34. 280, as cited in Costello, *St. Augustine on Inspiration and Canonicity of Scripture*, p. 58.

[39]See Rogers and McKim's references to Polman, p. 64, n. 121. For Polman's introductory commentary, see *The Word of God . . .* , p. 61.

[40]Ibid., p. 60. Polman writes regarding the science matter: "True, the Bible does not describe the Creation in detail, but merely tells us what the Holy Ghost in the Biblical author saw needful to report (*De Genesi ad litteram* 5. 23). What the Scriptures say on this subject is completely reliable, and even when they tell us that a single source watered the whole earth we have no reason for disbelief. . . . When the Bible tells us that there were waters above the firmament, waters there must have been. In any case, the authority of the Scriptures surpasses the capacity of all our reason (*De Genesi ad litteram*, 2. 9). This is equally true of the purely historical acounts" (*The Word of God . . .* , p. 52).

[41]Rogers and McKim, *Authority and Interpretation*, p. 65, n. 136.

[42]Vawter, *Biblical Inspiration*, pp. 38–39.

[43]The passage of St. Augustine which Rogers and McKim present comes from *The Harmony of the Gospels*, II, XXI, 51–52.

[44]Before his conversion, St. Augustine had been a Manichean; then he became a Neo-Platonist. Augustine believed that his knowledge of Platonism prepared him well for his eventual espousal of Christianity. After he had given himself to Christ, he had kind words for some aspects of Platonic thought whereas he criticized others. He especially appreciated *The Enneades* of Plotinus. The impact of Augustine's Platonism does not appear to have shaped his concept of biblical infallibility. He apparently worked with what we would call a correspondence theory of truth when he did his harmonization studies. Moreover, Plato himself did not disallow this theory of truth (see this study, chap. 1, n. 11). For background material on the relationship between "Platonism" and Augustine's epistemology, see: Charles Cochrane, *Christianity and Classical Culture: A Study of Thought and Action from Augustus to Augustine* (New York: Oxford University Press, 1963), pp. 432–55; Meyrick Carré, *Realists and Nominalists* (Oxford University Press, 1946). In his *Development of St. Augustine From Neoplatonism to Chris-*

tianity 386–391 A.D. (Washington, D.C.: University Press of America, 1980), pp. 235–61, Alfred W. Matthews carefully chronicles Augustine's growing awareness of incompatibilities between biblical Christianity and the tenets of Neoplatonism during the years 386–391. Matthews sets forth these incompatabilities especially on pages 260–61. See also his extensive bibliography regarding St. Augustine, pp. 277–311. Rogers and McKim's discussion of the relationship between Neoplatonism and Augustine needs to be rethought. In his *Evolution of Medieval Thought* (New York: Vintage Books, 1962), pp. 32–50, David Knowles describes well the essentially religious thrust of Augustine's interest in knowledge: "Augustine has a parallel ascent [compared to that of Plotinus]; the knowledge of creatures by science; the knowledge of Scripture and theology by wisdom; and the knowledge of the supreme, immutable Truth by intuition. Above all this is the mystical, ineffable union with God. In this ascent, however, he parts company with both Plato and Plotinus: with Plato, because Augustine's eye is from the beginning fixed on the journey to God, not on the formation of a citizen or a philosopher; with Plotinus, because Augustine relies from the beginning, and with growing insistence, upon a help and a light to which the human powers of the individual cannot attain, and to which they have no claim. By giving this spiritual, supernatural end and means to his teaching, Augustine was to influence both educational and spiritual teaching in the West for centuries" (p. 47). See especially: Gordon Lewis's forthcoming essay, "Faith and Reason in St. Augustine," in the *Trinity Journal.*

[45]For example, see *On Christian Doctrine,* Book 4, XXVII.

[46]Costello, *St. Augustine on Inspiration and Canonicity of Scripture,* pp. 6–7. Costello gives a good description of Augustine's perception of "the part of man in inspiration" (Ibid., pp. 17–23).

[47]Harald Hagendahl, *Augustine and the Latin Classics* (Stockholm: Almquist and Wiksell, 1967), I, pp. 561-62. See: Augustine's *On Christian Doctrine,* Book 4, VI, VII.

[48]Augustine expresses his concern for the "contradictions" in Scripture in various works ranging from *The Confessions* to *The Harmony of the Gospels.* He evidences a concern for the clarity of the style of Scripture in Letter 137, 18 (A.D. 412). Later Christian writers from John Calvin to Robert Boyle will interact with charges that the Bible's rhetorical style is deficient.

[49]J. N. D. Kelly analyzes well the correspondence between Augustine and Jerome in which the validity of Jerome's interpretation is weighed by both parties (*Jerome: His Life, Writings and Controversies* [New York: Harper and Row, 1975], pp. 263–72).

[50]Rogers and McKim cite Augustine's Letter 28 (p. 31): "It is one question whether it may be at any time the duty of a good man to deceive; but it is another question whether it can have been the duty of a writer of Holy Scripture to deceive: nay, it is not another question—it is no question at all. For if you once admit into such a high sanctuary of authority one false statement as made in the way of duty, there will not be left a single sentence of those books which, if appearing to any one difficult in practice or hard to believe, may not by the same fatal rule be explained away, as a statement in which, intentionally, and under a sense of duty, the author declared what was not true."

[51]In the corpus of Augustine's writings there are discussions of purposeful falsehoods, deceits, and lies. But Augustine's concept of truth is not exhausted by them. On occasion he will describe Christ as the Truth; on other occasions, he will evidently work with what we would call a correspondence or a coherence theory of truth. Moreover, his concern for "purposeful deceits" is not based solely on ethical consideration; he is also worried about the truthfulness of the biblical narratives themselves (that is, their veracity).

[52]In his *Harmony of the Gospels,* for example, Augustine seeks to resolve many textual problems without raising the issue of whether or not they stemmed from the possible willful deceits of the biblical authors. It is strange that G. W. Lampe does not acknowledge that Augustine's concern for harmonization in this work was based upon his desire to defend the infallibility of the Gospel accounts (G. W. Lampe, ed., *The*

Cambridge History of the Bible [Cambridge: Cambridge University Press, 1967], vol. 2, p. 180).

[53]James Samuel Preus, *From Shadow to Promise: Old Testament Interpretation From Augustine to the Young Luther* (Cambridge: Harvard University Press, 1969), p. 13. See: *On Christian Doctrine*, Book 1, XXXIX, 43.

[54]St. Augustine wrote: "Whoever, therefore, thinks that he understands the divine Scriptures or any part of them so that it does not build the double love of God and of our neighbor does not understand it at all" (*On Christian Doctrine*, Book 1, XXXVI, 40). For Augustine's attitudes toward the Scriptures and the church, see: Mark Noll, "Augustine on the Church, Its Nature, Authority, and Role in Salvation," *Trinity Journal* 5 (Spring 1976): 47–66.

[55]Augustine did not favor those who looked exclusively for the "historical truth" of a text; nor did he favor those who looked exclusively for its allegorical meaning. Interpreters should seek to find both. "Yet no one ought to suppose either that these things [Noah's ark and the deluge] were written for no purpose, or that we should study only the historical truth, apart from the allegorical meanings; or, on the contrary, that they are only allegories, and that there were no such facts at all, or that, whether it be so or no, there is here no prophecy of the church" (*City of God*, Book 15, XXVII). For Augustine's definition of literal signs and figurative signs, see *On Christian Doctrine*, Book 2, X. Augustine argued that it was imperative for an interpreter of Scripture to determine if a passage was figurative (*On Christian Doctrine*, Book 3, XXXIV). In *On Christian Doctrine*, Book 3, XXX-XXXVII, Augustine interacted carefully with the rules of the Donatist Tyconius (d. c. 400) regarding hermeneutics. See Preus, *From Shadow to Promise . . .*, pp. 9–12.

[56]*On Christian Doctrine*, Book 3, XXVII, 38: "When, however, from a single passage in the Scripture not one but two or more meanings are elicited, even if what he who wrote the passage intended remains hidden, there is no danger if any of the meanings may be seen to be congruous with the truth taught in other passages of the Holy Scriptures. For he who examines the divine eloquence, desiring to discover the intention of the author through whom the Holy Spirit created the Scripture, whether he attains this end or finds another meaning in the words not contrary to right faith, is free from blame."

[57]Augustine notes Jerome's apparent shift of opinion on this matter in Letter 180.5. See also: J. N. D. Douglas, *Jerome*, p. 272, n. 41. In Letter 82, paragraph 24 (A.D. 405) to Jerome, Augustine cited Ambrose (*Commentary on Galatians*) and Cyprian (Letter 70 to Quintus) as respected Christian scholars who supported his interpretation. In the preceding paragraph he argued that Jerome would not "be contented to be in error" with Origen and others who had misinterpreted the passage. Another issue also stimulated debate between St. Augustine and St. Jerome. Like some of his contemporaries, Augustine believed that the translators who created the Septuagint had been guided by the Holy Spirit; that each one of the famous seventy translators had arrived at the same translation of the Hebrew text, although they had done their work in isolation (*City of God*, Book XV, Chapter XIII). Their version possessed real authority; the Christian churches had used it in worship services and the New Testament authors had cited it along with the Hebrew text. At one stage in his career Augustine criticized St. Jerome for having translated his Vulgate from the Hebrew text rather than from the Septuagint (see Letter 28; A.D. 395). A few years later (see Letter 82; A.D. 405), he gave his approval to St. Jerome's translation even though it was based on the Hebrew text. In the *City of God*, (Book XVIII, Chapter XLIII) Augustine suggested that when the Hebrew text contained materials not in the Septuagint, they should be accepted; and in a reverse instance, if the Septuagint included materials not found in the Hebrew texts, they should be accepted. In computing some numbers in the Scriptures, he recommended that the Hebrew texts were probably more accurate than the extant Septuagint versions (*City of God*, Book XV, Chapter XIII). But so convinced was Augustine that the Septuagint possessed a genuine authority that he proposed (*City of God*, Book XVIII, Chapter XLIV) that some form of reconciliation must exist at a deep symbolic level between the Hebrew text's description

of the destruction of the Ninevites as lasting forty days versus the Septuagint's description that the destruction endured three days. In summary, St. Augustine believed that the Septuagint was an authoritative text, although he apparently moderated his enthusiasm for it later in his career. And he finally expressed his appreciation for Jerome's translation of the Old Testament based on the Hebrew text. Moreover, he was aware of copyist errors in the Septuagint copies with which he worked. In certain instances he was prepared to correct these copies by comparing them with the Hebrew text which he realized lay behind the Septuagint. St. Augustine's defense of the infallibility of the Scriptures became more difficult due to his misplaced confidence in the myth surrounding the Septuagint's creation under Ptolemy, a king of Egypt. It is also clear that he did not assume that his present-day copies of the biblical texts were without error. He wanted to establish the infallible originals by studying the Septuagint and the Hebrew texts for the Old Testament; he hoped to eliminate copyists' errors from the extant texts.

[58]Hans Küng, *Infallible? An Enquiry* (London: Collins, 1972), pp. 173–74; see Robert Preus's discussion of the oracle theme in Augustine in *Inerrancy*, 478, n. 17. Regarding Augustine's influence, see: Henri Marrou, *St. Augustine and His Influence Through the Ages*, translated by Patrick Hepburne-Scott and Edmund Hill (New York: Harper and Brothers, n.d.).

[59]H. Sasse, "Sacra Scriptura—Bemerkungen zur Inspirationslehre Augustins," *Festschrift Franz Dornsieff* (ed. Horst Kusch; Leipzeig: VEB Bibliographisches Institut, 1953), pp. 262–73. This influential essay has been translated into English: "Sacra Scriptura: Observations on Augustine's Doctrine of Inspiration," *The Reformed Theological Review* XIV (October 1955): 65–80. Roman Catholic scholars (Bruce Vawter, Oswald Loretz) cite this essay as an authoritative study.

[60]For our part, we do not believe that Augustine was caught up in a mantic theory of inspiration per se (see Costello, *St. Augustine on Inspiration and Canonicity of Scripture*, pp. 19–23).

[61]We do not know of any St. Augustine scholar whether Roman Catholic or Protestant who argues that St. Augustine restricted the concept of error in the Scriptures to purposeful deceits.

[62]Roman Catholic scholars have often done the best work in this field. We would surmise that their reviews of Rogers and McKim's discussion of biblical authority in the Middle Ages will be quite telling.

[63]My colleague Rodney Petersen has expertise in the area of medieval exegesis and biblical authority. I am indebted to him for the following survey of the issues evoked by medieval exegetes:

"Most of the current issues being raised which pertain to the interpretation of Scripture are not new. Many have been quite thoroughly discussed throughout the history of Christendom, although perhaps under a different guise. The roots of Biblical interpretation lie embedded in the Bible itself. Here the Sacred Writings of Israel are interpreted through the realization and confession of the messianic character of Jesus. Both his person and teaching, as well as the experience of those closest to him, as they worked with the implications of this messianic confession, became the normative basis for later Christian reflection.

"Early in the development of the church interpretative stress was seen to fall on either the historical, hence literal (Antiochene), meaning of the text or on the interpreted significance, hence spiritual (Alexandrine) implications. Such an understanding of the Bible was mediated variously to the medieval world, but especially through the 'four doctors' of the Latin church, Ambrose, Augustine, Jerome and Gregory the Great. Each of these stressed different items of concern (mediation, asceticism, mission, imminence, etc.) in an effort to understand the meaning of salvation. In each of these as well as other areas, the work of Augustine is of primary significance for later Biblical commentators. He continually laid stress upon an allegorical interpretation of Scripture which for him and his successors never nullified the literal understanding of the text. The integrity of the text, properly interpreted, was assumed; questions arose at the level of salvific significance.

"The meaning of Scripture could be affected by a variety of factors at a very basic level. The significance of the literal text could become caught between the perceived immutability of God (Anselm of Canterbury) and the experience of the believer in the context of historical change (Anselm of Havelberg). Questions pertaining to the degree of development and change acceptable to theology (*reformatio* or *instauratio*) are raised, together with Trinitarian implications, in this light. Questions like these often arose at times of social and ecclesiastical crisis, as well as with the introduction of new knowledge into the West. Then, too, there is the problem of the level at which the text is allegorized in order to deal with conflict in the world, whether such dualism remains at a moral or penetrates to an ontological level (various repetitions of Augustine's struggle with Manichaeism). A third question often raised about the meaning of the text in the medieval period concerned the extent to which its moral percepts were to be literally translated into daily life (Francis of Assisi). Periods of ascetic renewal follow upon times of moral laxity, a process which often bore political and apocalyptic implications, as men and women struggled to live by gospel counsel. Furthermore, there is the recurring question of the extent to which the Bible could be used to 'map' out one's approach to God—whether in spirit (Pseudo-Dionysius) or in time and nature (Eriugena). With implications for Christian mysticism and apocalypticism, such vertical and horizontal patterns of thought could have serious hermeneutical and sociological effects upon the nature of Christian hope. In addition to these four questions (and those which could be subsumed under them), there was, from the earliest days of the church, a competing tradition of final jurisdiction in Scriptural interpretation—whether found in the office of the bishop/presbyter or teacher of the church.

"While each of these and other questions are addressed repeatedly throughout the medieval period, different eras raised up one or the other for special attention. Following the formative periods of the early and then patristic church, such questions should be looked at during the Carolingian and Ottonian eras, the periods of early and heightened scholasticism, and, finally, at the times of protracted transition from the late medieval to modern world. In each of these periods one finds mediated a concern for the significance of Scripture, which concern never nullifies (except in cases of the most extreme mysticism) the literal sense of the Bible. As heirs of Augustine, the religious life is believed to be enriched because that which is sublime became concrete, accommodating itself to our limitations in a way which is always more, but never less than, the signs and symbols of history."

[64]Avery Dulles, "Scholasticism and the Church," *Theology Today* XXXVIII, 3 (October 1981): 341–42. Rogers writes: "We were vulnerable both to misrepresentations of the historical material in the sources and to the more precise knowledge of experts in the various specialties on which we touched. An example of that is Avery Dulles' proper demur from our interpretation of Aquinas' view of the faith-reason relationship. As he notes, we too much accepted the rationalistic interpretation of Aquinas held by Warfield and others of the old Princeton scholastic school. We need to have a fresh look at Aquinas, not filtered through his use by old Princeton, just as I came to a fresh view of the Westminster Divines when I read them firsthand instead of reading Warfieldian interpretations of them" (Jack Rogers, "A Response," *Theology Today*, p. 346).

[65]Wrote Wycliffe: "Whanne Christ seip in pe Gospel bope hevene and erpe shulen passe, but His wordis shulen not passe, He undirstandip bi His woordis His wit. And pus Goddis wit is Hooly Writ, pat my on no maner be fals" (Herbert Winn, ed., *Wyclif-Select English Sermons* [London: Oxford University Press, 1929], p. 19, "p" = th). James O'Connor alerted the author to the use made by Rogers and McKim of the Mallard article.

[66]J. A. Robson describes Wycliffe's commitment to biblical infallibility with these strong words: "In the case of Wyclif, of course, there was really no crisis; he was, unlike FitzRalph; a literal fundamentalist and his fundamentalism was the direct and inescap-

able consequence of his ultrarealism. Every word of Scripture was, and always had been, eternally true, in that it was an extension of the divine ideas" (*Wyclif and the Oxford Schools* [Cambridge: Cambridge University Press, 1966], p. 96). In his *John Wyclif and Reform* (Philadelphia: The Westminster Press, 1964), p. 83, John Stacey indicates that Wycliffe was a "fierce contender" for fundamentalism regarding his commitment to the complete infallibility of the Bible. On Wycliffe's life, see H. B. Workman, *John Wyclif* (2 vols.; Oxford: Oxford, 1926). A. G. Moland writes about the scope of the Bible's authority for some in the Middle Ages: "The extreme example is the view sometimes found that all knowledge is contained in the Bible" (Medieval Ideas of Scientific Progress, *Journal of the History of Ideas* XXXIX, 4 [Oct.–Dec. 1978]: 577).

[67]See especially: Beryl Smalley, *The Study of the Bible in the Middle Ages* (Notre Dame, Ind.: University of Notre Dame Press, 1970); Ceslaus Spicq, *Esquisse d'une histoire de l'exégèse latine au Moyen Age* (Paris: J. Vrin, 1944); the studies of Henri de Lubac, Pierre Benoît, Leon Sanders, and others. Selected journals that often deal with this question are *Archives d'histoire doctrinale et littéraire du Moyen Âge*, *Revue du Moyen Age latin*, *Revue Biblique*, *Speculum*, and *Zeitschrift für Kirchengeschichte*. Consult also: G. W. H. Lampe (ed.), *The Cambridge History of the Bible*; 2: *The West, From the Fathers to the Reformation* (Cambridge: Cambridge University Press, 1976); Jaroslav Pelikan, *The Growth of Medieval Theology (600–1300)* (Chicago: University of Chicago Press, 1978), pp. 34–42, 121–24, 221–23; Pelikan, *The Spirit of Eastern Christendom (600–1700)* (Chicago: University of Chicago Press, 1974); Etienne Gilson, *Reason and Revelation in the Middle Ages* (New York: Charles Scriber's Sons, 1966); Heiko Oberman, *The Harvest of Medieval Theology: Gabriel Biel and Late Medieval Nominalism* (Grand Rapids: Eerdmans, 1967); Steven Ozment (ed.), *The Reformation in Medieval Perspective* (Chicago: Quadrangle Books, 1971); David Lindberg (ed.), *Science in the Middle Ages* (Chicago: University of Chicago Press, 1978); Richard Dales, *The Scientific Achievement of the Middle Ages* (Philadelphia: University of Pennsylvania Press, 1978); Nicholas Steneck, *Science and Creation in the Middle Ages: Henry of Langenstein (d. 1397) on Genesis* (Notre Dame, Ind.: University of Notre Dame Press, 1976); Emile Bréhier, *La Philosophie due Moyen Age* (Paris: Albin Michel, 1971); Jeffrey B. Russell, *A History of Medieval Christianity Prophecy and Order* (Arlington Heights, Illinois: AHM Publishing Corporation, 1968); Marjorie Reeves, *Joachim of Fiore and the Prophetic Future* (New York: Harper and Row, 1977); Norman Cohn, *The Pursuit of the Millennium: Revolutionary Millenarians and Mystical Anarchists of the Middle Ages*, revised and expanded (New York: Oxford University Press, 1970); M. D. Chenu, *Nature, Man, and Society in the Twelfth Century*, translated by Jerome Baylor and Lester K. Little (Chicago: University of Chicago Press, 1968). In *Why God Became Man*, Anselm of Canterbury declares: "For I am sure that if I say anything that unquestionably contradicts Holy Scripture, it is false, and if I am aware of this I do not want to hold it" (cited in Eugene Fairweather [ed.], *A Scholastic Miscellany: Anselm to Ockham* [New York: Macmillan Company, 1970], p. 132). Anselm's sentiments were widely shared by theologians during the Middle Ages. Herman Sasse writes: ". . . during all these centuries no one doubted that the Bible in its entirety was God's Word, that God was the principal author of the Scriptures, as their human authors had written under the inspiration of God the Holy Spirit, and that, therefore, these books were free from errors and contradictions, even when this did not seem to be the case. The Middle Ages had inherited this view from the Fathers who had established it in numerous exegetical and apologetical writings" ("The Rise of the Dogma of Holy Scripture in the Middle Ages," *The Reformed Theological Review* XVIII, no. 2 [June 1959]: 45). We should always recall that more than 90% of the European population in the Middle Ages was caught up in an oral culture and could not read or write.

[68]In the history of biblical authority an Origen-Erasmus-Grotius-Jean Le Clerc connection developed. It often ran into conflict with an Augustine-Luther/Calvin-Westminster Divines connection. The impact of Origen's thinking upon Erasmus is well known.

Notes

CHAPTER III

[1]Important studies of Zwingli include: G. R. Potter, *Zwingli* (Cambridge: Cambridge University Press, 1976); Jaques Courvoisier, *Zwingli: A Reformed Theologian* (Richmond, Va.: John Knox Press, 1963), pp. 27–37; Jean Rilliet, *Zwingli: Third Man of the Reformation* (Philadelphia: Westminster Press, 1964); H. Wayne Pipkin, *A Zwingli Bibliography* (Pittsburgh: Pittsburgh Theological Seminary Press, 1971); Rupert E. Davies, *The Problem of Authority in the Continental Reformers* (Westport, Connecticut: Hyperion Press, 1979 [reprint of 1946 edition]), pp. 62–92; Zwingli, "Of the Clarity and Certainty of the Word of God," *Zwingli and Bullinger* (ed. G. W. Bromiley; Philadelphia: Westminster Press, 1953), pp. 49–95; Samuel Jackson (ed.), *Ulrich Zwingli (1484–1531) Selected Works* (Philadelphia: University of Pennsylvania Press, 1972). Consult the journal *Zwingliana* (Published in Zürich), and the works of Oskar Farner, Charles Garside, Jr., J. V. Pollet, and Gottfried W. Lochner. See also Paul Waggoner, "Zwingli's View of Scripture and Authority" (unpublished paper, Trinity Evangelical Divinity School, February 1981).

[2]Kenneth Davis, a leading Anabaptist scholar and the author of *Anabaptism and Asceticism: A Study in Intellectual Origins* (Scottsdale, Penn.: Herald Press, 1974), has indicated that many of the early Anabaptists believed in complete biblical infallibility (communications with J. Woodbridge, Spring, 1980). Professor Davis hopes to write on this subject. For background material on the Anabaptists, see: George H. Williams, *The Radical Reformation* (Philadelphia: Westminster Press, 1962); William Estep, *The Anabaptist Story* (Grand Rapids: Eerdmans, 1975); Fritz Blanke, *Brothers in Christ: The History of the Oldest Anabaptist Congregation, Zollikon, near Zurich, Switzerland* (Scottsdale, Pennsylvania: Herald Press, 1961).

[3]Some Reformed scholars believe that the central purpose or scope of the Scriptures is to bring glory to God.

[4]On this issue, consult: Rupert E. Davies, *The Problem of Authority in the Continental Reformers* (Westport, Connecticut: Hyperion Press, 1976 [reprint of 1946 edition]); for a sweeping view of the context for Roman Catholic and Protestant disagreements, see: Steven Ozment, *The Age of Reform, 1250–1550: An Intellectual and Religious History of Late Medieval and Reformation Europe* (New Haven: Yale University Press, 1980).

[5]See, for example, H. O. Old, *The Patristic Roots of Reformed Worship* (Zürich: Theologischer Verlag Zürich, 1975).

[6]The Reformers carefully refrained from separating "Word" from "Spirit." The Holy Spirit confirms biblical authority to the believer through the Word itself. They accused

certain Anabaptists of allegedly defending inspired individual revelations. See, for example, John. S. Oyer, *Lutheran Reformers Against Anabaptists: Luther, Melanchthon and Menius and the Anabaptists of Central Germany* (The Hague: Martinus Nijhoff, 1964), pp. 226–31. On the other hand, Luther struck out at those Christians who interpreted the Bible in such a literalistic fashion (according to the "letter") that they did not look for Christ behind the words of Scripture or sense the power of the Spirit which works through them. See: Gerhard Ebeling, *Luther: An Introduction to His Thought*, translation by R. A. Wilson (Philadelphia: Fortress Press, 1970), pp. 93–109. Although Luther speaks about the Word of God in several ways (the preached word, Christ . . .), there is little doubt that he also identified the Bible as the Word of God. It does not become the Word of God; it is the Word of God. Evangelical and non-evangelical historians alike are subjecting neoorthodox interpretations of Luther and Calvin to closer scrutiny. Regarding Luther, see this chapter, n. 13. Regarding Calvin, see Richard Muller, "The Foundation of Calvin's Theology, Scripture as Revealing God's Word," *The Duke Divinity School Review* 44, 1 (Winter 1979): 19: "Calvin's view of Scripture and doctrine, which was designed to cut through a mass of medieval speculations, will support none of Niesel's neo-orthodox conundrums in driving a wedge between Christ as Word of God and Scripture as Word in the sense of witness." Karl Barth himself frankly acknowledged that the Reformers espoused a belief in verbal inspiration (*Doctrine of the Word of God*, part 2, p. 520, noted in John Gerstner, "The View of the Bible held by the church: Calvin and the Westminster Divines," *Inerrancy* (ed. Norman Geisler; Grand Rapids: Zondervan, 1979), pp. 389–90.

[7]Roman Catholics claimed that representatives of the church had the sole right to interpret Scripture. Luther reacted strongly against this notion. See Luther's *Appeal to the German Nobility* (1520) in which he argued that the second wall behind which "Romanists" hide is the following: ". . . if it were proposed to admonish them with the Scriptures, they objected that no one may interpret the Scriptures but the Pope." See: Theodore Casteel, "Calvin and Trent: Calvin's Reaction to the Council of Trent in the context of his Conciliar Thought," *Harvard Theological Review* 63 (1970): 91–117. For the Catholic viewpoint, see George Tavard, "Tradition in Early Post-Tridentine Theology," *Theological Studies* 23 (1962): 377–405.

[8]Cited in Ernst F. Winter, ed., *Erasmus—Luther Discourse on Free Will* (New York: Frederick Ungar Publishing Co., 1961), p. 59.

[9]Ibid,. pp. 59–60. Earlier Erasmus declared: "I know, when investigating truth, there is no harm in adding to the diligence of one's predecessors. I admit that it is right that the sole authority of Holy Scriptures surpasses the voices of all mortals. But we are not involved in a controversy regarding Scripture. The same Scripture is being loved and revered by both parties. Our battle concerns the sense of Scripture" (Ibid., p. 15). Erasmus advocated the principle of "humility" in submitting to the interpretation of past Catholic exegetes. But he did not always submit.

[10]Cited in John C. Olin (ed.), *Christian Humanism and the Reformation: Selected Writings of Erasmus* (New York: Fordham University Press, 1975), pp. 84–85. Several Christians in Erasmus's own day questioned his commitment to complete biblical infallibility. In a conflict with Spanish monks Erasmus claimed that he had proposed a limited biblical infallibility viewpoint "per fictionem." He claimed complete infallibility "in truth." Professor Berndt Moeller argues that Erasmus "held fast to the complete infallibility of the Bible" ("Scripture, Tradition, and Sacrament in the Middle Ages and in Luther," *Holy Book and Holy Tradition* [ed. F. F. Bruce and E. G. Rupp; Grand Rapids: Eerdmans, 1968], p. 127). Jacques Chomarat dissents from this opinion ("Les *Annotations* de Valla, celles d'Erasme et la grammaire," *Histoire de l'exégèse au XVIe siècle* [ed. Olivier Fatio and Pierre Fraenkel; Genève: Droz, 1978], pp. 209–10). For background on Erasmus's perspectives on language and theology, consult: Marjorie O'Rourke Boyle, *Erasmus on Language and Method in Theology* (Toronto: University of Toronto Press, 1977); Jerry Bentley, "Biblical Philology and Christian Humanism: Lorenzo Valla and Erasmus

as Scholars of the Gospels," *Sixteenth Century Journal* VIII, 2 (1977): 9–28.

[11]David K. Lotz, "*Sola Scriptura*: Luther on Biblical Authority," *Interpretation* XXXV, no. 3 (July 1981): 258–73. Regarding Luther's principles of biblical interpretation, consult Berndt Moeller's essay, "Scripture, Tradition and Sacrament in the Middle Ages and in Luther," pp. 128–34; John Pilch, "Luther's Hermeneutical 'Shift,'" *Harvard Theological Review* 63 (1970): 445–48; Darrell R. Reinke, "From Allegory to Metaphor: More Notes on Luther's Hermeneutical Shift," *Harvard Theological Review* 66 (1973): 386–95.

[12]Lotz, "*Sola Scriptura* . . . ," p. 273. Lotz concludes his essay with these remarks.

[13]Ibid., p. 263. Willem J. Kooiman's analysis in *Luther and the Bible* (Philadelphia: Muhlenberg Press, 1961), pp. 236–37, appears to include some of the presuppositions Lotz's criticisms target.

[14]Ibid., p. 269. Luther also approached the Scriptures in a "devotional" fashion. See his comment on a "correct way of studying theology" (*Luther's Works: Career of the Reformer* IV, vol. 34, pp. 285–87). See Woodbridge, "The Spiritual Counsel of Pastor Martin Luther," forthcoming essay. For Luther's attitudes toward "Scholasticism," consult Ozment, *The Age of Reform 1250–1550*, pp. 231–39.

[15]Lotz argues that Luther affirmed biblical inerrancy ("*Sola Scriptura* . . . ," pp. 267–68, p. 268, n. 29), but that he did not base the authority of the Bible upon its infallibility per se. Lotz's point is well taken. However, his criticism that so-called "biblicists" believe in the inerrancy of Scriptures before they direct their faith to Christ is unwarranted.

[16]Paul Althaus, *The Theology of Martin Luther* (Philadelphia: Fortress Press, 1966), p. 6.

[17]Luther repeatedly described the Bible as an infallible authority in contradistinction to fallible councils and popes. Members of councils and popes could err because they are human; the Bible does not err because it is God's Word.

[18]Cited in Robert Preus, "The View of the Bible Held by the Church: The Early Church Through Luther," *Inerrancy*, p. 380 (W^2 9. 356). Preus relies heavily upon M. Reu and W. Walther in his discussion of Luther. His discussion of Luther should be studied with care.

[19]Cited in Paul Althaus, *The Theology of Martin Luther*, p. 6, n. 12 (*Weimar Ausgabe* hereafter [WA] 7.315).

[20]Cited in Preus, "The View of the Bible . . . ," p. 380 (WA 54, 158). In this passage Luther does not speak about "errors" in terms of the biblical authors' "purposeful deceits"; rather he assumes that the words of the Bible are God's words and that to challenge these words as deceptive is tantamount to charging God with deception and fraud.

[21]Ibid. (W^2 20. 798).

[22]WA 40, ii, 52, 19–20, Luther also wrote: "For if they believed they were God's words they would not call them poor, miserable words but would regard such words and titles as greater than the whole world and would fear and tremble before them as before God himself. For whoever despises a single word of God does not regard any as important (from Luther's *Vom Abendmahl Christi*, cited in M. Reu, "Luther and the Scriptures," *The Springfielder* (1960): 32. Or he declared: "Not only the words but also the diction used by the Holy Ghost and the Scripture is divine" (WA 40, iii, 254).

[23]*Luther's Works*, 37.308. Luther attempted to find Christ in every single word of the Old Testament. See: Joseph Friedmann, "Luther, Forster, and the Curious Nature of Wittenberg Hebraica," *Bibliothèque d'humanisme et renaissance* 42, 3 (1980): 611–19. Consult also: Arnold Ages, "Luther and the Rabbis," *The Jewish Quarterly Review* VIII, 1 (July 1967): 63–68. In 1540 Luther declared: "If I were younger I would want to learn this language [Hebrew] because without it one can never rightly understand the sacred Scripture" (LW, 54, pp. 375–76). Unfortunately he depended too much on the deficient learning of Johannes Forster (1495–1556), professor of Hebrew at the University of Wittenberg.

[24]Rogers and McKim, *The Authority and Interpretation of the Bible*, pp. 77–79.

[25]Ibid., p. 133, n. 112. Reinhold Seeberg, *The History of Doctrines* (Grand Rapids: Baker 1978 [reprint]), II, p. 300.

[26]M. Reu. *Luther and the Scriptures* (Columbus: Wartburg, 1944). This study has been reprinted in *The Springfielder* (1960).

[27]Reu, "Luther and the Scriptures," p. 41.

[28]Writes Reu: "If Luther, indeed, has never directly admitted that an actual mistake is to be found in a Scripture passage, and if instead, when an incorrect historical allusion or a contradiction of another Scripture passage seems to be evident, he sought some expedient that might remove the difficulty and frequently in so doing so ventured to propose daring hypotheses, he did not mean by his expressions, 'that is a matter of no importance,' or, 'that does not affect the matter,' that it was a matter of indifference to him as to whether an actual error occurred or not. . . . In these statements Luther does not say that it is a matter of indifference to him whether they contain errors or not but only that his faith would not be endangered, if, in spite of his best efforts, he would be unable to solve the apparent contradictions or *to prove the inconsequence of all skeptical questions.* He dismisses the matter if he cannot prove it conclusively, but his inability to do so neither commits him to the opinion that these passages really contain error, nor is his faith in salvation thereby imperiled" (Ibid., pp. 49–50).

[29]Ibid., p. 58. See: Willem Jan Kooiman, *Luther and the Bible*, pp. 74–75; W. Schwarz, *Principles and Problems of Biblical Translation: Some Reformation Controversies and Their Background* (Cambridge: At the University Press, 1955), pp. 167–212.

[30]Brian Gerrish, whose authority Rogers and McKim also invoke, takes a different stance than Heick. He argues that Reu generally understood correctly Luther on infallibility. Gerrish does not believe that Seeberg's list of critical opinions demonstrates that Luther admitted the reality of "errors" in the original autographs: "Of the examples given by Seeberg one (the first) relates to textual or 'lower' criticism; three (nos. 4, 6 and 8) relate to authorship; and four (nos. 5, 9, 10, 11) to canonicity. Only three (nos. 2, 3 and 7) appear to relate to errors in the original text of the canonical writings, and there are some Luther scholars (M. Reu, for example) who find it possible to maintain that even these three are inconclusive. . . . Certainly, Luther is extremely reluctant to admit error in Scripture, and on the whole I think that Reu has understood him correctly. It seems, in fact, that Luther never really questioned the medieval theory of inspiration, although he did provide a way to escape from it" ("Biblical Authority and the Continental Reformation," *Scottish Journal of Theology* 10 [1957]: 345–46). David Lotz also accepts Reu's assessment of Luther's commitment to biblical inerrancy ("*Sola Scriptura* . . . ," p. 268, n. 29). See: Martin Scharlemann, "Reu and the Doctrine of the Holy Scriptures," *Concordia Journal* 5, no. 1 (January 1979): 12–20.

[31]J. Theodore Mueller, "Luther and the Bible," *Inspiration & Interpretation* (ed. John Walvoord; Grand Rapids: Eerdmans, 1957), pp. 87–114.

[32]One can find a convenient listing of scholars who affirm that Calvin believed in "complete" or "limited" biblical infallibility in J. K. S. Reid, *The Authority of Scripture: A Study of the Reformation and Post Reformation Understanding of the Bible* (New York: Harper & Brothers, n.d.), pp. 54–55; see also: H. Jackson Forstman, *Word and Spirit: Calvin's Doctrine of Biblical Authority* (Stanford: Stanford University Press, 1962), pp. 1–6; Richard Stauffer, *Dieu, la création et la providence dans la prédication de Calvin* (Berne: Peter Lang, 1978), p. 72.

[33]Ford Lewis Battles wrote the foreword for Rogers and McKim's study. He translated Calvin's *Institutes* (McNeill edition) and wrote an important article on the concept of accommodation in Calvin: "God was Accommodating Himself to Human Capacity," *Interpretation* 31 (1977): 19–38. To our knowledge, he was not an advocate of "Neoorthodoxy." John McNeill authored, among other essays, *The History and Character of Calvinism* (New York: Oxford University Press, 1967) and "The Significance of the Word of God for Calvin" *Church History* 28 (June 1959): 131–46. T. H. L. Parker's *John Calvin: A*

Biography (Philadelphia: Westminster, 1975) is important for its dating of events in Calvin's life. François Wendel's *Calvin: The Origins and Development of His Religious Thought* (New York: Harper and Row, 1963) is one of the finest analyses of Calvin's thought save for the author's discussion of Calvin and biblical authority. See also: Hans-Joachim Kraus, "Calvin's Exegetical Principles," *Interpretation* 31 (1977): 8–18. For Calvin's interaction with various classical philosophies, see Charles Partee, *Calvin and Classical Philosophy* (Leiden: E. J. Brill, 1977). Partee writes: "Calvin insists that he is not Platonic or of some other sect opposed to Christ. Calvin eschews Plato as a source of his theology, but he admits that Plato knows something about holiness. It is not always possible, in specific instances, to ascertain whether Calvin's knowledge is derived from a direct reading of the philosopher cited or mediated to him through secondary sources, but Calvin is certainly influenced by various philosophical currents of his time, especially Platonism and Stoicism" (p. 111). On the other hand, Calvin did not turn his back completely on Aristotle. See: Irena Backus, "'Aristotelianism' in some of Calvin's and Beza's expository and exegetical writings . . . ," *Histoire de l'exégèse au XVIe siècle*, pp. 351–60.

[34]Scholars have argued strenuously about Calvin's view of the Holy Spirit's interaction with external biblical evidences in confirming biblical authority. For a good discussion of the question, see: Kenneth Kantzer, "John Calvin's Theory of the Knowledge of God and the Word of God" (Ph.D. Dissertation, Harvard, 1950), pp. 427–62.

[35]Richard Muller, "The Foundation of Calvin's Theology: Scripture as Revealing God's Word," p. 22. Regarding verbal inspiration, Muller observes: "I am tempted to say in conclusion that Calvin would have agreed with later doctrines of verbal inspiration but would have questioned the advisability of grounding the authority of Scripture solely on an objective statement of its divine origin which must remain forever external to the believer" (Ibid.).

[36]Gerrish, "Biblical Authority and the Continental Reformation," pp. 354–55. Gerrish cites B. B. Warfield concerning the "original document" hypothesis.

[37]Forstman, *Word and Spirit . . .* , p. 65.

[38]John Calvin, *Commentaries on the Epistles to Timothy, Titus, and Philemon* (ed. William Pringle; Edinburgh: The Calvin Translation Society, 1856), pp. 248–49.

[39]Calvin, *Commentary on a Harmony of the Evangelists, Matthew, Mark, and Luke* (ed. William Pringle; Edinburgh: The Calvin Translation Society, 1845–46), vol. 1, p. 127.

[40]McNeill, "The Significance of the Word of God," pp. 131–46.

[41]Kenneth Kantzer, "Calvin and the Holy Scriptures," *Inspiration and Interpretation*, pp. 137–42.

[42]Calvin, *Commentaries on the Epistle of Paul the Apostle to the Romans* (ed. John Owen; Edinburgh: Calvin Translation Society, 1849), p. 117.

[43]Calvin, *Calvin's Commentaries: The Epistle of Paul the Apostle to the Hebrews* (ed. David Torrance; Grand Rapids: Eerdmans, 1963), p. 136. Italics mine. The John Owen translation of this passage limits the specific context for Calvin's remark: "But the Apostle followed the Greek translators when he said, 'A body hast thou prepared'; for in quoting these words the Apostles were not so scrupulous . . ." p. 227.

[44]Calvin on occasion defended the common style of the Bible against charges by those who compared it to the standards of Ciceronian rhetoric, which some Renaissance humanists appreciated. In his defense, Calvin by no means advocated the form/function distinction between words and saving message that Rogers and McKim have attributed to him. See: W. Robert Godfrey, "Biblical Authority in the Sixteenth and Seventeenth Centuries: A Question of Transition," forthcoming article in *Scripture and Truth* (ed. D. A. Carson and J. D. Woodbridge; Grand Rapids: Zondervan, 1983).

[45]Calvin, *Commentary on Hebrews* (Torrance edition), p. 23.

[46]Calvin, *The Epistles of Paul The Apostle to the Romans and to the Thessalonians* (ed. David Torrance and Thomas Torrance; Grand Rapids: Eerdmans, 1961), p. 225. The author is indebted to Mark Rothemel for several key insights into Rogers and McKim's use of Calvin's commentaries.

[47]Calvin, *Commentary Upon the Acts of the Apostles* (ed. Henry Beveridge; Edinburgh: Calvin Translation Society, 1844), p. 265. See also page 182 of the Torrance edition. As W. Robert Godfrey points out, the Latin edition does not indicate that the error should be attributed to Luke (forthcoming essay, "Biblical Authority in the Sixteenth and Seventeenth Centuries . . ."). Rogers and McKim's discussion is apparently based on John McNeill's misreading of the same passage (McNeill, "The Significance of the Word of God," p. 143).

[48]See W. Robert Godfrey's discussion of Calvin's comments on this in "Biblical Authority in the Sixteenth and Seventeenth Centuries. . . ."

[49]This discussion concerns Calvin's commentary on Gen. 1:16.

[50]Calvin, *Commentaries on the First Book of Moses Called Genesis* (ed. John King; Edinburgh: Calvin Translation Society, 1847), I, p. 87. It should be noted that Calvin does not intimate that Moses was bound by the thought patterns of his times and culture: "Nor did Moses truly wish to withdraw us from this pursuit [astronomy] in omitting such things as are peculiar to that art; but because he was ordained a teacher as well of the unlearned and rude as of the learned, he could not otherwise fulfill his office than by descending to this grosser method of instruction. Had he [Moses] . . . spoken of things generally unknown, the uneducated might have pleaded in excuse that such subjects were beyond their capacity. Lastly, since the Spirit of God here opens a common school for all, it is not surprising that he should chiefly choose those subjects which would be intelligible to all" (Ibid.). Calvin's expression, "Had he [Moses] spoken of things generally unknown," carries with it the implication that he could have so spoken. Moreover Moses was writing under the inspiration of the Holy Spirit.

[51]Calvin's commentary on Genesis, for example, reflects the author's unquestioning confidence in the truthfulness of Moses' account of creation.

[52]Calvin commented upon Psalm 93:1 using what Edward Rosen calls "pre-Copernican" categories (E. Rosen, "Calvin's Attitude Toward Copernicus," *Journal of the History of Ideas* 21 [1960]: 438–39).

[53]Rogers and McKim, *The Authority and Interpretation of the Bible*, p. 142, n. 254.

[54]Calvin, *The Epistles of Paul the Apostle to the Romans and to the Thessalonians* (ed. David Torrance and Thomas Torrance; Grand Rapids: Eerdmans, 1960), p. 114.

[55]See this chap., n. 44.

[56]Calvin, *The First Epistle of Paul The Apostle to the Corinthians* (ed. David Torrance and Thomas Torrance; Grand Rapids: Eerdmans, 1960), pp. 208–9.

[57]Edward Dowey, *The Knowledge of God in Calvin's Theology* (New York: Columbia University Press, 1952), p. 91. Emphasis added by Dowey. Professor Dowey may have changed his evaluation of Calvin and Scripture in more recent writings.

[58]Davies, *The Problem of Authority in the Continental Reformers*, p. 116. Emile Doumergue's list of "errors" that Calvin allegedly admitted has played a similar role as Seeberg's list of "errors" that Luther allegedly admitted.

[59]Martin Luther, *Luther's Works Table Talk* (ed. Theodore Tappert; Philadelphia: Fortress, 1967), pp. 54, 358–59.

[60]Rogers and McKim, *The Authority and Interpretation of the Bible*, p. 166.

[61]Alexandre Koyré, *The Astronomical Revolution: Copernicus-Kepler-Borelli* (Ithaca: Cornell University Press, 1973), p. 74.

[62]Ibid.

[63]Ibid., p. 75. Koyré's discussion and the bibliography he cites should be studied with care.

[64]For other perspectives on this issue, see: Klaus Scholder, *Ursprünge und Probleme der Bibelkritik im 17 Jahrhundert* . . . (München: Kaiser, 1966), pp. 56–65.

[65]Edward Rosen, "Calvin's Attitude toward Copernicus," *Journal of the History of Ideas* 21 (1960): 431–41; Rosen, "A Reply to Dr. Ratner: Calvin's Attitude toward Copernicus," *Journal of the History of Ideas* 22 (1961): 386–88. Rosen argues that Calvin was a pre-Copernican but not an anti-Copernican. Ratner suggests that Calvin was an anti-

Copernican ("Some Comments on Rosen's 'Calvin's Attitude Toward Copernicus,'" *Journal of the History of Ideas* 22 (1961): 382–85. In their discussion of the relationship between the Bible and science, Rogers and McKim do not carefully define what "science" means in a sixteenth-century context.

[66]Stauffer has emerged as one of the leading Calvin scholars in the world due to his systematic study of Calvin's published and unpublished sermons. See his *Dieu, la création et la providence dans la prédication de Calvin* (Berne: Peter Lang, 1978).

[67]Edward Rosen seeks to sort out the origins of this comment in his "Calvin's Attitudes Toward Copernicus," pp. 433–38.

[68]In his *Religion and the Rise of Modern Science* (Grand Rapids: Eerdmans, 1972), R. Hooykaas also argues that Calvin never referred to Copernicus (p. 121). Hooykaas, a fine scholar, has surprisingly misunderstood Calvin's concept of accommodation and biblical infallibility. He assumes that Calvin may have admitted the possibility of a factual error in the original text (Acts 7:16) (p. 120). This is a tenuous piece of evidence upon which to base an interpretation. We discussed Calvin's treatment of that passage earlier in this chapter (n. 47).

[69]According to Rosen, Professor Ratner found it "incredible that Calvin 'never heard' of Copernicus ..." (Rosen, "A Reply to Dr. Ratner ...," p. 386). We too find that idea a difficult supposition, even though Rosen defends it.

[70]Cited in Dowey, *The Knowledge of God in Calvin's Theology*, p. 140, n. 443. See Calvin, *Commentaries on the First Book of Moses Called Genesis. 1.61*, where the Reformer takes note of Saint Augustine's warning to Christians not to "push their inquiries respecting the infinity of duration any more than respecting the infinity of space."

[71]Cited in Hugh Kearney, *Science and Change 1500–1700* (New York: McGraw Hill, 1974), p. 104. Perhaps the most extensive discussion of the reception of the Copernican hypothesis is Jerzy Dobrzycki (ed.), *The Reception of Copernicus' Heliocentric Theory* (Boston: D. Reidel Publishing Company, 1974).

[72]See Kristian Moesgaard, "Copernican Influence on Tycho Brahe," *The Reception of Copernicus' Heliocentric Theory*, pp. 48–51.

[73]Cited in John L. Russell, "The Copernican System in Great Britain," *The Reception of Copernicus' Heliocentric Theory*, p. 196.

[74]Kearney, *Science and Change 1500–1700*, p. 104. Barbara Biénkowska summarizes the penetration of the Copernican viewpoint into Poland. "At first it was presented as a new system, from the logical point of view absurd and erroneous as inconsistent with the 'letter' of the *Bible*, later as a probable hypothesis, then as a perfect hypothesis, and finally as the only true system of the universe" ("From Negation to Acceptance: The Reception of the Heliocentric Theory in Polish Schools in the 17th and 18th Centuries," *The Reception of Copernicus' Heliocentric Theory*, p. 89).

[75]Cited in Edward Rosen, "Copernicus and Renaissance Astronomy," *Renaissance Men and Ideas* (ed. Robert Schwoebel; New York: St. Martin's Press, 1971), p. 100. In the introduction to his famous *New Astronomy*, Johannes Kepler (1571–1630) argued that Copernicus's views were compatible with scriptural teachings (Ibid., pp. 99–101).

[76]*The Castle of Knowledge* (London: Reginalde Wolfe, 1556), p. 82. A second edition appeared in 1596. For information on Robert Recorde (c. 1510–1558), see John Russell, "The Copernican System in Great Britain," pp. 189–91.

[77]In the Middle Ages Christian scholars had attempted to mesh their "scientific" enterprises with the Scriptures. Nicholas Steneck writes: "Commenting on Genesis and on the minute details that go into bringing a universe into being is, in short, part of the laboratory procedure of medieval science ..." (*Science and Creation in the Middle Ages: Henry of Langenstein* [d. 1397] *on Genesis* [Notre Dame: University of Notre Dame Press, 1976], p. 55). For a good bibliography on medieval science, see Richard Dales's *Scientific Achievement of the Middle Ages* (Philadelphia: University of Pennsylvania Press, 1978), pp. 177–82. See also the significant studies of Wesley Stevens on "science" in the Carolingian period.

[78]One of the best studies on exegetical work in the sixteenth century is the previously noted *Histoire de l'exégèse au XVIe siècle* (ed. Olivier Fatio and Pierre Fraenkel; Genève: Droz, 1978). See also Susi Hausammann, *Römerbriefauslegung zwischen Humanismus und Reformation Eine Studie zu Heinrich Bullingers Römerbriefvorlesung von 1525* (Zürich: Zwingli Verlag, 1970); John E. Bigane, III, *Faith, Christ or Peter: Matthew 16:18 in Sixteenth Century Roman Catholic Exegesis* (Washington, D.C.: University Press of America, 1981).

Notes

CHAPTER IV

[1]For a good introduction to the sixteenth century, see Roland Bainton, *The Reformation in the Sixteenth Century* (Boston: Beacon Press, 1952). Steven Ozment's *Age of Reform 1250–1550: An Intellectual and Religious History of Late Medieval and Reformation Europe* (New Haven: Yale University Press, 1980) provides a more long-range background for sixteenth-century religious history. Consult also: Jean Delumeau, *Le catholicisme entre Luther et Voltaire* (Paris: Presses universitaires de France, 1971); Hermann Tüchle, C. A. Bowman, Jacques Le Brun, *Réforme et contre-réforme* 3 *Nouvelle histoire de l'église* (Paris: Seuil, 1968), pp. 539–80 (an extensive bibliography). On Roman Catholic spirituality, see Louis Cognet, *Post-Reformation Spirituality* (New York: Hawthorn Books, 1959). Today scholars are more prone to speak of a Catholic Reformation and a Protestant Reformation. See: Pierre Chaunu, *Le temps des réformes: La crise de la chrétienté L'éclatement (1250–1550)* (Paris: Fayard, 1975).

[2]Regarding the Council of Trent, consult: Hubert Jedin, *A History of the Council of Trent* (New York: Nelson, 1957, 1961); Ozmont, *The Age of Reform 1250–1550 ...*, pp. 406–9; Marvin R. O'Connell, *The Counter Reformation, 1559–1610* (New York: Harper and Row, 1974), pp. 84–103.

[3]C. V. Wedgewood, *The Thirty Years War* (New York: Anchor Books, 1961); Phyllis Crew, *Calvinist Preaching and Iconoclasm in the Netherlands 1544–1569* (Cambridge: Cambridge University Press, 1978); Natalie Davis's essay, "The Rites of Violence" in her volume *Society and Culture in Early Modern France* (Stanford: Stanford University Press 1975), pp. 152–87; Robert Mandrou (ed.), *Histoire des Protestants de France* (Toulouse: Privat, 1977), pp. 45–116; consult the several studies of Janine Estèbe on the Saint Bartholomew's massacres (1572). Roman Catholics and Protestants also criticized each other in print. For a discussion of the *Magdeburg Centuries* (1559–1574) associated with the name of the Lutheran Matthias Flacius Illyricus and the *Annales* of the Roman Catholic Baronius, see: Cyriac K. Pullapilly, *Caesar Baronius: Counter-Reformation Historian* (Notre Dame, Ind.: University of Notre Dame Press, 1975). Protestants threw themselves into the study of patristics in the last half of the sixteenth century as they looked for arguments with which to counter the Roman Catholic claim that the church's present beliefs were the same as those of the Fathers. The *Centuries* put Catholic scholars on the defensive as E. A. Ryan notes (*The Historical Scholarship of Saint Bellarmine* [New York: Fordham University Press, 1936], pp. 12–13).

[4]In the letter to Martin Dorp (1515), which we cited in Chapter III, Erasmus de-

scribed his relationship to Valla in these terms: "Certainly I consider Valla deserving of the highest praise; he was a rhetorician more than a theologian, who had the diligence in treating of Sacred Scripture to compare the Greek with the Latin, although there are not many theologians who have read the Bible from cover to cover. Yet I disagree with him in a number of places, especially in those which have theological implications" (John C. Olin, ed., *Christian Humanism and the Reformation: Selected Writings of Erasmus* [New York: Fordham University Press, 1975], p. 89). In 1514 Dorp, representing theologians at Louvain, had written to Erasmus in an attempt to persuade him to refrain from his New Testament textual work. See also Jacques Chomarat, "Les *Annotations* de Valla, celles d'Erasme et la grammaire," *Histoire de l'exégèse au XVIe siècle* (ed. Olivier Fatio and Pierre Fraenkel; Genève: Droz, 1978), pp. 202–28; Richard Waswo, "The Reaction of Juan Luis Vives to Valla's Philosophy of Language," *Bibliothèque d'humanisme et renaissance* XLII (1980): 595–609. Another important influence on Erasmus's thinking were the writings of Lefèvre d'Étaples. Consult, for example, John Payne, "Erasmus and Lefèvre d'Étaples as Interpreters of Paul," *Archiv für Reformationsgeschichte* 65 (1974): 54–83. Erasmus also speaks about Lefèvre d'Étaples in his letter to Dorp.

[5]In 1518, Cajetan, the papal legate at the Augsburg discussions, pointed out to Luther the "error" in Matt. 27:9 regarding a quotation from Zechariah ascribed to Jeremiah.

[6]See the Council of Trent Decree concerning the canonical Scriptures, April 8, 1546 (Philip Schaff, ed., *The Creeds of Christendom* [Grand Rapids: Baker, n.d. (reprint)], II, pp. 79–83). On the other hand, several Roman Catholics like Sixtus of Sienna evidenced a certain tolerance in the way they treated textual matters relating to biblical infallibility. Consult John W. Montgomery's helpful essay, "Sixtus of Siena and Roman Catholic Biblical Scholarship in the Reformation Period," in his *Ecumenicity, Evangelicals, and Rome* (Grand Rapids: Zondervan, 1969), pp. 47–69.

[7]Bruce Vawter, *Biblical Inspiration* (Philadelphia: Westminster, 1972), pp. 63–68. Other matters such as Lessius's attitude toward the inspiration of canonical Scriptures were also hotly contested. See especially: Sebastiano Pagano, "Some Aspects of the Debate on Inspiration in the Louvain Controversy (1587–1588)," *Catholic Biblical Quarterly* 14 (October 1952): 336–49; 15 (January 1953): 46–59.

[8]Cited in Richard Popkin, *The History of Scepticism: From Erasmus to Descartes* (New York: Harper and Row, 1968), p. 69. For the context of this statement see Ruth Kleinman, *Saint François de Sales and the Protestants* (Genève: Droz, 1962), pp. 62–63. François de Sales also declared: "Is it possible . . . that the Church has been so mistaken and that the Huguenots . . . have so happily encountered truth everywhere that they have never erred in the understanding of Scripture?" (Ibid., p. 145).

[9]This is not to deny the impact of Aristotelianism upon the thought patterns of several Roman Catholic apologists. Consult Robert Richgels, "Scholasticism Meets Humanism in the Counter Reformation: The Clash of Cultures in Robert Bellarmine's Use of Calvin in the *Controversies*," *Sixteenth Century Journal* 6 (1975): 53–66. In fact some of the Aristotelian apologists resorted to the Pyrrhonical apologetic as well.

[10]Popkin, *The History of Scepticism*, p. 68.

[11]The Jesuit François Veron (1575–1625) borrowed this tactic from another Jesuit, Jean Gontery (1562–1616). Louis Bredvold notes that Veron's *machine de guerre de nouvelle invention* "had its effect upon thousands and caused his name to be remembered, with both reverence and execration, for a century" (*The Intellectual Milieu of John Dryden* [Ann Arbor: The University of Michigan Press, 1966 (reprint of 1934 edition)], p. 80). See: Bibliothèque nationale D 54285: François Veron, *Briefve mèthode pour reduire les devoyez et convaincre les ministres de la parole de Dieu réformée* (Lyon: Jean Lautret, 1618); B. N. D 54291: Veron, *Combat contre tous les Ministres de France Specialement contre le Sieur du Moulin, et ses colleagues de Charenton* (Paris: Cotteria, 1620).

[12]Cited in Popkin, *The History of Scepticism*, p. 71.

[13]B. N. D²6979: Jean Daillé, *La Foy fondée sur les saintes Escritures contre les nouveaux Methodistes* (Charenton: Samuel Perier, 1656 [2nd ed.]), p. 2.

[14]Even Amyraut stressed reason's rights in the context of debate with Roman Catholic fideists. Notes Brian Armstrong: "Rex [Walter] and Sabean [David] have shown that his [Amyraut's] *De l'élévation de la foy et l'abaissement de la raison en la créance des mystères de la religion* of 1640 is an attack on the fideism of the Roman Catholic theologians by means of an assertion of the reliability of reason" (Armstrong, *Calvinism and the Amyraut Heresy* [Madison: University of Wisconsin Press, 1969], p. 273).

[15]Popkin, *The History of Scepticism*, pp. 71–72.

[16]B. N. D 2204: Baile, *Catechisme et abbregé des controverses de nostre temps* (Paris: Pierre Chevalier, 1607), pp. 19–20. See especially George Tavard, "Scripture and Tradition among Seventeenth-Century Recusants," *Theological Studies* 25, 3 (September, 1964): 343–85.

[17]Rogers and McKim, *The Authority and Interpretation*, pp. 464–65.

[18]Ibid., p. 122.

[19]Ibid., pp. 465–66.

[20]Ibid., pp. 121–22. The authors do not cite article 20 in their presentation of the Scots Confession, 1560 (p. 465). This article can be found in Schaff (ed.), *The Creeds of Christendom*, III, pp. 465–66. On John Knox's commitment to biblical infallibility see Robert Greaves, "The Nature of Authority in the Writings of John Knox," *Fides et Historia* 10, 2 (Spring 1978): 43.

[21]Many Protestant writers of the sixteenth and seventeenth centuries identified "men" as those who could "err" (e.g., not tell the truth on all occasions), whereas they thought the writers of Scripture under the inspiration of the Holy Spirit were men who did not err.

[22]B. N. D²34002: Pierre Viret, *Sur les conciles et les commandements* ... (Genève: n.d.), p. 19v.

[23]Ibid., p. 21v.

[24]B. N. D²4274: Pierre du Moulin, *Du juge des controverses* (Sedan: Jean Iannon, 1630). On Du Moulin, see Lucien Rimbault, *Pierre du Moulin 1568–1658: Un Pasteur classique à la âge classique* (Paris: Vrin, 1966). On Reformed apologetics in the seventeenth century, see the excellent study by Walter Rex, *Essays on Pierre Bayle and Religious Controversy* (The Hague: Martinus Nijhoff, 1965).

[25]Wrote Du Moulin: "Our adversaries especially want to attack the original Hebrew and Greek texts which they have denigrated and have attempted to render suspect, as being corrupted. They have ordered that the Latin Vulgate version, received in the Roman Church, be the only one held as authentic (*Du juge des controverses* ..., p. 19)."

[26]For Rogers and McKim's treatment of Pierre du Moulin, see pp. 163–64.

[27]See the notice about William Whitaker in Sidney Lee (ed.), *Dictionary of National Biography* (New York: Macmillan Company, 1900), LXI, pp. 21–23.

[28]Bellarmine reportedly kept a portrait of Whitaker, so much did he admire the man's learning and ingenuity (William Whitaker, *A Disputation on Holy Scripture* ... [ed., William Fitzgerald; Cambridge: Cambridge University Press, 1849], p. x).

[29]*Histoire critique du Vieux Testament* (Rotterdam: Reinier Leers, 1685), p. 472.

[30]In Lee (ed.), *Dictionary of National Biography*, LXI, p. 22, Whitaker is described in this fashion: "No English divine of the sixteenth century surpassed Whitaker in the estimation of his contemporaries."

[31]Philip Hughes, *The Theology of the English Reformers* (Grand Rapids: Eerdmans, 1966), p. 16. This work was directed at Robert Bellarmine and Thomas Stapleton. It was later bound with another volume of Whitaker, *On the Authority of the Scripture* (1594). On Whitaker's relationship with Stapleton, see: Marvin O'Connell, *Thomas Stapleton and the Counter-Reformation* (New Haven: Yale University Press, 1964), pp. 74–77.

[32]Whitaker, *A Disputation on Holy Scripture*, pp. 660–61.

[33]Jewel is quite explicit: "Many think the apostle's speech is hardly true of the whole

scripture, that all and every part of the scripture is profitable. Much is spoken of genealogies, and pedigrees, of lepers, of sacrificing goats and oxen, &c: these seem to have little profit in them, but to be vain and idle. If they shew vain in thine eyes, yet hath not the Lord set them down in vain. 'The words of the Lord are pure words, as the silver tried in a furnace of earth fired seven times.' There is no sentence, no clause, no word, no syllable, no letter, but it is written for thy instruction: there is not one jot but it is sealed and signed with the blood of the Lamb. Our imaginations are idle, our thoughts are vain: there is no idleness, no vanity in the word of God. Those oxen and goats which were sacrificed teach thee to kill and sacrifice the uncleanness and filthiness of thy heart. . . . That leprosy teacheth thee to know the uncleanness and leprosy of thy soul. Those genealogies and pedigrees lead us to the birth of our Saviour Christ. So that the whole word of God is pure and holy; no word, no letter, no syllable, no point or prick thereof, but is written and preserved for thy sake" (A Treatise of the Holy Scriptures, in The Works of John Jewel, Bishop of Salisbury [Cambridge: The University Press, 1850], IV, p. 1175). For a discussion of Jewel, see W. M. Southgate, John Jewel and the Problem of Doctrinal Authority (Cambridge, Mass.: Harvard University Press, 1962). Jewel had a great appreciation for the patristic writers' understanding of Scripture.

[34]Whitaker, A Disputation on Holy Scripture, pp. 36–37.

[35]Ibid., p. 37.

[36]Ibid.

[37]Ibid., p. 38.

[38]Ibid., pp. 294–95.

[39]Ibid., p. 295.

[40]See Jill Raitt, The Eucharistic Theology of Theodore Beza (Chambersburg, Pa.: American Academy of Religion, 1972); Brian Armstrong, Calvinism and the Amyraut Heresy. John Patrick Donnelly, "Italian Influences on the Development of Calvinist Scholasticism," Sixteenth Century Journal 7 (April 1976): 81–101; Donnelly, Calvinism and Scholasticism in Vermilgi's Doctrine of Man and Grace (Leiden: E. J. Brill, 1976).

[41]For example, Roger Nicole's perspectives concerning Amyraut's thought are quite different from those of Brian Armstrong. Consult Nicole, "Moyse Amyraut (1596–1664) and the Controversy on Universal Grace: First Phase (1634–1637)" (Ph.D. dissertation, Harvard University, 1966). Armstrong attempts to fend off Nicole's interpretation in Calvinism and the Amyraut Heresy, pp. 286–87.

[42]See W. Robert Godfrey's forthcoming essay, "Biblical Authority in the Sixteenth and Seventeenth Centuries: A Question of Transition" in Scripture and Truth (ed. D. A. Carson and J. D. Woodbridge).

[43]Rogers and McKim, The Authority and Interpretation of the Bible, pp. 147–65.

[44]Ibid., pp. 202–3.

[45]Ibid., pp. 218–23.

[46]The authors attempt on several occasions to make the doctrine of inerrancy depend on one form of Aristotelian thought or another; they never do so in a compelling way. See for example their discussion of John Owen, p. 222.

[47]The authors are less than fair in their treatment of Theodore Beza: "Beza was a major influence at the Synod of La Rochelle in 1571. The Synod produced a new confession of faith that contained scholastic terminology appearing to contradict the Second Helvetic Confession on the subject of communion. Ramus was infuriated by the confession and wrote to Bullinger denouncing its innovations. The debate over these matters was suddenly cut short by the Massacre of St. Bartholomew's Day on August 24, 1572, in which Ramus and many other French Protestant leaders were killed. The opposition to Beza's scholasticizing was decimated . . ." (p. 164). The authors do not tell us that in his own correspondence with Bullinger, Beza indicated that he was quite willing to give up the controverted word substance. Robert Kingdon writes: "He [Beza] insists that its use was required only to undercut the wild doctrines of a group of Italian troublemakers in Lyon. He declares himself personally willing to forego use of the word, if the description

of what takes place in the sacrament is expressed with the care which the Zurichers normally use" (Robert Kingdon, *Geneva and the Consolidation of the French Protestant Movement, 1564-1572* [Madison: The University of Wisconsin Press, 1967], p. 104). Rogers and McKim's portrayal of the relationship between Ramus and Beza is misleading. Kingdon's book gives a competent analysis of the multiple issues that troubled that relationship.

[48]Fatio, *Méthode et théologie: Lambert Daneau et les débuts de la scolastique réformée* (Genève: Droz, 1976), pp. ix-xiii. Fatio, one of the best historians of Reformed thought, has in mind H. E. Weber's *Reformation, Orthodoxie und Rationalismus* (Gütersloh, 1937); Ernst Bizer's *Frühorthodoxie und Rationalismus in Theologische Studien*, Heft 71 (Zürich, 1963); W. Kickel's *Vernunft und Offenbarung bei Theodor Beza* (Neukirchen, 1967) among other works. Rogers and McKim rely on some of the very studies whose presuppositions Fatio challenges. For a review of Fatio's important book in English, see Richard Muller's analysis in *The Westminster Theological Journal* XLI, 1 (Fall 1978): 215-17.

[49]Robert Preus, *The Theology of Post Reformation Lutheranism: A Study of Theological Prolegomena* (St. Louis: Concordia, 1970); Preus, *The Inspiration of Scripture: A Study of the Theology of the Seventeenth Century Lutheran Dogmaticians*, 2nd. ed. (Edinburgh: Oliver and Boyd, 1957).

[50]Preus writes: "There is nothing new about the doctrine of the truthfulness of Scripture as taught by the Lutherans during the late period of orthodoxy. The same position was shared by Gerhard, Flacius, Luther, the Scholastics, and the early church fathers. What is new is a rather marked preoccupation with the doctrine and a greater emphasis on it by Calov, Scherzer, Dannhauer, Quenstedt, and others at about the middle of the 17th century" (*The Theology of Post Reformation Lutheranism*, p. 347; see n. 259, p. 397 for documentation concerning this contention). It is true that some of the later seventeenth-century Lutheran theologians, such as George Calixt, used the criteria of "antiquity" and "perpetuity" to judge the truth and divine origin of religion. See Werner Elert, *The Structure of Lutheranism: The Theology and Philosophy of Life of Lutheranism, Especially in the Sixteenth and Seventeenth Centuries* (Saint Louis: Concordia, 1962), I, p. 209. The doctrine of *Sola Scriptura* was thereby imperiled.

[51]This is a Thèse de Doctorat ès Sciences Religieuses. The thesis deserves publication; Robinson writes judiciously and with a mastery of his subject matter.

[52]For example, as Sarah Hutton has pointed out, Platonism was compatible with the thought of the Dutch Arminians known for their rationalistic tendencies: "Its Dutch aspect suggests a connection between Arminianism and Platonism which fits well with Rosalie Colie's observations of the strong links between the Cambridge Platonists and the Dutch Remonstrants" ("Thomas Jackson, Oxford Platonist, and William Twisse, Aristotelian," *Journal of the History of Ideas* 39, 4 [October-December 1978]: 652). Consult Rosalie Colie, *Light and Enlightenment: A Study of the Cambridge Platonists and the Dutch Arminians* (Cambridge: Cambridge University Press, 1957).

[53]Dibon notes that in the universities of the United Provinces toward 1620 there was a "strong tendency to the 'aristotelico-ramiste' conciliation" in logic (*La philosophie néerlandaise au siècle d'or* [Paris: Elsevier, 1954], I, p. 258). On Ramism, see Walter Ong, *Ramus: Method and the Decay of Dialogue: from the Art of Discourse to the Art of Reason* (Cambridge, Mass.: Harvard University Press, 1958).

[54]Rogers, *Scripture in the Westminster Confession* (Grand Rapids: Eerdmans, 1967), p. 224.

[55]Dibon writes concerning the Dutch theologians: "The historical Aristotle, to whom our professors maintain their fidelity and whom they do not fail to oppose to the fictional Aristotle of the scholastic tradition, remains, concerning the issue of 'lumière naturelle,' the master thinker, but not an infallible master" (*La philosophie néerlandaise au siècle d'or*, I, p. 258).

[56]Ibid., p. 259. Dibon observes: "It is striking to see with what frequency there ap-

pears in the writings of philosophers as well as theologians friend Plato, friend Aristotle, but greater friend, truth."

[57]Ibid., p. 248.

[58]In his *Pia desideria* (1675) Jacob Spener criticizes sharply those German Lutheran theologians of his day who had become caught up in writing showy metaphysical tractates. Other theologians and pastors were more obviously concerned about the health of the Lutheran churches when they wrote.

[59]This kind of blanket charge is not appropriate, unless the authors can document it; they do not do so in their essay.

[60]Geoffrey Bromiley, *Historical Theology: An Introduction* (Grand Rapids: Eerdmans, 1978), p. 328. Bromiley specifically challenges (pp. 327–28) the kinds of criticism Rogers and McKim make concerning Lutheran and Reformed theologians.

[61]Rogers and McKim, *The Authority and Interpretation of the Bible*, p. 198, n. 251. Cf. Geoffrey Bromiley, "The Church Doctrine of Inspiration," *Revelation and the Bible: Contemporary Evangelical Thought* (ed. Carl F. H. Henry; Grand Rapids: Baker Book House, 1958), pp. 212–14.

[62]Basil Hall, "Biblical Scholarship: Editions and Commentaries," *The Cambridge History of the Bible: The West from the Reformation to the Present Day* (ed. S. L. Greenslade; Cambridge: At the University Press, 1976), I, p. 63. Hall's essay (pp. 38–93) provides a helpful backdrop concerning textual criticism by humanists in the sixteenth century.

[63]Philip Schaff, ed., *The Creeds of Christendom: The Greek and Latin Creeds* (Grand Rapids: Baker, n.d. [reprint]), II, pp. 79–83.

[64]Whitaker, *A Disputation on Holy Scripture*, p. 135. John Jewel argued that God's Word had been preserved so well that "it yet continueth still without adding or altering of any one sentence, or word or letter" ("A Treatise of the Holy Scripture . . . ," *The Works of John Jewel*, IV, p. 1165). Some Englishmen apparently did think that their Bibles perfectly reflected the originals.

[65]Wrote Whitaker: "We must hold, therefore, that we have now those very ancient Scriptures which Moses and the other prophets published, although we have not, perhaps, precisely the same forms and shapes of the letters" (*A Disputation on Holy Scripture*, p. 117).

[66]For apologetic reasons Roman Catholics frequently argued that the Jews had not preserved the Hebrew text in its basic integrity; Protestants countered that the Jews had been careful to do so. See, for example, William Whitaker's discussion of this point (this chapter, n. 67).

[67]Elsewhere Whitaker declared: "Now then, if the originals of sacred Scripture have not been so disgracefully corrupted by any malice of Jews or adversaries, as some people have ignorantly suspected; and if no mistakes have crept into the originals, but such as may casually be introduced into any book (which our opponents expressly allow) . . ." (Ibid., p. 161).

[68]See Grotius's *Truth of the Christian Religion, A New Edition*, trans. by John Clarke (Cambridge: J. Hall, 1840), p. 126.

[69]Jean Morin (1591–1659) was raised in a Protestant home but converted to Roman Catholicism. See his *Exercitationes biblicae de hebraei graecique testus sinceritate* (1633). Consult: Paul Auvray, "Jean Morin, 1591–1659," *Revue Biblique* 66 (1959): 397–414.

[70]*Histoire critique du Vieux Testament*, p. 465.

[71]Ibid., p. 1.

[72]On Cajetan and Pagnini's dilemmas, see: Basil Hall, "Biblical Scholarship: Editions and Commentaries," pp. 45, 64–65.

[73]Le Brun, "Sens et portée du retour aux origines dans l'oeuvre de Richard Simon," *XVIIe siècle* XXXIII (Avril–Juin 1981): 185–98. This article will appear in an English translation in the *Trinity Journal*. In the preface to his *Histoire critique du Nouveau Testament* (Rotterdam: Reinier Leers, 1689), Simon argues that Christians since the earliest

times had attempted to eliminate mistakes from the copies of the biblical texts. This enterprise Simon calls criticism. He writes: "The Church has had since the first centuries of Christianity scholars who have applied themselves with care to the correction of errors which through the passage of time slipped into the Sacred Books. This work which demands an exact knowledge of these Books, and great research in manuscript copies, is called criticism [*critique*], because one determines the best lessons which one ought to conserve in the text. Origen became duly distinguished by this kind of study, not only among the Greeks, but even throughout the East, where the Bibles he had corrected were preferred by common agreement to all the others." Simon then sketches out a brief history of *critique*. He was apparently the first Frenchman to use this French word in relation to the study of the Bible's texts. Simon's use of the word *critique* in the seventeenth century should be considered by scholars who are prone to speak of a "precritical" period even in the eighteenth century; the latter expression should not be used without careful explanation.

Notes

CHAPTER V

[1]Hugo Grotius (1583–1645) was a political theorist of reputation. He was associated with the political and theological cause of the Dutch Remonstrants (Arminians). In his *Truth of the Christian Religion* (1627) Grotius advocated a doctrine of accommodation which resembled that of Faustus Socinus: the biblical authors could make "minor" errors because they had adjusted their writings about the external world to beliefs current in their day. See: Grotius, *The Truth of the Christian Religion* (ed. Jean LeClerc; Cambridge: J. Hall, 1840). Socinus had described accommodation in these terms: "Christ and the apostles were influenced by the opinions of men, and in certain matters they are able to adapt and accommodate themselves to those opinions that flourished at that time. As a result, some of the divine writers upheld the truth better than others do, and sometimes in a minor way a writer has been mistaken about those things that only slightly deal with what we are to believe or do" (cited in quotation of Calovius in Robert Preus, *The Theology of Post Reformation Lutheranism: A Study of Theological Prolegomena* [St. Louis: Concordia, 1970], p. 190). This statement of Socinus is found in *De Auctoritate S. Scripturae*, Cap. I. See George H. Williams, ed., *The Polish Brethren* (2 vols.; Missoula, Mont.: Scholars Press, 1980).

[2]Richard Popkin, "Scepticism, Theology and the Scientific Revolution in the Seventeenth Century," *Problems in the Philosophy of Science* (ed. I. Lakatos and Alan Musgrave; Amsterdam: North Holland Publishing Company, 1968), III, pp. 21–25.

[3]In his *Divinae fidei analysis* (1652) Holden restricted "not only inerrancy but inspiration itself to the doctrinal matters of Scripture..." (Vawter, *Biblical Inspiration* [Philadelphia: Westminster, 1972], p. 134). Professor Jacques Le Brun, (Hautes Etudes) Paris, is presently studying the impact of Holden's writings upon Richard Simon. See the controverted passages of Holden's *Divinae fidei analysis* I.v. and II.iii. Holden was one of the first to limit infallibility to matters of doctrine.

[4]On Spinoza's perspectives concerning biblical criticism, consult: Sylvain Zac, *Signification et valeur de l'interprétation de l'Écriture chez Spinoza* (Paris: Presses universitaires de France, 1965); Leo Strauss, *Spinoza's Critique of Religion* (New York: Schocken, 1965); A. Malet, *Le Traité Theologico-Politique de Spinoza et la pensée biblique* (Paris: Belles Lettres, 1966).

[5]I hope to write a technical study on the history of biblical criticism in the seventeenth and eighteenth centuries. Since 1973 I have been doing research in this area and have focused my attention on the writings of Richard Simon, Pierre Bayle, Jean Le Clerc, and Spinoza.

[6]Nonetheless, scholars who have sought to ferret out the origins of the "Enlightenment" have often downplayed the role of shifting attitudes toward biblical authority. For a survey of the historiography on the origins of the French Enlightenment, see: Ira Wade, *The Intellectual Origins of the French Enlightenment* (Princeton: Princeton University Press, 1971). The controversial issue of the "dechristianization" of Europe is broached in a significant essay by Jean Delumeau, "Au sujet de la déchristianisation," *Revue d'histoire moderne et contemporaine* XXII (Janvier–Mars 1975): 52–60.

[7]W. Schwarz summarizes the traditional method of exegesis that the humanists modified: "The method of Bible exegesis was evolved through long experience. Its basic principle was the fourfold sense of the text: the literal sense explains the historical contents, the allegorical sense elucidates matters of faith by revealing the allegory implied in the Biblical text, the moral sense indicates rules of human conduct, whilst the anagogical sense deals with the future to be hoped for" (*Principles and Problems of Biblical Translation: Some Reformation Controversies and Their Background* [Cambridge: At the University Press, 1955], p. 47).

[8]Erasmus, Reuchlin, and others were particularly concerned about errors in the Vulgate (Ibid., pp. 92–166). They were frequently hesitant to specify "errors" in the "originals." Sometimes in their editing of classical works, humanists created new "errors"; these errors were solidified by being put in printed editions of texts. See the important study by E. J. Kenney, *The Classical Text Aspects of Editing in the Age of the Printed Book* (Berkeley: University of California Press, 1974).

[9]Contemporaries made this distinction. Sometimes intellectual *libertines* were falsely accused of moral improprieties. See the entire issue of the *XVIIe siècle* 32. 2 (Avril–Juin 1980), devoted to an important discussion of *libertinage* by René Pintard, Roger Zuber, Georges Couton, Pierre Rétat, Bernard Toranne and others. See also Lucien Fèbvre, *Le problème de l'incroyance au 16e siècle: La religion de Rabelais* (Paris: Albin Michel, 1968).

[10]Françoise Charles-Daubert, "Raison, révélation, libertinage," *Revue des sciences philosophiques at théologiques* 64 (Juillet 1980): 401–8.

[11]On Mersenne, see Robert Lenoble, *Mersenne; ou, la naissance du mécanisme* (Paris: Vrin, 1943); Lenoble, *Esquisse d'une histoire de l'idée de nature* (Paris: Albin Michel, 1969).

[12]Richard Popkin, *The History of Scepticism From Erasmus to Descartes* (New York: Harper and Row, 1968), pp. 197–217.

[13]Wade, *The Intellectual Origins . . .* , pp. 53–55. See, for example, Henri Busson, *La religion des classiques (1660–1685)* (Paris: Presses universitaires de France, 1948).

[14]Simon, *Histoire critique du Vieux Testament* (Rotterdam: Reinier Leers, 1685), p. 465. On Jean Morin, see this essay, chap. 4, n. 69.

[15]On diverse aspects of the tangled and sometimes painful relationships between Christians and Jews, see: Jacques Le Brun (ed.), *Les chrétiens devant le fait juif* (Paris: Editions Beauchesne, 1979). Luther's attitudes toward Jews took a very bad turn in the last years of his life. In the late seventeenth century Richard Simon still believed that anti-Jewish sentiments held back Christians from learning about the culture of Jews in the Old Testament. According to Simon, this information was critical if one were to understand the New Testament. See: M. Yardini, "La vision des Juifs et du judaisme dans l'oeuvre de Richard Simon," *Revue des études juives* CXXIX (1970): 197–203.

[16]Basil Hall, "Biblical Scholarship: Editions and Commentaries," *The Cambridge History of the Bible: The West from the Reformation to the Present Day* (ed. S. L. Greenslade; Cambridge: At the University Press, 1976), III, pp. 43–44.

[17]Ibid., p. 44. See Jerome Friedman, "Sixteenth-Century Christian-Hebraica: Scripture and the Renaissance Myth of the Past," *Sixteenth Century Journal* XI, 4 (Winter 1980): 67–85.

[18]John Robinson, "The Doctrine of Holy Scripture in Seventeenth Century Reformed Theology" (Thèse de Doctorat ès Sciences Religieuses, The University of Strasbourg,

1971), p. 106 (this is Polanus's perception of Levita's position). For background on the Massoretic text, see: Christian Ginsburg, *Introduction to the Massoretico-critical Edition of the Hebrew Bible* (London: Trinitarian Bible Society, 1897).

[19]Robinson, "The Doctrine of Holy Scripture . . . ," p. 108.

[20]Richard Simon describes the flap which occurred because Father Jean Morin helped in the publication of Cappel's later work *Critica sacra (1650)*. Protestant apologists such as Bootius accused Cappel of having consorted "avec le P. Morin pour detruire les Oringinaux de la Bible. . ." (*Histoire critique du Vieux Testament*, p. 477).

[21]Don Allen, *The Legend of Noah: Renaissance Rationalism in Art, Science, and Letters* (Urbana: University of Illinois Press, 1949), pp. 51–52.

[22]On Aben Ezra, see article "Ibn Ezra, Abraham," *Encyclopaedia Judaica* (New York: Encyclopaedia Judaica Company, 1971), Vol. 8, pp. 1163–70.

[23]Some doubt remains about Aben Ezra's intentions in raising questions about the Mosaic authorship of the Pentateuch. Did he do so to provoke research or to undermine biblical authority? Richard Simon believed that Aben Ezra merely "wondered" about the objections he proposed against a full Mosaic authorship of the Pentateuch.

[24]Baruch Spinoza, *The Chief Works of Benedict de Spinoza* (ed. R. H. M. Elwes; London: George Bell and Sons, 1883), I, pp. 7–8. On the spread of Spinoza's thought, see Jean Orcibal, "Les Jansénists face à Spinoza," *Revue de littérature comparée* 23 (1949): 441–68; Paul Vernière, *Spinoza et la pensée française avant la Révolution*, (2 vols; Paris: Presses universitaires de France, 1954). Rosalie Colie, "Spinoza and the Early English Deists," *Journal of the History of Ideas* XX (January 1959): 23–46. See also this chapter, n. 62.

[25]Woodbridge, "The Reception of Spinoza's *Tractatus Theologico-Politicus* by Richard Simon (1638–1712)," paper delivered in May 1980 at the Lessing Akademie, Wolfenbüttel, West Germany; paper to be published by the Lessing Akademie of West Germany. See Simon, *Histoire critique du Vieux Testament*, Book I, Chapter VII, and his *De l'inspiration des livres sacrez* (Rotterdam: Reinier Leers, 1687), pp. 43–49.

[26]In the sixteenth century the exegetical studies of several rabbis obliged some Christian theologians to reconsider their own approaches to Scripture. Were they interpreting correctly messianic passages of the Scriptures? Then, again, the influence of Rabbi David Kimchi's works is evident in the writings of Michel Servetus. Consult: Jerome Friedman, "Servetus and the Psalms: The Exegesis of Heresy," *Histoire de l'exégèse au XVIe siècle* (ed. Olivier Fatio and Pierre Fraenkel; Genève: Droz, 1978), p. 173. For a more positive contribution of Jewish exegetical studies to Christians' research, see: A. F. Von Gunten, "La contribution des 'Hebreux' à l'oeuvre exégétique de Cajétan," *Histoire de l'exégèse au XVIe siècle*, pp. 46–83. For an earlier period, see: Eugene Merrill, "Rashi, Nicholas of Lyra, and Christian Exegesis," *The Westminster Theological Journal* XXXVIII (Fall 1975 to Spring 1976): 66–79.

[27]This is clear from the records of the Company of Pastors, State Archives, Geneva. The present author has studied the originals of the proceedings of the Company of Pastors for the decade, 1670–1679.

[28]Archives de Genève, Company of Pastors R. 13 fol. 599 (28 September 1677).

[29]The studies of Elizabeth Labrousse and Walter Rex devoted to Pierre Bayle introduce the thinking of the theologians of Geneva (1670s and 1680s).

[30]Popkin, "Scepticism, Theology, and the Scientific Revolution," pp. 17–18. On the role of printing in the emergence of "modern science," see: Elizabeth Eisenstein, *The printing press as an agent of change: Communications and cultural transformations in early-modern Europe* (New York: Cambridge University Press, 1980), pp. 685–708 (note also her excellent bibliography).

[31]Popkin, "Scepticism, Theology, and the Scientific Revolution," p. 18. Regarding La Peyrère, see: David R. McKee, "Isaac de la Peyrère, a Precursor of Eighteenth Century Deists," *PMLA* 59 (1944): 456–85. Richard Popkin continues to do research on the career of La Peyrère.

[32]Consult the Latin edition: *Prae-adamite* (1655: Bibliothèque nationale A 10951).

[33]B.N. M. 18646: I. de la Peyrère, *Relation de l'Islande* (Paris: L. Billaine, 1663); B.N. M. 18667: La Peyrère, *Relation de Groenland* (Paris: Augustin Courbé, 1647).

[34]Popkin, "Scepticism, Theology, and the Scientific Revolution," p. 19.

[35]B.N. D. 40449: La Peyrère, *Lettre de la Peyrère, à Philotime* (Paris: Augustin Courbé, 1657).

[36]Simon wrote at least seven letters to La Peyrère in the years 1670–1671 (*Lettres choisies*, 1730 edition). Simon tried to deny any dependence upon La Peyrère.

[37]Allen, *The Legend of Noah . . .* , p. 71.

[38]Ibid., p. 74.

[39]Ibid., pp. 89–90. See, for example, Edmond Halley's *Some Considerations about the Cause of the universal Deluge, laid before the Royal Society, on the 12th of December 1694*, in *Science and Religious Belief 1600–1900: A Selection of Primary Sources* (ed. D. C. Goodman; Dorchester: The Open University Press, 1973), pp. 243–50.

[40]For a sensitive history of the early modern "scientists," see Robert Mandrou, *Des humanistes aux hommes de science XVIe et XVIIe siècles* (Paris: Seuil, 1973).

[41]The first edition of this book was published by John Bill. See the forthcoming edition of Richard Simon's *Additions*, which were appended to it in the 1670s (ed. Jacques Le Brun and John Woodbridge; Paris: Presses universitaires de France, 1982). On travel literature, consult among others, Geoffrey Atkinson, *The Extraordinary Voyage in French Literature before 1700* (New York: Columbia University, 1920); Pierre Martino, *L'Orient dans la littérature française au XVIIe et au XVIIIe siècle* (Paris: Hatchette, 1906); plus the hundreds of travel reports from the sixteenth and seventeenth centuries. Concerning new perspectives on knowledge, see George Sarton, *The Appreciation of Ancient and Medieval Science During the Renaissance (1450–1600)* (Philadelphia: University of Pennsylvania Press, 1955); H. T. Pledge, *Science Since 1500* (London: Her Majesty's Stationery Office, 1966); D. W. Waters, *The Art of Navigation in England in Elizabethan and Early Stuart Times* (New Haven: Yale University Press, 1958); Marie Boas, *The Scientific Renaissance 1450–1630* (London: Collins, 1962); Mark H. Curtis, *Oxford and Cambridge in Transition (1558–1642)* (Oxford: Clarendon Press, 1959); the multiple works of Margaret Jacob, Christopher Hill, John Redwood, Herbert Butterfield, Roger Hahn, William Shea, and others. Consult especially Richard S. Brooks, *The Interplay Between Science and Religion in England 1640–1720: A Bibliographical and Historiographic Guide* (Evanston: Garrett-Evangelical Theological Seminary, 1975), which updates considerably the bibliography out of which Rogers and McKim work. The study of the history of science has become a genuine industry. Scholars are much concerned with its relationship to Protestantism, Neo-Platonism, the Hermetic tradition, and other themes. Rogers and McKim do not give much indication of keeping abreast with its surging advances.

[42]See Jerome J. Langford's discussion of Christians who objected to Galileo's theories on Scriptural grounds (*Galileo, Science and the Church* [New York: Desclée Company, 1966], pp. 50–78).

[43]Ibid., pp. 70–74.

[44]Cited in Stillman Drake, *Galileo at Work* (Chicago: University of Chicago Press, 1978), p. 224.

[45]Ibid., p. 226.

[46]Ibid., pp. 226–29.

[47]Cited in *Discoveries and Opinions of Galileo* (ed. Stillman Drake; New York: Doubleday and Company, 1957), p. 183. Nevertheless Galileo leaves the impression elsewhere in this letter that our understanding of nature if properly demonstrated should not be put in question by referring to biblical passages. Citing Augustine, he argued that the chief purpose of the Bible is to reveal salvation truths. Galileo felt obliged to address squarely those opponents who used the Bible's infallibility in their arguments against him: "The reason produced for condemning the opinion that the earth moves and the sun stands still is that in many places in the Bible one can read the sun moves

and the earth stands still. Since the Bible cannot err, it follows as a necessary consequence that anyone takes an erroneous and heretical position who maintains that the sun is inherently motionless and the earth movable" (Ibid., p. 181). Galileo hastened to confess his own commitment to biblical infallibility. The issue, he continued, concerned a proper interpretation of an infallible Bible.

[48]Ibid., p. 194. It is important to observe that Galileo cited Augustine's commentary on Gen. 1:21: "It is to be held as an unquestionable truth that whatever the sages of this world have demonstrated concerning physical matters is in no way contrary to our Bibles; hence whatever the sages teach in their books that is contrary to holy Scriptures may be concluded without any hesitation to be quite false." In a word, Galileo believed Augustine saw some correlation between the teachings of the Bible and science (see this essay, chap. 2, n. 40).

[49]Langford, *Galileo, Science, and the Church*, p. 73.

[50]On April 12, 1615, Cardinal Bellarmine addressed an important letter to Foscarini (d. June 10, 1616) who had written a book defending the thesis that the Copernican system did not contradict Scripture. In the letter Bellarmine complimented Foscarini and Galileo for saying that they approved the Copernican system hypothetically but not absolutely. He also discussed the value of "saving the appearances." On the other hand Bellarmine assumed that the Copernican system contradicted scriptural teaching and the common agreement of the holy Fathers: "Second, I say that, as you know, the Council [of Trent] prohibits expounding the Scriptures contrary to the common agreement of the holy Fathers. And if Your Reverence would read not only the Fathers but also the commentaries of modern writers on Genesis, Psalms, Ecclesiastes, and Josue, you would find that all agree in explaining literally (*ad litteram*) that the sun is in the heavens and moves swiftly around the earth, and that the earth is far from the heavens and stands immobile in the center of the universe. Now consider whether in all prudence the Church could encourage giving to Scripture a sense contrary to the holy Fathers and all the Latin and Greek commentators. Nor may it be answered that this is not a matter of faith, for if it is not a matter of faith from the point of view of the subject matter, it is on the part of the ones who have spoken" (cited in Langford, *Galileo, Science and the Church*, pp. 60–61). For a discussion of the 1616 decree of the Sacred Congregation of the Holy Office, once again consult: Langford, *Galileo, Science and the Church*, pp. 79–104.

[51]Nonetheless, Bacon makes declarations that do not fully support a radical compartmentalization: "And again, the scope or purpose of the Spirit of God is not to express matters of nature in the Scriptures, otherwise than in passage [in passing], and for application to man's capacity and to matters moral and divine" (*The Advancement of Learning: Divine and Human* [1605] in *Selected Writings of Francis Bacon* [ed. Hugh Hick; New York: Random House, 1955], pp. 386–87). This passage and several others like it should be studied in their full contexts. Their meaning is difficult to determine. See: Michael Hattaway, "Bacon and 'Knowledge Broken': Limits for Scientific Method," *Journal of the History of Ideas* XXXIX, 2 (April–June 1978): 183–97.

[52]It appears that Socinus, Grotius, and perhaps Galileo began to fashion a doctrine of accommodation different from the one proposed by Augustine and Calvin. "Accommodation" began to account for "genuine discrepancies" between what the Bible taught and what "scientists" believed to be the case. We do not know what knowledge Grotius and Galileo had of Socinus's thinking in this regard. Rogers and McKim do not discriminate between varying ways scholars spoke about accommodation. In the nineteenth century Charles Hodge noted that Semler and others had defined the concept of it in a "rationalistic" fashion; Hodge did not approve this definition.

[53]See Kepler's discussion of this topic in his *Astronomia Nova* (Heidelberg, 1609), a pertinent selection of which appears in *Science and Religious Belief 1600–1900: A Selection of Primary Sources*, pp. 19–25.

[54]In *The printing press as an agent of change . . .* , Elizabeth Eisenstein studies in

some detail the role of printing in disseminating the thought of Copernicus and Galileo.

[55]Popkin, *The History of Scepticism from Erasmus to Descartes*, p. 177.

[56]Ibid., p. 200.

[57]See Cornelia Serrurier's essay, "Descartes l'homme et le croyant," in *Descartes et cartésianisme hollandais* (Paris: Presses universitaires de France, 1950), pp. 45–70.

[58]Even before Spinoza's *Tractatus* (1670), Meyer, a doctor in Amsterdam had published the *Philosophia Scriptura interpres* (1666) in which he argued that the Bible is infallible but that it should be interpreted by reason (which emanates from God). Balthasar Bekker (1634–1698) went further and argued that reason should judge faith. Scripture does not contradict reason. These men, Cartesians both, were precursors and intermediaries for Spinoza. See: Francisque Bouillier, *Histoire de la philosophie cartésienne* (Paris: Charles Delagrave, 1868), I, pp. 309–13.

[59]On Grotius, see: Werner Kümmel, *The New Testament: The History of the Investigation of Its Problems* (Nashville: Abingdon, 1970), pp. 33–39.

[60]It does appear that Stillingfleet, a noted Anglican, was prepared to speak about an infallibility limited to "doctrine" (Dennis Okholm, "Religious Authority in Seventeenth-Century England: The Understanding and Use of Reason and Scripture in the Writings and Sermons of Four Bishops" [M.A. Thesis in Church History, Trinity Evangelical Divinity School, 1977], p. 104). Okholm discusses Stillingfleet's position and those of John Tillotson, Simon Patrick, and Gilbert Burnet. Stillingfleet's stance is quite different from that of fellow Anglicans, Whitaker and Jewel, who lived one hundred years earlier. See especially, Henry Van Leeuwen, *The Problem of Certainty in English Thought 1630–1690* (The Hague: Nijhoff, 1963).

[61]See: John C. Biddle, "John Locke's Essay on Infallibility: Introduction, Text, and Translation," *Journal of Church and State* 19, 2 (Spring 1977): 301–27. Locke declares: "However, the most certain interpreter of Scripture is Scripture itself, and it alone is infallible" (Ibid., p. 327). It should be noted that Locke discussed the Bible's infallibility in the context of whether or not the pope was an infallible interpreter. Rogers and McKim's proposal that the concept of inerrancy emerged when churchmen began to judge the Bible by Locke's concept of reason betrays an unfamiliarity with Locke's thinking about these issues. Locke still held to the complete infallibility of the Bible in the early 1680's (see this chapter, n. 97). He may have continued to hold this belief even longer. See J. T. Moore, "Locke's Analysis of Language and the Assent to Scripture," *Journal of the History of Ideas* XXXVII (Oct.–Dec. 1976): 707–14.

[62]For photos of these false covers, see: *Spinoza troisième centenaire de la mort du philosophe* (Paris: Institut Néerlandais, 1977), p. 59.

[63]Many Protestant printers in the United Provinces and elsewhere were engaged in illicit smuggling activities with business contacts in Roman Catholic France. On the topic of the illegal book trade during this period, see: Raymond Birn, "La contrebande et la saisie de livres à l'aube du siècle des lumières," *Revue d'histoire moderne et contemporaine* XXVIII (Janvier–Mars 1981): 158–73; Anne Sauvy, *Livres saisis à Paris entre 1678 et 1701* (La Haye: Nijhoff, 1972).

[64]Reinier Leers of Rotterdam published several of the works of Simon, Bayle, Malebranche and other luminaries in the Republic of Letters. His publishing activities and personal religious beliefs would be the worthy subject matter of a full length monograph.

[65]On Bayle, see Paul Dibon, ed., *Pierre Bayle, le philosophe de Rotterdam* (Amsterdam: Elzevier, 1959); Elisabeth Labrousse, *Pierre Bayle* (2 vols.; La Haye: Nijhoff, 1963–1965); and the studies of Pierre Rétat, Jacques Solé, and others. For a sophisticated analysis of Leibniz's thought, see Yvon Belaval, *Leibniz critique de Descartes* (Paris: Gallimard, 1960). Consult also the works on other early modern students of the Bible: Alphonse Dupront, *Pierre Daniel Huet et l'exégèse comparatiste au XVIIe siècle* (Paris: Leroux, 1930); Leonard E. Doucette, *Emery Bigot: Seventeenth Century French Humanist* (Toronto: University of Toronto, 1970); see also books and articles on Henri Justel, E. Du

Pin, Scaliger, Menage, Hobbes, Limborch, Bekker, Arnauld, Pierre Nicole, John Dryden, Dom Calmet, and other members of the Republic of Letters.

[66]Jean Le Clerc critiques Simon's *Histoire critique du Vieux Testament* in an important volume, *Sentimens de quelques théologiens de Hollande . . .* (1685). A flurry of volumes by the two disputants followed.

[67]On the career of Richard Simon, see Paul Auvray, *Richard Simon (1638–1712)* (Paris: Presses universitaires de France, 1974); Jean Steinmann, *Richard Simon et les origines de l'exégèse biblique* (Paris: Desclée de Brouwer, 1960); Henri Margival, *Essai sur Richard Simon et la critique biblique au XVIIᵉ siècle* (Genève: Slatkine, 1970 [reprint]); Auguste Bernus, *Richard Simon et son histoire critique du Vieux Testament* (Genève: Slatkine, 1969 [reprint]); F. Saverio Mirri, *Richard Simon e il metodo storico-critico de B. Spinoza* (Firenze: Felice Le Monnier, 1972).

[68]Spinoza was prepared to dismiss passages in the Bible that did not accord with his standards of right morality or of reason. Other critics of the Bible judged harshly the moral lapses of biblical figures. In the late seventeenth and in the eighteenth centuries they frequently targeted David who was a "man after God's heart" and yet a man who had committed adultery and was a party to murder. This form of moral criticism was used with telling effectiveness. The orthodox did not respond to it as well as they might have.

[69]Pierre-Marie Beaude discusses this approach in his "L'accomplissement des prophéties chez Richard Simon," *Revue des sciences philosophiques et théologiques* 60 (Janvier 1976): 3–35.

[70]In principle Simon upheld the tradition of the Roman Catholic Church as an authoritative interpretative guide for reading Scripture. In practice he on occasion challenged traditional interpretations of the Bible. Moreover, in his *Brerewood Additions* Simon actually wrote a polemic with Protestant sentiments; he did so for money.

[71]The doping practice occurred especially during Simon's writing duel with Jean Le Clerc in the mid 1680s. He broke out with some kind of skin infection because he ate too much chocolate. His doctor put him on a fish diet that evidently cleared up the problem. Simon may have relied on chocolate earlier in his career as well.

[72]On Simon's clash with Bossuet in 1702, consult: Woodbridge, "Censure royale et censure épiscopale: Le conflit de 1702," *Dix-huitième siècle* 8 (1976): 333–55.

[73]An extensive list of works drawn up to counter Simon can be found in Auguste Bernus, *Notice bibliographique sur Richard Simon* (Bâle: H. Georg, 1882).

[74]Nonetheless Simon believed the original autographs to have been infallible. See Jacques Le Brun, "Sens et portée du retour aux origines dans l'oeuvre de Richard Simon," *XVIIᵉ siècle* 33 (Avril–Juin 1981): 185–98.

[75]Simon was in many regards a Molinist in theology. The correspondence between Bossuet and the "Great Arnauld" reveals their mutual disdain for Simon's anti-Augustinianism and lack of respect for Catholic tradition (C. Urbain and E. Levesque [eds.], *Correspondance de Bossuet* [Paris: Hachette, 1910], V, pp. 406–7 [a letter of July 1693 from Arnauld to Bossuet]). Regarding the Vulgate, Simon repeated time and time again his belief that it was the best version and the "authentic" one, but that it was not infallible. Moreover, even though the Fathers of the Council of Trent authorized the Vulgate, they did not forbid other versions such as the ones he was thinking about drawing up (*Histoire critique du Vieux Testament*, pp. 242–70). Because Simon was bold enough to point out discrepancies between the Vulgate and the extant Hebrew versions, he became terribly suspect for certain orthodox Catholics (*Histoire critique du Vieux Testament*, pp. 259–61). On the multiple concepts of Catholic tradition in the seventeenth century, see: Georges Tavard, *La tradition au XVIIᵉ siècle en France et en Angleterre* (Paris: Cerf, 1969).

[76]The Spinoza-Simon association crops up in the correspondence of both Protestants and Catholics. See the letter of the Benedictine Martianay to Estiennot (October 1, 1690) in Emile Gigas (ed.), *Lettres des Bénédictins de la Congrégation de St. Maur 1652–*

1790 (Copenhague: G. E. Gad, 1892), II, pp. 165–67, and the letter of Pierre Bayle to Minutoli (January 1, 1680) in Emile Gigas (ed.), *Choix de la correspondance inédite de Pierre Bayle, 1670–1700* ... (Copenhague: G. E. Gad, 1890), I, pp. 154–55. One of Simon's earliest critics, Ezekiel Spanheim, saw Simon as a scholar aiding Spinoza's cause. See Spanheim's "Lettre à un ami ..." (1678) published in Simon's *Histoire critique du Vieux Testament* (1685 edition), pp. 569–70. In 1678 Bossuet believed that Simon might be a partisan of Spinoza.

[77]Paul Auvray has argued that Richard Simon wrote the *Histoire critique du Vieux Testament* (1678) without a basic knowledge of the contents of Spinoza's *Tractatus* (1670). Consult: Auvray, "Richard Simon et Spinoza," in *Religion, érudition et critique à la fin du XVIIe siècle et au début du XVIIIe* (Paris: Presses universitaires de France, 1968), pp. 201–14.

[78]Woodbridge, "The Reception of Spinoza's *Tractatus Theologico-Politicus* by Richard Simon (1638–1712)," paper delivered in May 1980 at the Lessing Akademie, Wolfenbüttel, West Germany (to be published by the Lessing Akademie).

[79]In the 1678 Preface to the *Histoire critique du Vieux Testament* Simon writes: "With this same principle one will respond very easily to all the false and pernicious principles that Spinoza has claimed can be drawn from these changes or additions, with which to deny the authority of the Divine books, as if the changes were purely human...."

[80]Simon, *Histoire critique du Vieux Testament*, pp. 17–21, 31–40, 46–51.

[81]Ibid., pp. 15–21.

[82]The best monograph on the career of Jean Le Clerc is Annie Barnes' *Jean Le Clerc (1657–1736) et la république des lettres* (Paris: Droz, 1938). See also René Voeltzel, "Jean Le Clerc (1657–1736) et la critique biblique" in *Religion, érudition et critique à la fin du XVII siècle et au début du XVIII*, pp. 33–52; Abraham des Amorie van de Hoeven, *De Joanne Clerico et Philippo Limborch dissertationes duaes* (Amsterdam, 1843); Jean Le Clerc, *Joannis Clerici Philosophiae et S. Linguage ... Vita et Opera* (Amsterdam: J. L. de Lormo, 1711); Theodore Parrhase (Jean Le Clerc), *Parrhasiana* (2 vols; Amsterdam: Héritiers d'Antoine Schelte, 1699–1701); E. J. Kenney, *The Classical Text*, pp. 40–44. As to the animosity between the two men, it had a context. Simon and Le Clerc had earlier engaged in a caustic interchange. Simon wrote a piece, *Novorum Bibliorum polyglotorum synopsis* (signed Adamantius; published by Frederic Arnoldi [in reality by Reiner Leers], 1684) in which he asked fellow members in the Republic of Letters to give him suggestions on the prospectus for a new polyglot Bible. The young Le Clerc took Simon up on his offer and sent him an evaluation (through the good auspices of the Rotterdam publisher Reinier Leers). Disliking the sharp tone in this letter, Simon criticized Le Clerc harshly in yet another piece. We should situate the great debate of 1685–1687 in the context of festering animosities from an earlier year.

[83]Astruc, *Conjectures sur les mémoires originaux dont il paroit que Moyse s'est servi pour composer le Livre de la Genèse* (Brussels [Paris], 1753), pp. 7, 9, 454–55, 476–77. See also: Adolphe Lods, "Astruc et la critique biblique de son temps," *Revue d'histoire et de philosophie religieuses* (1924): 123–27. Astruc saw himself as advancing Le Clerc and Simon: "Dans le fonds, je pense comme ces Auteurs, mais je porte mes conjectures plus loin & je suis plus decidé" (*Conjectures sur les mémoires originaux ...* , p. 9).

[84]On Voltaire's Old Testament studies, see: Bertram Schwarzbach, *Voltaire's Old Testament Criticism* (Genève: Droz, 1971). Voltaire was apparently familiar with the Simon-Le Clerc debate.

[85]The first edition of Simon's *Histoire critique du Vieux Testament* (1678) was rudely suppressed due to the efforts of Bossuet. This edition was burned (1678) with probably no more than six or seven copies being saved from the flames. Poorly made editions of the volume appeared in Holland in the early 1680s. However the standard edition was published by Reinier Leers at Rotterdam in 1685. His denials notwithstanding, Simon undoubtedly contributed to the creation of this edition.

[86]In December of 1685, Louis Maimbourg wrote telling comments to Le Clerc about the impact of the *Sentimens* ... : "... Dieu soit loué le temps est proche du grand jour que nous attendons après une nuit si longue et si obscure: et c'est sans flaterie Monsieur que j'en ay cru voir l'aurore dans ce docte Ouvrage avec toutes ses couleurs les plus vives et lest plus charmantes" (University of Amsterdam C 89); in the same month Jean Robert Chouet of Geneva wrote: "... jamais Lecture de Roman ne m'a tant plu. J'ai pourtant eu de la peine a en être le Maistre; il me les a fallu prester à cent personnes, et dans ce moment mesme ils courent de coste et d'autre. Vous ne devez pourtant douter, Monsieur, que les pensées de vos Lettres ne soient fort différentes; car comme vous ne censurez pas seulement le P. Simon, maisbien d'autres gens encore, vous devez vous attendre à essuier de chagrin d'une Armée d'Auteurs ..." (University of Amsterdam C37). Some of Le Clerc's correspondence for this time frame is also found in the Archives de Bessinge (Tronchin).

[87]Bayle lamented, "All your Treatise on the inspiration of the prophets and of the Apostles can do is sow a thousand doubts and a thousand seeds of atheism in people's minds" (my translation; University of Amsterdam K3b, Bayle to Le Clerc, July 18 [1685?]). The Bayle-Le Clerc interchange over Scriptural issues (1685–1687) warrants a lengthy discussion which we cannot give here. In the *Nouvelles de la République des Lettres*, Bayle's reviews favored Simon's theses much to Le Clerc's anger and disgust (see: *N.R.L.*, July 1685, Article III). Much intrigue hovers behind Bayle's writing and rewriting of his reviews regarding Le Clerc's 1685–1687 publications. Genuine animosities were engendered between the two men due to these reviews. See Martin Klauber's M.A. thesis in Church History (Trinity Evangelical Divinity School, 1981) on the Le Clerc interchange.

[88]Jean Senebier, *Histoire littéraire de Genève* (Genève: Barde, Manget & compagnie, 1786), II, pp. 291–92. The references are to Johann A. Fabricius and Richard Simon. In his volume *Parrhasiana*, I, pp. 367–75, Le Clerc named others who had attacked him for his *Sentimens* ... : Matthais Honcamp, Mr. Maius, Mr. Vander Waeyen....

[89]One of LeClerc's correspondents, Jean Robert Chouet, told the young author about Bossuet's reaction as recounted to Chouet by an abbé from Dijon: "Mons. de Meaux [Bossuet] m'a écrit ces jours passés, qu'il avoit leu son Livre, et qu'il n'en estoit point satisfait. Ce Prelat croit qu'il est l'un des [plus] grands Sociniens qui est au monde, et qui ne donne aucun frein ni aucunes bornes à ses pensées" (University of Amsterdam C37, Chouet to Le Clerc, December 19, 1685).

[90]Le Clerc declares: "Trois de nos Amis se sont vus tous les jours, pendant quelques semaines, dans la Bibliothèque de M.O. pour lire cet Ouvrage ensemble, apres l'avoir lu chacun en particulier; & comme ils m'ont fait l'honneur de me recevoir dans leurs Conférences, je puis vous rendre un assez bon compte de ce qu'on y a dit (*Sentimens* ... , p. 2).

[91]Le Clerc, *Sentimens* ... , p. 129.

[92]Ibid., pp. 219–45 (Letter 11), pp. 246–86 (Letter 12). On the authorship and content of these letters, see: Jean Roth, "Le Traité de l'inspiration de Jean Le Clerc," *Revue d'histoire et de philosophie religieuses* (1956): 50–60. We are assuming that Le Clerc wrote these letters whose authorship is contested. He denied repeatedly that either Noël Aubert de Versé or Pierre Allix had a hand in their creation, as rumor had it (see Le Clerc's denial concerning Aubert de Versé in *Parrhasiana* ... , I, p. 375, and Pierre Allix's letter to Le Clerc [University of Amsterdam C2a, January 19, 1686]).

[93]Le Clerc had probably read Spinoza's *Tractatus theologico-politicus* as early as 1681 (University of Amsterdam K24c, Le Clerc to Limborch, December 6, 1681). However Erasmus and Grotius were his real mentors. He cites them repeatedly in his writings. On October 21, 1695, he wrote the following to Count Pembroke: "L'on pourroit nommer plusieurs, mais *Erasme* et *H. Grotius* qui sont deux hommes incomparables, suffisent pour me Consoler. Jamais personne ne travailla plus qu'eux à éclaircir l'Ecriture Sainte ..." (University of Amsterdam, III D 24, "Epistolae ad Anglos," p. 22). Le Clerc re-edited both Erasmus's works and those of Grotius.

[94]Le Clerc, *Sentimens* . . . , p. 231.

[95]Printed in the year 1690. This volume consists of Letters 11 and 12 from the *Sentimens . . . and Letters 3, 4, 5 from the Défense des sentimens*. . . . A British Museum notice suggests that John Locke, one of Le Clerc's close friends, may have been translator (an intriguing supposition, but not yet demonstrated). There was also a German translation of the *Sentimens . . . : Briefe eniger Holländischer Gottesgelehrtern* . . . (n. p., 1779).

[96]Le Clerc, *Five Letters concerning the Inspiration* . . . , pp. 7–8. A Cartesian emphasis upon clear and distinct ideas may be connected in some way to this statement. A few Protestant theologians wanted to abandon the analogy of faith test for the "clear and distinct" ideas test as they weighed the "truthfulness" of their exegesis. On the other hand, various forms of Cartesian thought were under mounting attack in these days (see: Richard Watson, *The Downfall of Cartesianism, 1673–1712* [The Hague: Nijhoff, 1966]).

[97]John Locke followed the Simon-Le Clerc debate very carefully. He made annotated remarks on several of the four volumes. His own views on verbal inspiration were troubling him by 1685. On September 26, 1685, Locke wrote an important letter to Philip van Limborch about his personal misgivings regarding Le Clerc's *Sentimens*. . . . Included in this letter were statements of this kind: "If everything in holy writ is to be considered without distinction as equally inspired of God, then this surely provides philosophers with a great opportunity for casting doubt on our faith and sincerity. If, on the contrary, certain parts are to be considered as partly human writings, then where in the Scriptures will there be found the certainty of divine authority, without which the Christian religion will fall to the ground? . . . But since there are in fact a number of other passages [in Le Clerc's *Sentimens* . . .] upon the general infallibility and inspiration of Holy Scripture, and to which I confess that I cannot find an answer, I earnestly beg that you will not find it too troublesome to explain to me your own feelings on the matter. Many things that I have come across in the canonical books, long before I read this treatise, have kept me in doubt and anxiety, and you will be doing me a most welcome service if you can relieve me of these scruples" (John Locke, *The Correspondence of John Locke* [ed. E. S. De Beer; Oxford: Oxford University Press, 1976] vol. 2, pp. 748–51). The Simon and Le Clerc debate did not strengthen Locke's beliefs in verbal inspiration and the Bible's complete infallibility. Le Clerc's in-coming correspondence confirms the fact that a good number of readers accepted his "conjectured" ideas. Interestingly enough, Jean Le Clerc later published a volume *Genesis sive Mosis Prophetae liber primus* (Amstelodomi: n.p., 1693) in which he argued clearly for the Mosaic authorship of the Pentateuch. See his "Dissertatio de Scriptore pentateuchi Mose," which is found in this volume. Le Clerc's reversal is quite startling. It may not have been only coincidence that he was seeking a job at an English university when he published this piece.

[98]See Simon's discussion of the hermeneutical principles of both Protestants and Socinians in his *Histoire critique du Vieux Testament*, pp. 427–54.

[99]The present author is doing research on the German reactions to the writings of Jean Le Clerc, Richard Simon, and Spinoza. Simon's writings were reviewed more extensively in Germany than in any other area. And yet we know little about the ties between various strands of biblical criticism in Germany (Lessing, Reimarus, Semler) in the eighteenth century and various strands of biblical criticism in the United Provinces or France in the late seventeenth century.

[100]Several volumes and essays are particularly instructive in this regard: Don C. Allen, *The Legend of Noah: Renaissance Rationalism in Art, Science and Letters* (Urbana: University of Illinois Press, 1949); Klaus Scholder, *Ursprünge und Probleme der Bibelkritik im 17 Jahrhundert* . . . (München: Kaiser, 1966); Jacques Le Brun, "Das Entstehen der historischen Kritik im Bereich der religiosen wissenschaften im 17. Jahrhundert," *Trierer Theologische Zeitschrift* 89, 2 (April, Mai, Juin 1980): 100–117.

Notes

CHAPTER VI

[1]See W. R. Godfrey's essay, "Reformed Thought on the Extent of the Atonement to 1618," *The Westminster Theological Journal* XXXVII (Fall 1974 to Spring 1975): 133–71, which is taken from chap. 2 of his Ph.D. dissertation, "Tensions within International Calvinism: The Debate on the Atonement and the Synod of Dort, 1618–1619," Stanford University, 1974.

[2]For details on this European-wide controversy, see: John Woodbridge, "The 'Great Manuscript Chase,' The Eucharistic Controversy and Richard Simon," unpublished paper delivered at the national meeting of the Evangelical Theological Society, Deerfield, Illinois, December 1978.

[3]Leszek Kolakowski, *Chrétiens sans Église La conscience religieuse et le lien confessionel au XVIIe siècle* (Paris: Gallimard, 1969). It should be pointed out that although Protestants and Catholics often competed with each other, they did sometimes live together in comparative peace. Consult, for example: Caroline Hibbard, "Early Stuart Catholicism: Revisions and Re-Revisions," *The Journal of Modern History* 52, no. 1 (March 1980): 1–34. Several plans of union were discussed between Protestants and Catholics in the seventeenth century. The most famous discussion ensued between Leibniz and Bossuet. On another plan, see Richard Stauffer, *L'affaire d'Huisseau Une controverse protestante au sujet de la "Réunion des chrétiens" (1670–1671)* (Paris: Presses universitaires de France, 1969). Huisseau suggested that reunion could be based on the fact that both parties accepted an infallible Bible.

[4]For an excellent discussion of the tensions within English Puritanism during the 1640s, see: John Wilson, *Pulpit in Parliament Puritanism During the English Civil Wars 1640–1648* (Princeton: Princeton University Press, 1969), pp. 230–35. Wilson notes the rising tide of discord regarding millenarian issues among Puritans. We are using the controversial expression *Puritan* in a loose sense in this study. Some individuals at the Westminster Assembly apparently did not appreciate being called Puritans. For a general background study on Puritans and the Bible, see John Coolidge, *The Pauline Renaissance in England Puritanism and the Bible* (Oxford: Clarendon Press, 1970). Consult also: Paul Christianson, *Reformers and Babylon: English apocalyptic visions from the reformation to the eve of the civil war* (Toronto: University of Toronto Press, 1976).

[5]Grand Rapids: Eerdmans, 1967.

[6]Rogers, *Scripture in the Westminster Confession . . .*, p. 416.

[7]John Gerstner, "The Church's Doctrine of Biblical Inspiration," *The Foundation of*

Biblical Authority (ed. James M. Boice, Grand Rapids: Zondervan, 1978), pp. 42–45. Rogers and McKim, *The Authority and Interpretation of the Bible*, pp. xxiv, n. 11; 250, n. 32; 373, n. 95.

[8]Consult B. B. Warfield, *The Westminster Assembly and Its Work* (New York: Oxford University Press, 1931). See also Charles Briggs, *Whither? A Theological Question for the Times* (New York: Scribner, 1889); Briggs, *General Introduction to the Study of Holy Scripture* (Edinburgh: T & T Clark, 1899).

[9]Rogers and McKim, *The Authority and Interpretation of the Bible*, pp. 206–8. Rogers and McKim also rest their case upon the disjunction that because one Westminster Divine, Samuel Rutherford, did not view the Scriptures to be completely infallible, the Westminster Divines did not esteem the Scriptures to be completely infallible (inerrant). This is an awkward extrapolation because it makes one man's views (which Rogers and McKim have probably misinterpreted) the basis for interpreting a Confession (approved by many). See this chapter, n. 40.

[10]Rogers, *Scripture in the Westminster Confession*, pp. 90–95. See Keith Sprunger, "John Yates of Norfolk: The Radical Puritan Preacher as Ramist Philosopher," *Journal of the History of Ideas* XXXVII (Oct.–Dec. 1976): 697–706.

[11]On the career of William Ames, see Keith Sprunger, *The Learned Doctor William Ames: Dutch Backgrounds of English and American Puritanism* (Urbana: University of Illinois Press, 1972) and the many books of Perry Miller.

[12]William Ames, *The Marrow of Theology* (trans. and ed. John Eusden; Boston: Pilgrim Press, 1968 [reprint]), pp. 185–86.

[13]Geoffrey Bromiley, *Historical Theology: An Introduction* (Grand Rapids: Eerdmans, 1978), p. 327.

[14]Ames, *The Marrow of Theology*, pp. 188–89. In paragraph 27, Ames distinguishes between interpreters and prophets. For him interpreters were translators/copyists who could err. Prophets were the biblical authors who did not err. Ames's distinction is found in earlier English writers of the sixteenth century.

[15]Perkins, *The Works of William Perkins* (ed. Ian Breward; Appleford . . . , England: The Sutton Courtenay Press, 1970), pp. 549–50. On Perkins's theology see: H. C. Porter, *Reformation and Reaction in Tudor Cambridge* (Hamden, Conn.: Archon Books, 1972 [reprint], pp. 288–313.

[16]Perkins, *The Works of William Perkins*, p. 552.

[17]Ibid., p. 48. Perkins notes that the Bible "agrees with itself most exactly and the places that seem to disagree may easily be reconciled" because "the scope of the whole Bible is Christ with his benefits" (Ibid., p. 47). Perkins attempted to avoid an extreme literalism by observing that the words and letters of Scripture should not be interpreted in isolation; their "sense" or focus is important. Perkins writes: ". . . for Christ in Scripture expoundeth himself" (Ibid., p. 47).

[18]Ibid., p. 334. Perkins cites Ps. 12:6 as his proof text for this claim. It should be noticed that he indicates that the Scriptures are free from both deceit and error (contra Rogers and McKim's definition of infallibility for the Puritans).

[19]Ibid., pp. 39–40.

[20]See the significant essay by Philip Hugues, "The Inspiration of Scripture in the English Reformers Illuminated by John Calvin," *The Westminster Theological Journal* 23 (May 1961): 129–50.

[21]Rogers, *Scripture in the Westminster Confession* . . . , p. 306.

[22]Rogers, "Biblical Authority and Confessional Change," *Journal of Presbyterian History* 59, 2 (Summer 1981): 133.

[23]For a good survey of the way multiple forms of Newton's thought penetrated the Republic of Letters, see Robert Schofield, "An Evolutionary Taxonomy of Eighteenth Century Newtonianisms," *Studies in Eighteenth Century Culture* (ed. Roseann Runte; Madison: The University of Wisconsin Press, 1978), vol. 7, pp. 175–92. Voltaire introduced one form of Newtonianism into France in the 1730s. T. Kuhn's "revolutions" or paradigm

shifts seem less than adequate as an interpretive model for understanding the historical complexities associated with reception of diverse aspects of Newtonian thought. See also I. Berhard Cohen, "The Eighteenth Century Origins of the Concept of Scientific Revolution," *Journal of the History of Ideas* XXXVII (April–June 1976), 257–88; Richard Westfall, "The Changing World of the Newtonian Industry," *Journal of the History of Ideas* XXXVII (January–March 1976): 175–84.

[24]For a discussion of the reception of Copernican ideas in Protestant as opposed to Catholic countries, see Elizabeth Eisenstein, *The printing press as an agent of change: Communications and cultural transformations in early-modern Europe* (Cambridge: Cambridge University Press, 1980), pp. 636–60. For an incisive critique of the literature on Puritanism and "science," consult: Robert Greaves, "Puritanism and Science: The Anatomy of Controversy," *Journal of the History of Ideas* XXX (July–September 1969): 345–68.

[25]See this essay, chap. 3, n. 76.

[26]On this debate, see the somewhat polemical essay by Grant McColley, "The Ross-Wilkins Controversy," *Annals of Science* 3 (1938): 153–89.

[27]Barbara Shapiro, *John Wilkins 1614–72: An Intellectual Biography* (Berkeley: University of California Press, 1969), pp. 52–53.

[28]The authors cite (pp. 225–26, n. 117) Proposition III from Richard Westfall's *Science and Religion in Seventeenth-Century England* (Ann Arbor: University of Michigan Press, 1973), p. 34 and Proposition II from R. Hooykaas's *Religion and the Rise of Modern Science* (Grand Rapids: Eerdmans, 1972), p. 116.

[29]Wilkins, *A Discourse Concerning a New Planet* (London: John Maynard, 1640) Proposition III.

[30]Ibid., Proposition II.

[31]Wilkins believed that Moses and Joshua had learned "sciences" in a time when they were taught in a rude and imperfect manner. Moses and Joshua were susceptible to the errors common in their day. Joshua was perhaps unskilled in astronomy "having the same grosse conceit of the Heavens as the vulgar had." Wilkins summarizes his thinking: "From all which it may be inferred, that the ignorance of such good men and great scholars concerning these philosophical points, can be no sufficient reason, why after examination we should deny them, or doubt of their Truth" (*A Discoverie Concerning a New Planet*, Proposition I).

[32]Cited in McColley, "The Ross-Wilkins Controversy," p. 162 (from Ross's *The New Planet No Planet* [1646], p. 13).

[33]Ibid., pp. 162–63.

[34]Rogers and McKim, *The Authority and Interpretation of the Bible*, p. 206. The authors note that Rutherford declared that the Bible was our rule (1) "in fundamentals of salvation" and (2) "in all morals of both first and second table." They do not point out, as Rogers does in his thesis (p. 367), that the Bible is also a rule for Rutherford, (3) "in all institutions" and (4) "in circumstances of worship." It appears that Rutherford's discussion of art and science has some special relationship to Roman Catholic claims (p. 367, n. 525). What that relationship is, Rogers does not explain. Nevertheless it is apparently a key that unlocks the import and meaning of Rutherford's discussion.

[35]Wilkins, *A Discourse Concerning a New Planet*, Proposition IV.

[36]See this chapter, the citation for n. 29.

[37]Wilkins writes: "True indeed, for Divinity we have an infallible rule that do's plainly inform us of all necessary Truth" (*A Discourse Concerning a New Planet*, Proposition I).

[38]Earlier Roman Catholics and Protestants had on occasion argued that the Bible was a rule giving us pertinent knowledge in all areas. Several called it an encyclopedia. Wilkins does not want to make this claim. But he is willing to argue that the Bible does give us infallible information even when it treats topics incidentally.

[39]This is our supposition. We do not know in fact if Rutherford was aware of

Wilkins's discussion of a *rule*. The concept of rule in the 1640s needs to be studied with care.

[40]Rutherford apparently espoused a view of verbal inspiration. For background on Samuel Rutherford (1600–1661), see Marcus Loane, *Makers of Religious Freedom in the Seventeenth Century: Henderson-Rutherford-Bunyan-Baxter* (Grand Rapids: Eerdmans, 1961), pp. 59–103.

[41]Regarding John Lightfoot, consult: Chaim Eliezer Schertz, "Christian Hebraism in Seventeenth-Century England as Reflected in the Works of John Lightfoot" (Ph.D. in Church History at New York University, 1977; Ann Arbor: University Microfilms International, 1981). Eliezer suggests that Lightfoot allowed for a few minor errors in the text, despite his "fundamentalism" (contra the conclusions of B. B. Warfield's lengthy analysis of Lightfoot found in *The Westminster Assembly and Its Word*, pp. 280–333). Regarding James Ussher, consult: R. Buick Knox, *James Ussher: Archbishop of Armagh* (Cardiff: University of Wales Press, 1967). Knox writes: "Therefore he [Ussher] gave great attention to constructing a chronological system from the raw materials provided in the Bible; he set himself to this task with confidence because he was sure that the Biblical data were true in their most literal sense and that when reference to a year occurs this signifies a year of three hundred and sixty-five days" (p. 105).

[42]See this chapter, n. 6.

[43]Recently, Rogers has written along the same line: "I tell my students that the Bible functions at two levels. One is what we called, in our book, the central saving message. The other might be termed the surrounding cultural milieu. Accepting the first demands faith. Understanding the second requires scholarship. I learned this distinction from the Puritan divines who in their Westminster Confession of Faith point to both factors" ("A Response," *Theology Today*, XXXVIII, No. 3 [October 1981], p. 347.) He claims that "verbal inerrancy" was fashioned in the late seventeenth century (Ibid., p. 344), that is, after the Westminster Divines had met.

[44]Leslie Stephens and Sidney Lee (eds.), *Dictionary of National Biography* (London: Smith, Elder, 1908), III, p. 272. See the many references to Gouge in Wilson, *Pulpit in Parliament*, pp. 65, 72, 93. . . .

[45]Gouge sat on the committee that worked on the first chapter of the Confession that deals with Scripture. On his role at the Assembly, see Rogers, *Scripture in the Westminster Confession*, p. 128. Rogers describes Gouge's relationship to Ramism in these terms: "William Gouge, a prominent member of the Westminster Assembly, defended Ramism at Cambridge where he lectured on logic and philosophy" (Ibid., p. 89).

[46]William Gouge, *A Commentary on the Whole Epistle to the Hebrews* in *Gouge on Hebrews* (Edinburgh: James Nichol, 1867), III, p. 138. The author is indebted to Joseph Prillwitz whose paper (Trinity Evangelical Divinity School, March 10, 1978) on Gouge and the Westminster Confession is the source for some of his citations by Gouge.

[47]Ibid., I, p. 29.

[48]Gouge, *The Whole Armour of God or a Christian's Spiritual Furniture to Keep Him Safe from all the Assaults of Satan* (London: John Beale, 1637), pp. 330–31. Gerald Cragg observes that Gouge believed the Bible could genuinely mislead: "Gouge realized that the Bible could mislead as well as guide. The Word of God, he pointed out, is 'that part of God's will which is in the holy scriptures he caused to be recorded. . . . This Word is properly and truly the right sense and meaning of the Scriptures; for except that be found out, in many words there may seem to be matter of falsehood' " (*Freedom and Authority: A Study of English Thought in the Early Seventeenth Century* [Philadelphia: Westminster Press, 1975], p. 142). Gouge is saying that if the Bible is not properly interpreted, it may appear to have errors. He is not saying that the Bible actually contains falsehood.

[49]Roger Nicole believes that Rogers has dismissed too rapidly the documentation that Warfield assembled concerning the Westminster Divines and Holy Scripture: "It is surprising that in his thesis Rogers gave only a very cursory review of Warfield's work on

the Westminster Standards, much briefer in fact than that devoted to the work of Charles A. Briggs, although the latter was flawed by some incredibly inept mistakes such as interpreting as a 'Westminster divine's own view what are really the words of his opponent.' It seems incredible that Rogers judged he could safely bypass all the evidence amassed by Warfield, presumably on the grounds that some members of the assembly were not Aristotelian in their philosophical presuppositions and that our primary source of reference . . ." (A. A. Hodge and B. B. Warfield, *Inspiration* [Grand Rapids: Baker, 1979 (reprint)], p. 98 [from Nicole's Appendix 6, "The Westminster Confession and Inerrancy," pp. 97–100]).

[50]B. B. Warfield, *The Westminster Assembly and Its Work*, pp. 264–73.

[51]Schertz, "Christian Hebraism in Seventeenth-Century England . . . ," pp. 85–89.

[52]Ibid., p. 87.

[53]Baxter, *The Practical Works of Richard Baxter* (London: George Virtue, 1838), III, pp. 92–93. Baxter later became a strong critic of Spinoza's *Tractatus* (1670). See: Rosalie Colie, "Spinoza in England, 1665–1730," *Proceedings of the American Philosophical Society* 107, no. 3 (June 1963): 189–92. Consult also Baxter's discussion of the Bible in *The Autobiography of Richard Baxter* (ed. N. H. Keebie; London: Dent, 1974), pp. 109–12, 212–13.

[54]Bishop Ussher viewed the Hebrew text (which he called the "Hebrew verity") as the most reliable text. He tried to recover it through lower textual critical work. B. B. Warfield indicates that Ussher's "Body of Divinity" (1645) was a significant source in the framing of the Westminster Confession's discussion of Scripture. Consult: Warfield, *The Westminster Assembly and Its Work*, pp. 176–90. Ussher, a distinguished Hebraist, was apparently a defender of complete biblical infallibility.

[55]The basic premise of lower textual criticism is to recover as much as possible the "authentic" text of a document. Erasmus had proposed this as an essential aspect of the Christian humanist's program. Richard Simon assumed that the originals had been lost by Tertullian's day (that late second century). Citing Augustine's own efforts, he urged that the "critic" attempt to approach the "lost originals" as much as possible through textual criticism.

[56]Baxter's contention was seconded by other Protestant writers as well. Much like his contemporary William Ames, John Smyth, a Cambridge graduate (1593) and a separatist had written: "Men are of two sortes: Inspired or ordinary men. Men inspired by the Holy Ghost are the Holy Prophets &. Apostles who wrote the Holy Scriptures by inspiration: 2 Pet. 1.21, 2 Tim. 3.16, Rom. 1.2, namely the Hebrue of the ould testament &. the greeke of the new testament. The Holy Scriptures viz. the Originalls Hebrew &. Greek are given by Divine Inspiration &. in their first donation were without error most perfect &. therefore Canonicall" (Smyth, 1:279) (as cited in L. Russ Bush and Tom J. Nettles, *Baptists and the Bible: The Baptist doctrines of biblical inspiration and religious authority in historical perspective* [Chicago: Moody, 1980], p. 28). See also the opinion of Thomas Grantham (1634–1692) about the Holy Writings and the "Greek copies" (Ibid, p. 41).

[57]The correspondence of the participants at Westminster might reveal genuine insights about the dynamics of their meetings and about the connotative freight of the expressions they used in their statements regarding Holy Scripture. By studying this correspondence, we might make advances on the studies by Warfield and Rogers. Surprisingly, much research remains to be accomplished in this area.

[58]Stanley Gundry has written extensively on John Owen's view of Scripture. See his essay, "John Owen on Authority and Scripture" in a forthcoming I.C.B.I volume edited by John Hannah. Gundry demonstrates conclusively that Rogers and McKim have presented a deficient interpretation of John Owen. He elucidates carefully Owen's commitment to complete biblical infallibility.

[59]Leon M. Allison, "The Doctrine of Scripture in the Theology of John Calvin and Francis Turretin" (Th.M. Thesis; Princeton Theological Seminary, 1958).

[60]On p. 196, n. 177, Rogers and McKim attempt to substantiate their claim by refer-

ring to Allison's thesis, "The Doctrine of Scripture ...," pp. 92–93. Allison makes the following comment: "It seems to be a reasonable conjecture that Turretin did not consider Calvin to be a good authority to bring forth in his discussion of the Scripture. It is quite possible that Turretin had come to the conclusion that Calvin's concept of the Scripture was quite different from his own" (p. 92). What Allison conjectures, Rogers and McKim state as fact. Moreover they ignore Allison's analysis (pp. 97–98) of the commonalities between Calvin's views on Scripture and Turretin's perspectives (including their shared doctrine of "a verbally inerrant Scripture").

[61]W. R. Godfrey presents a set of pertinent criticisms directed at Rogers and McKim's "misrepresentation" of Turretin's thought in his forthcoming essay, "Biblical Authority in the Sixteenth and Seventeenth Centuries: A Question of Transition," *Scripture and Truth* (eds. D. A. Carson and J. D. Woodbridge; Grand Rapids: Zondervan, 1983). We cite but one of Godfrey's criticisms: "For Rogers and McKim, Turretin's formalization of Scripture's authority climaxes in his abandoning the idea of accommodation. They declare that accommodation "was entirely absent from Turretin" (p. 177). But here again Turretin is misrepresented. He declared clearly: "When God understands, he understands himself, as he is finite, and so infinitely; but when he speaks, he speaks not to himself, but to us, i.e., in accommodation to our capacity, which is finite. . . ." Or, Rogers and McKim argue that Turretin did not establish the believer's conviction of the Bible's authority in the witness of the Holy Spirit. In fact Turretin makes the witness of the Holy Spirit just such an efficient cause: "It is a question of the principle, or efficient cause, of faith by which we believe the divine quality of Scripture, that is, of whether or not the Holy Spirit produces it in us" (Francis Turretin, *The Doctrine of Scripture: Locus 2 of Institutio theologiae elencticae*, trans. John W. Beardslee, III [ed. John W. Beardslee, III; Grand Rapids: Baker, 1981], p. 73). A reading of Turretin's discussion of this matter makes one wonder how our authors came to their judgment. There are several other key points about Turretin's theology of the Bible that they simply misinterpret. Turretin gives this very important survey of the status of the infallibility issue in his day: "To deal with them [contradictions], the scholars (*doctores*) follow various paths. Some think the question may be easily handled by granting that the sacred writers could have made mistakes, by failure of memory, or in unimportant details. This argument is used by Socinus when he treats the authority of Scripture, by Castellio in his *Dialogue*, and by others. But this does not counter the argument of the atheists; it joins them in a blasphemous manner. Others hold that the Hebrew and Greek sources have been corrupted in places, through the malice of Jews and heretics, but that the correction is easy by means of the Vulgate and the infallible authority of the church. We will argue against it in a later section, when we discuss the purity of the sources. Others concede that small errors have appeared in Scripture, and remain, which cannot be corrected by reliance on any manuscript or by collation, but which are not to be ascribed to the sacred writers, but explained partly by the ravages of time and partly by the faults of copyists and editors, and which do not destroy the authority of Scripture because they occur only with regard to unnecessary or unimportant statements. Scaliger, Cappel, Amama, Voss, and others are of this opinion. Finally, others uphold the integrity of Scripture and do not deny that various seeming contradictions—not, however, true or real ones—occur; (they believe) that these passages are difficult to understand but not altogether contradictory and impossible. This is the more common opinion of the orthodox, which we follow as the more safe and the more true" (Ibid., pp. 58–59). It is interesting to note that Turretin associated the position of Rogers and McKim with that of Socinus.

[62]See, for example, E. de Budé, *Vie de François Turrettini, théologien genevois 1623–1687* (Lausanne: G. Bridel, 1871).

[63]Walter Rex portrays Turretin in this fashion: "Indeed, aside from the specific doctrines disputed with the Salmurians and his political theories, Turretini is in general far from being the rigid, backward conservative depicted by historians. On the contrary, we see in his theology an example of the final triumph of one part of the liberal

rationalist tradition, which has now been joined—in external form and emphasis at least—by the conservative tradition also" (Rex, *Essays on Pierre Bayle and Religious Controversy* [The Hague: Nijhoff, 1965], p. 139). It is possible that Rex's description does not adequately capture Turretin's person and thought. Nevertheless, it points out the deficiencies of those portraits that are presently being painted by historians.

[64]Rogers and McKim note (p. 174) that Turretin cited Aquinas explicitly only once in his discussion of Scripture (whereas he cited Calvin 0 times, Jerome 26, and Augustine 20 . . .). They deduce from these figures that Turretin did not respect Calvin as a source. But if one relies upon their kind of extrapolation from these data, it would be proper to conclude that Turretin was not much interested in Aquinas, but favored Jerome and Augustine. We find this kind of argumentation less than satisfactory. Once again, W. R. Godfrey's essay underscores the need for a fresh estimate of Francis Turretin's person and work, a study based on research in primary sources.

[65]Consult the papers for the conference on "Rationality in the Calvinian Tradition," held August 3–5, 1981, at the Institute for Christian Studies, Toronto, Canada. Regarding Roman Catholic thinking, consult the entire edition of the *Revue des sciences philosophique et theologique* 64, 3 (Juillet 1980) devoted to "révélation et rationalité au XVIIe siècle"; George Tavard, *The Seventeenth-Century Tradition: A Study in Recusant Thought* (Leiden: Brill, 1978).

[66]A comparative study of Francis Turretin and his son Jean-Alphonse Turretin might reveal a shift between one man's emphasis on "regenerated reason's" circumscribed role in religious affairs and the other's emphasis on "reason's" rights to judge special revelation. For background on the philosophical and theological issues under consideration in Geneva during the 1670s and 1680s, see: Michael Heyd, "From a Rationalist Theology to Cartesian Voluntarism: David Derodon and Jean-Robert Chouet" *Journal of the History of Ideas* XL (Oct.–Dec. 1979): 527–42. On Jean Alphonse Turretin and biblical criticism, see Werner Kümmel, *The New Testament: The History of the Investigation of Its Problems* (Nashville: Abingdon, 1972), pp 58–60.

[67]Rosalie Colie's *Light and Enlightenment: A Study of the Cambridge Platonists and the Dutch Arminians* (Cambridge: Cambridge University Press, 1957) is the book with which any study of this topic should begin. See also Frederick Powicke, *The Cambridge Platonists: A Study* (Hamden, Conn.: Archon Books, 1971 reprint).

[68]In the mid-century English Puritans were very much exercised by the emergence of the Quakers and others who allegedly appealed to extrabiblical "revelations" (Christopher Hill, *Change and Continuity in Seventeenth Century England* [Cambridge, Mass.: Harvard University Press, 1975] pp. 40–41). Interestingly enough, scholars are becoming more aware of mystic strains within Puritanism itself. Consult the superb review of literature devoted to "Enthusiasm" by Michael Heyd: "The Reaction to Enthusiasm in the Seventeenth Century: Towards an Integrative Approach," *Journal of Modern History* 53, 2 (June 1981): 258–80.

[69]Several studies of Paul Dibon explicate this topic with genuine finesse. See in particular, his *La philosophie néerlandaise au siècle d'or* . . . (2 vols.; Paris: Elsevier, 1954).

Notes

CHAPTER VII

[1]For a significant interpretation of the expressions, *Enlightenment, Lumières, Illuminismo, Illustración, Aufklärung*, see Michel Baridon, "Lumières et Enlightenment Faux parallèle ou vrai dynamique du mouvement philosophique?" *Dix-huitième siècle* 10 (1978): 45–69.

[2]Basing their discussion on secondary works, Rogers and McKim indicate that for Robert Boyle the "Bible was seen less as a record of God's relationship to people than as a further and higher revelation of His power" (p. 228). A careful reading of Boyle's *Treatises on the High Veneration Man's Intellect Owes to God: On Things Above Reason: and on the Style of the Holy Scriptures* (London: John Batchard and Son, 1835) does not sustain their analysis. Boyle very carefully undertakes to refute the claims of those who believe that the different writing styles of the biblical authors do not lend credence to the divine inspiration of the Bible. Boyle apparently espoused complete biblical infallibility. See Paul Waggoner, "Robert Boyle on Science, History, and Scripture" (unpublished paper; Trinity Evangelical Divinity School, May 22, 1981).

[3]Rogers and McKim make what are misleading statements about Isaac Newton (p. 232): "When Newton equated Christ with reason, he eliminated all supernatural elements from Christianity." Today scholars are much more aware of Newton's biblicism. He used it to support his alleged Arianism and he demonstrated it in his studies of biblical prophecy. Moreover, Richard Brooks argues forcefully against the thesis of Richard Westfall, John Dillenberger, and others that Newton posited separated compartments in the structure of reality (natural philosophy and revealed religion). Consult: Brooks, "The Relationships between Natural Philosophy, Natural Theology, and Revealed Religion in the Thought of Newton and their Historiographic Relevance" (Ph.D. dissertation in Religion, History; Northwestern University, 1976; Ann Arbor: Xerox University Microfilms, 1976), p. 112, n. 2. For Newton's biblicism, see Brooks's chapter, "Newton's Attitudes Towards Revealed Religion" pp. 86–110. P. M. Heimann also criticizes Richard Westfall and others concerning their presentation of Boyle and Newton: "Newton and Boyle are regarded as having 'prepared the ground for the deists of the Enlightenment'; for 'deism, the religion of reason, steps full grown from the writings of the Christian *virtuosi.*' This historiography is doubly misleading: in its account of doctrines of providence in the thought of Boyle and Newton, and of the consequent characterization of eighteenth-century history" ("Voluntarism and Immanence: Conceptions of Nature in Eighteenth-Century Thought," *Journal of the History of Ideas* XXXIX, 2 [April-

June 1978]: 271). Rogers and McKim's analysis is essentially based on the Westfall historiography to which Heimann refers. The authors are apparently unfamiliar with the very beneficial efforts by scholars to evaluate Bayle, Newton, Locke, Boyle, and others in the context of their own times. Distinctions must be made between what thinkers themselves advocated and the perceptions of their thought by later writers. These distinctions are especially significant when one attempts to discover the origins of the Enlightenment. On the issue of miracles and science, see R. M. Burns, *The Great Debate on Miracles: from Joseph Glanvill to David Hume* (Lewisburg, Pa.: Bucknell University Press, 1981).

[4]We have already referred to the fact that John Locke (until at least 1685) espoused complete biblical infallibility (contra the infallibility of papal interpreters) (see chap. 5, n. 97). Rogers and McKim seriously distort Locke's concept of the relationship between reason and special revelation in the 1690s when they declare (p. 233), "Reason became the judge of revelation." John C. Biddle, a Locke expert, writes more carefully: "The attempt to support revelation by arguments of natural reason seemed to Locke to be both impossible and impious. He considered such doctrines as the nature of the Trinity and the afterlife to be above man's reason, and viewed all desires for their rational demonstration as a subversion of faith in revelation.... Thus, although Toland and later Deists drew heavily upon his philosophy, Locke seems not to have been an intentional party to their emphasis on reason and natural religion. Rather, as an opponent of the Deists and a defender of Revelation, he sought a simple, moral Christianity based on faith" (John C. Biddle, "Locke's Critique of Innate Principles and Toland's Deism," *Journal of the History of Ideas* XXXVII [July-September 1976]: 422). It is true that Locke received rude criticism ranging from Stillingfleet's barbs to Leibniz's insinuation that he was inclined to Socinianism.

[5]On the outlawed pastors of the Church of the Desert and their interaction with the *Siècle des lumières*, see: John Woodbridge, "L'influence des philosophes français sur les pasteurs réformés du Languedoc pendant la deuxième moitié du dix-huitième siècle" (Thèse: Doctorat de troisième siècle; Université de Toulouse, 1969). These pastors often studied at the French Seminary in Lausanne, Switzerland. In the 1750s one of their professors (whom we have not been able to identify) presented fourteen proofs to demonstrate that the Scriptures contain no errors (University of Geneva Public Library Collection Antoine Court 23, fols. 18–32). He argued that the Holy Spirit is necessary to convince us of the divinity of the Holy Scriptures (fol. 31). Those who believe that the Bible has errors are "Catholics, Enthusiasts, and Deists" (fol. 32). On Jacob Vernes (1728–1791), see Paul Chaponnière, "Un pasteur Genevois ami de Voltaire: Jacob Vernes," *Revue d'histoire littéraire* 36, 2 (avril-juin 1929): 181–201; Edouard Dufour, "Jacob Vernes 1728–1791, Essai sur sa vie et sa controverse apologétique avec J. J. Rousseau" (Thèse: Bachelier en Théologie; Faculté de l'Université de Genève; Genève, 1898). On Jacob Vernet (1698–1788), see *Mémoire historique sur la vie et les ouvrages de M. J. Vernet* (Paris, 1790). Consult also: Paul Chaponnière, *Voltaire chez les Calvinistes* (Paris: Perrin, 1936). On the religious world of eighteenth-century Germany, see in particular: Walter Grossmann, *Johann Christian Edelmann: From Orthodoxy to Enlightenment* (The Hague: Mouton, 1976). Grossmann provides marvelous background material on "radical pietism" and Lutheran orthodoxy in his study of Edelmann's relationship to Lessing and Reimarus. See Lessing's attack on biblical inerrancy in Gotthold Lessing, "On the Proof of the Spirit and of Power," *Lessing's Theological Writings* (ed. Henry Chadwick; Stanford: Stanford University Press, 1967), p. 55. Consult also: Thomas Saine, "Gotthold Ephraim Lessing's Views on Theological Issues as Reflected in his Early Book Reviews," *Studies in Eighteenth Century Culture* (ed. Roseann Runte; Madison: The University of Wisconsin Press, 1979), vol. 9, pp. 269–84. Orthodox Lutherans were prominent defenders of complete biblical infallibility. The present author is doing research on the reception of the biblical criticism of Spinoza, Simon, and Le Clerc in eighteenth-century Germany. The research must take into consideration the impact of radical pietism upon developments in biblical criticism. Another

work of note on intellectual life in Germany is Friedhelm Radandt, *From Baroque to Storm and Stress* (New York: Barnes and Noble, 1977). Concerning Roman Catholicism in the eighteenth century, see L. J. Rogier and G. de Berthier de Sauvigny, *Siècle des lumières, révolutions, restaurations (1715–1848)* (Paris: Seuil, n.d.).

[6]Numerous theologians in England, Germany, and elsewhere wrote huge tomes in which they attempted to demonstrate that the Christian faith in general and specific Christian doctrines in particular were rational. In emphasizing the evidences for Christianity and its "reasonableness" against "rationalist" opponents, these Christians (Butler, Paley, and others) sometimes downplayed the role of the Holy Spirit in confirming the authority of the Bible to the believer. They demonstrated a confidence in the persuasive value of rational argumentation that was noticeably greater than the more restrained appraisals of some of their Protestant predecessors who believed that the natural man cannot understand the things of God without the Holy Spirit's intervention. These apologists were sometimes quite careful in their arguments to fend off "rationalism." In a lecture delivered on July 5, 1696, at Cambridge University, the distinguished textual critic, Richard Bentley affirmed his belief in the mysteries of the Christian religion "... because they are plainly taught in the word of God, who can neither err nor deceive, and this we affirm to be a reasonable conclusion, though it carry us even to the confines of Heaven, beyond the limits of Reason" (Bentley, *Of Revelation and the Messias* [sic] [London: H. Mortlock, 1696], p. 11 as cited in Stewart Stout, "The Place of Special Revelation in the Early Boyle Lectures" [unpublished paper; Trinity Evangelical Divinity School, June 5, 1981]). For a representative discussion of the career of a deist, see Thomas L. Bushell, *The Sage of Salisbury, Thomas Chubb 1679–1747* (London: Vision, 1968). For a representative discussion of the career of a leading *philosophe* who ultimately defended atheism, see Arthur Wilson, *Diderot* (New York: Oxford University Press, 1972). We should recall that polemicists hung expressions like *deist, atheist,* and *Socinian* upon their opponents in ways that were often unfair. For a representative discussion of the career of a theologian who took a more mystical approach to the Bible, see Bernard Dupriez, *Fénelon et la Bible Les origines du mysticisme fénelonien* (Paris: Bloud et Gay, 1961).

[7](New Haven: Yale University Press, 1974). This volume should be studied with care. Peter H. Reill reviews the literature on hermeneutics in Germany in the eighteenth century in his "History and Hermeneutics in the *Aufklärung:* The Thought of Johann Christoph Gatterer," *Journal of Modern History* 45, 1 (March 1973): 24–51.

[8]In the 1770s and 1780s several Swiss theologians such as David Levade (professor of theology at the French seminary in Lausanne) appealed to Rousseau's subjective apologetic in their defense of the Christian religion: "Incrédules! Ecoutez, non point les conseils du Maître que nous adorons, et que vous rejettez, mais ecoutez les conseils que vous donne un philosophe [Rousseau] bien plus éloigné de vos fontaines que des nôtres" (*Sermons prononcés dans les Eglises d'Amsterdam et de Lausanne* [Lausanne, 1791], p. 37; see also p. 17, n. a; pp. 27–28, nn. a and b; p. 48 n. b; pp. 54, 64, 65, 91, 94, 99, 106, 119, 143). For Christians' use of Rousseau's subjective apologetic, see Albert Monod, *De Pascal à Chateaubriand Les défenseurs françois du Christianisme de 1670 à 1802* (New York: Burt Franklin, 1971 [1916]), pp. 409, 402–24.

[9]Ridicule had been used as a favorite vehicle for those who wanted to impugn the truth claims of Christianity in days before Voltaire chose it as a major weapon. See John Redwood, *Reason, Ridicule and Religion: The Age of Enlightenment in England 1660–1750* (Cambridge: Harvard University Press, 1976). Concerning Voltaire and biblical criticism, see Bertram Schwarzbach, *Voltaire's Old Testament Criticism* (Genève: Droz, 1971). In his "Important Study by Lord Bolingbroke ... (1736)," Voltaire cited Jean Le Clerc as one who had overthrown the Mosaic authorship of the Pentateuch (*Voltaire on Religion: Selected Writings,* tr. Kenneth Appelgate [New York: Frederick Ungar Publishing Co., 1974], p. 98). The standard work on Voltaire and religion is René Pomeau's *La religion de Voltaire* (Paris: Nizet, 1969 [re-edition]). It includes material on Voltaire's attitudes toward

the Bible. See the important biographies of Voltaire: Theodore Bestermann, *Voltaire* (Oxfordshire: University of Chicago Press, 1976); Hadyn Mason, *Voltaire* (Baltimore: Johns Hopkins Press, 1981). Bestermann's editions of Voltaire's correspondence are invaluable tools for studying the *philosophe*. For a review of the state of biblical criticism in France for the year 1778 (the year both Voltaire and Rousseau died), consult: Marie-Hélène Contoni, "La critique biblique en 1778," *Dix-huitième siècle* 11 (1979): 213–33. Contoni has done very sophisticated research on biblical criticism in eighteenth-century France. Concerning Jean-Jacques Rousseau and religion, see Jacques-François Thomas, *Le pélagianisme de J.-J. Rousseau* (Paris: Nizet, 1956); Pierre Maurice Masson, *La religion de J. J. Rousseau* (3 vols.; Paris: Hachette, 1916); Ronald Grimsley, *Rousseau Religious Writings* (Oxford: Clarendon Press, 1970).

[10]A sampling of the rich bibliography on the Enlightenment might include the following: Paul Raabe and Wilhelm Schmidt-Biggemann (eds.), *Aufklärung in Deutschland* (Bonn: Hohwacht Verlag, 1979); Franco Venturi, *Italy and the Enlightenment: Studies in a Cosmopolitan Century* (ed. Stuart Woolf; New York University Press, 1972); the entire edition of the 1978 *Dix-huitième siècle* devoted to the topic "Qu'est-ce que les lumières?" the transactions of the five International Congresses on the Enlightenment and the publications of the Voltaire Foundation, Oxfordshire, England. See, too, the major interpretations of the Enlightenment by Peter Gay, Lester Crocker, Daniel Mornet, Norman Hampson, Ernst Cassirer (including his study of I. Kant), Robert Darnton, René Pomeau, Theodore Bestermann. Consult also several significant theses: Roger Mercier, *La réhabilitation de la nature humaine (1700–1750)* (Villemomble, France: La Balance, 1960); Robert Mauzi, *L'ideé du bonheur au XVIIIe siècle* (Paris: Armand Colin, 1960); Daniel Roche, *Le siècle des lumières en province Académies et académiciens provinciaux, 1680–1789* (2 vols.; Paris: Mouton, 1978). On the subject of dechristianization in the eighteenth century, see the significant works of Michel Vovelle which include *Piété, baroque, et déchristianisation en Provence au XVIIIe siècle* (Paris: Plon, 1973) and *Religion et révolution la déchristianisation de l'an II* (Paris: Hachette, 1976).

[11]On the founding of Princeton Seminary, see Mark Noll, "The Founding of Princeton Seminary," *The Westminster Theological Journal* 42 (Fall 1979): 72–110. Noll writes: "The Princeton Theology was conservative, at least in part, because the founders saw the creation of a seminary as one means to combat cultural chaos" (p. 109).

[12]Archibald Alexander was well versed in a broad spectrum of theological writings. James Alexander wrote about his father's theological culture: "In some departments of learning he was no doubt surpassed by many of his brethren; but it is believed that none of his coevals had read more extensively in the theology of the sixteenth and seventeenth century, including Romanist and Lutheran, as well as Reformed divines" (James Alexander, *The Life of Archibald Alexander, D. D.* [New York: Charles Scribner, 1854], p. 296).

[13]See Sydney Ahlstrom, "The Scottish Philosophy and American Theology," *Church History* 24 (September 1955): 257–72; Theodore Bozeman, *Protestants in an Age of Science: The Baconian Ideal and Antebellum American Religious Thought* (Chapel Hill: University of North Carolina Press, 1977); John C. Vander Stelt, *Philosophy and Scripture: A Study in Old Princeton and Westminster Theology* (Marlton, N.J.: Mack Publishing Company, 1978).

[14]See this essay, chap. 6, nn. 11–14.

[15]John Gerstner, "The View of the Bible Held by the Church: Calvin and the Westminster Divines," *Inerrancy* (ed. Norman Geisler; Grand Rapids: Zondervan, 1979), pp. 400–407. Gerstner cites John E. Smith, the General Editor of *The Works of Jonathan Edwards* (New Haven: Yale University Press, 1959), in this regard: "The central problem is this: Edwards, on the one hand accepted totally the tradition established by the Reformers with respect to the absolute primacy and authority of the Bible, and he could approach the biblical writings with that conviction of their inerrancy and truth which one usually associates with Protestant fundamentalism" (Ibid., p. 407).

[16]In his diary (May 2, 1709) William Byrd of Westover noted: "In the evening we talked about religion and my wife and her sister had a fierce dispute about the infallibility of the Bible" (cited in Carl Bode, ed., *American Literature: The 17th and 18th Centuries* [New York: Washington Square Press, 1973], p. 230). Or Samuel Willard, who wrote the most extensive theology text by an American Puritan, declared: "Truth is self-consenting, but error is self-contradictory. There is a sweet harmony in the whole Word of God. There are no contradictions to be found there. If any shall judge that there are such, the mistake is not in the Scriptures, but in their deceived understandings" (cited in Ernest B. Lowrie, *The Shape of the Puritan Mind: The Thought of Samuel Willard* [New Haven: Yale University Press, 1974], pp. 35–36).

[17]On the career of Timothy Dwight, a president of Yale College (1795–1817), see Stephen Berk, *Calvinism versus Democracy: Timothy Dwight and the Origins of American Evangelical Orthodoxy* (Hamden, Conn.: Anchor Books, 1974). Upon his assumption of the presidency at Yale College, Dwight addressed the question, "Are the Scriptures of the Old and New Testaments the Word of God?" In a sermon he taught: ". . . each inspired man [among the Apostles] was, as to his preaching or his writing, absolutely preserved from error" (Dwight, *Theology Explained and Defended in a Series of Sermons by Timothy Dwight . . .*, [ed. Seveno Dwight; Edinburgh, 1831], pp. XXIII-XXIV). Samuel Hopkins, whom Berk calls "the progenitor of the metaphysical New Divinity," espoused complete biblical infallibility. Hopkins writes: "Many have thought they have found numerous contradictions in the Bible; and its enemies have eagerly searched to find them, and have used all their art and plausible coloring to make them appear to be real contradictions, and urged them with all their power against revelation. But this has turned to the advantage of the Holy Scriptures, and been the occasion of making their consistency and harmony more evident and certain than if no such accusation had been brought against them. For the objections of this kind have been critically examined, and found to be entirely groundless. And since all the wit and art of men of the best abilities, and under the greatest advantages to try, cannot find any real contradictions in them, and those which have been most plausibly urged, or have had the greatest appearance of inconsistencies, at first view, appear upon careful and thorough examination, to be perfectly consistent, this has cast new light on the subject, and made it more abundantly evident and certain that there is, indeed, no inconsistency to be found in them" (*System of Doctrines* [1792] in *The Works of Samuel Hopkins, D. D.* [Boston: Doctrinal Tract and Book Society, 1852] I, pp. 22–23). Like many others, Hopkins also proposes: "Therefore, if any real, material contradictions or inconsistencies can be found in this book, it will be sufficient reason for rejecting it, as not from God" (Ibid., p. 22).

[18]The most adequate discussion of the American Enlightenment is found in Henry May, *The Enlightenment in America* (New York: Oxford University Press, 1979). See, too: G. Adolf Koch, *Religion of the American Enlightenment* (New York: Thomas Y. Crowell Company, 1968); Sydney Ahlstrom, *A Religious History of the American People* (New Haven: Yale University Press, 1974), pp. 366–68. For a general background on the period, see Garry Wills, *Inventing America: Jefferson's Declaration of Independence* (New York: Vintage Books, 1979). Several scholars are presently studying the impact of the Scottish Enlightenment upon the thinking of the founding fathers.

[19]Samuel Taylor Coleridge, *Confessions of an Inquiring Spirit* (Boston: James Munroe and Company, 1841). On Coleridge, see among other studies, Basil Willey, *Nineteenth Century Studies: Coleridge to Matthew Arnold* (New York: Harper and Row, 1966), pp. 1–50.

[20]Coleridge, *Confessions of an Inquiring Spirit*, pp. 79–80.

[21]Ibid., p. 81.

[22]This commitment to complete biblical infallibility continued for many decades. In 1893, Thomas Huxley commented about the longstanding commitment of some of his fellow citizens to complete biblical infallibility: "The doctrine of biblical infallibility . . . was widely held by my countrymen within my recollection: I have reason to think that

many persons of unimpeachable piety, a few of learning, and even some of intelligence, yet uphold it. But I venture to entertain a doubt whether it can produce any champion whose competency and authority would be recognised beyond the limits of the sect, or theological coterie, to which he belongs. On the contrary, apologetic effort, at present, appears to devote itself to the end of keeping the name of 'Inspiration' to suggest the divine source, and consequently infallibility, of more or less of the biblical literature, while carefully emptying the term of any definite sense. For 'plenary inspiration' we are asked to substitute a sort of 'inspiration with limited liability,' the limit being susceptible of indefinite fluctuation in correspondence with the demands of scientific criticism" (cited in John C. Greene, "Darwin and Religion," *European Intellectual History since Darwin and Marx* [ed. W. Warren Wagar; New York: Harper and Row, 1966], pp. 15–16). To our mind George Marsden, a fine historian, has perhaps exaggerated some of the conceptual differences which existed between English and American Evangelicals toward biblical authority (Marsden, "Fundamentalism as an American Phenomenon: A Comparison with English Evangelicalism," *Church History* 46, 2 [June 1977]: 215–32). See James Moore, *The Post-Darwinism Controversies . . .* (London: Cambridge University Press, 1979). Moore proposes the paradoxical thesis that the orthodox were better prepared to accept Darwin's thought than Protestant liberals. Moore's bibliography on this topic is superb. For general background on religion in nineteenth-century Europe, see Bernard Reardon, *Religious Thought in the Nineteenth Century Illustrated from Writers of the Period* (Cambridge: At the University Press, 1966), pp. 1–35; Alec Vidler, *The Church in an Age of Revolution: 1789 to the Present Day* (Baltimore: Penguin, 1971).

[23]Cited in William Lee, *The Inspiration of Holy Scriptures, Its Nature and Proof* (New York: Thomas Whittaker, 1854), p. vii.

[24]Noah Porter, later a president at Yale, described Thomas Arnold in this way: "Such a man was the late Dr. Arnold, an eminent and inspiring example to all scholars and all teachers, the record of whose life should be held in the memory of all such, till a brighter example shall rise" ("The Youth of the Scholar,"*Bibliotheca Sacra and Theological Review* 3 [1846]: 121). Regarding Thomas Arnold, see: Arthur P. Stanley, *The Life and Correspondence of Thomas Arnold* (2 vols.; Boston: Ticknor and Fields, 1868).

[25]Cited in Basil Willey, *Nineteenth Century Studies . . .* , p. 264.

[26]T. F. Curtis, *The Human Element in the Inspiration of the Sacred Scriptures* (New York: D. Appleton & Company, 1867), p. 20. Curtis discusses Coleridge's *Letters of an Inquiring Spirit* at length. Coleridge became more acquainted with the writings of German critics through his contacts with William Taylor of Norwich. On Taylor's role in introducing German higher criticism to England, see Merton Christensen, "Taylor of Norwich and the Higher Criticism," *Journal of the History of Ideas* XX (April 1959): 179–85. On the relationship between "European" and "American" Romanticism, see Sydney Ahlstrom, "The Romantic Religious Revolution and the Dilemmas of Religious History," *Church History* 46, 2 (June 1977): 149–70.

[27]Curtis, *The Human Element in the Inspiration of the Sacred Scriptures*, p. 19. Curtis noted: "Few men have been more influential in forming the present state of religious thought in England, than the late Dr. Arnold, of Rugby (Ibid., p. 103).

[28]Lee, *The Inspiration of Holy Scripture*, p. viii. Lee was also concerned about negative impact of J. D. Morell's *The Philosophy of Religion* (London: Longman, Brown, Green, and Longmans, 1849).

[29]Noah Porter, "Coleridge and his American Disciples," *Bibliotheca Sacra and Theological Review* 4 (1847): 117–71. See also another lengthy article devoted to Coleridge: Lyman Atwater, "Coleridge," *The Biblical Repertory and Princeton Review* 20 (1848): 143–86. Theodore Bozeman describes well the impact of the "non-Baconian philosophical movement": "Then, during the 1830s, a fresh sense of intellectual emergency was created within Old-School ranks by the emergence of an emphatically non-Baconian philosophical movement. Quickly replacing Unitarianism as the leading challenge to traditional belief was the new Transcendentalism, which troubled con-

servatives associated with J. G. Fichte, G. W. F. Hegel, Friedrich Schleiermacher, Samuel Taylor Coleridge, Ralph Waldo Emerson, J. D. Morell, and other figures" *(Protestants in an Age of Science . . .*, p. 135).

[30]T. F. Curtis, *The Human Element in the Inspiration of Sacred Scriptures*, p. 37.

[31]Professor Ian Rennie has recently made this point in his paper, "An Historical Response to Jack Rogers' 'Mixed Metaphors, Misunderstood Models, and Puzzling Paradigms . . .,'" conference paper for "Interpreting an Authoritative Scripture," Conference held June 22–26, 1981, Institute for Christian Studies, Toronto, Canada. Rennie argues (pp. 6–8) that verbal inspiration developed in sixteenth-century Germanic circles whereas plenary inspiration was a common view among English Protestants during the seventeenth through nineteenth centuries. According to Rennie, those who advocated "verbal inspiration" tended to be both theological and social conservatives who assumed defensive postures. His analysis deserves an in-depth analysis that we cannot give it here (but see this essay, chap. 8, n. 51).

[32]Professor Rennie notes that whether they were proponents of "plenary" or "verbal" inspiration, most Evangelicals assumed that the Bible was "inerrant," "infallible," "without error," "without mistake" (Ibid., pp. 6, 10). As we shall see many of them circumscribed this infallibility by associating it with the original autographs. Moreover, they included science within the purview of this infallibility. In his excellent study *Protestants in an Age of Science*, Theodore Bozeman describes the concord Old-School Presbyterians believed to exist between Scriptural teachings and diverse sciences during the ante-bellum period. See also E. Brooks Holifield, *The Gentlemen Theologians: American Theology in Southern Culture, 1795–1860* (Durham, N.C.: Duke University Press, 1978), pp. 96–100. Holifield writes (p. 100): "The Southern pastors could therefore appeal to the scientists as guardians of Scriptural infallibility, but as the condition of their guardianship the geologists demanded a subtle rationalizing of the text, which the ministers began to interpret in accordance with the latest findings of nineteenth-century science." In a similar fashion "scientists" in the sixteenth and seventeenth centuries frequently sought to demonstrate an accord between biblical infallibility and the findings of their investigations (see Richard Popkin, "Scepticism, Theology and the Scientific Revolution in the Seventeenth Century," *Problems in the Philosophy of Science* [eds. I. Lakatos and Alan Musgrave; Amsterdam: North Holland Publishing Company, 1968] 3, pp. 21–25). It should be pointed out that some Christians declined to affirm complete biblical infallibility.

[33]These Evangelicals generally defined biblical infallibility in a similar fashion as later Evangelicals defined inerrancy. In a blurb for William Newton Clarke's *Sixty Years with the Bible: A Record of Experience* (New York: Charles Scribner's Sons, 1910), a reviewer noted that Clarke had given up "the common view [complete biblical infallibility] which all evangelicals held a half century ago. . . ." Clarke himself wrote: "I have dated this conviction against the inerrancy of the Bible here in the Seventies, and here it belongs . . ." (Ibid., p. 108). Interestingly enough, Clarke indicates that he gave up the doctrine of inerrancy before the date Ernest Sandeen indicates that it was fully crafted (1881).

[34]Cited in John H. Leith, ed., *Creeds of the Churches* (New York: Anchor Books, 1963), pp. 334–35.

[35]Norman Maring, "Baptists and Changing Views of the Bible, 1865–1918," *Foundations* 1, 3 (July 1958): 52. Less creedally oriented churches refrained from establishing statements where biblical authority was defined with precision. Their members usually read the Bible as if it were infallible, however.

[36]L. Russ Bush and Tom J. Nettles, *Baptists and the Bible: The Baptist doctrines of biblical inspiration and religious authority in historical perspective* (Chicago: Moody Press, 1980), pp. 157–70 (Dagg), 203–11 (Boyce), 211–18 (Manly, Jr.), 273–83 (Hovey).

[37]Cited in G. F. Wright, *Charles Grandison Finney* (Boston: Houghton, Mifflin, 1891), p. 183. See Finney's letter on this subject in the *Oberlin Evangelist* (June 23, 1841): 100–101.

[38]Charles Finney, *Skeleton Lectures* (1840; published 1841), p. 52. See David Callen's M.A. thesis in Church History devoted to Charles Finney's perception of biblical authority (Trinity Evangelical Divinity School, 1982). The author is indebted to Mr. Callen for the Finney data. Finney apparently shared with the Princetonians and others a commitment to aspects of Common Sense Realism.

[39]Samuel Wakefield, *A Complete System of Christian Theology* (Cincinnati: Cranston and Stowe, 1869), pp. 77–78. Wakefield viewed his study as an introductory theological text to supplement Watson's *Theological Institutes* (1825) used by mature theologians. Wakefield notes his debt to John Dick and Thomas Horne, both of whom were advocates of complete biblical infallibility in the original autographs. Richard Watson (1781–1833), whose *Institutes* became a standard expression of Methodist doctrine, had earlier defended complete biblical infallibility. The views of John Wesley deserve some commentary. Wesley speaks a language which approximates verbal dictation. Moreover he espoused the position that there are no errors within Scripture. He declared: "All Scripture is given by inspiration of God ... consequently, all Scripture is infallibly true" (cited in A. Skevington Wood, *The Burning Heart: John Wesley, Evangelist* [Grand Rapids: Eerdmans, 1967], p. 214 [see pp. 209–19]). Wesley read Soame Jenyn's *View of the Internal Evidences of the Christian Religion* in *The Evangelical Family Library* 14 (New York: The American Tract Society, n.d.). Jenyns had conjectured a theory (similar to Rogers and McKim's proposal) that the biblical authors recounted stories "accommodated to the ignorance and superstition of the times and countries in which they were written ..." (p. 214). He continued: "In the sciences of history, geography, astronomy, and philosophy, they appear to have been no better instructed than others, and therefore were not less liable to be mislead by the errors and prejudices of the times and countries in which they lived" (p. 215). To these claims Wesley responded: "He [Jenyns] is undoubtedly a fine writer; but whether he is a Christian, Deist, or Atheist I cannot tell. If he is a Christian, he betrays his own cause by averring, that 'all Scripture is given by inspiration of God; but the writers of it were sometimes left to themselves, and consequently made some mistakes.' Nay, if there be any mistakes in the Bible, there may as well be a thousand. If there be one falsehood in that book, it did not come from the God of Truth" (*The Works of John Wesley* [Grand Rapids: Zondervan, n.d.], vol. 4, p. 82 [journal entry August 24, 1776]). It is interesting to note that Archibald Alexander appreciated Jenyns's emphasis upon the "internal evidences" for the Christian religion. Wesley wrote to William Warburton on November 26, 1772, regarding Warburton's *On the Offices and Operations of the Holy Spirit* (1750). Warburton had argued that the human authors made "no considerable errors" when they operated under a "virtual" influence of the Holy Spirit. Wesley responded: "Nay, will not the allowing there is any error in Scripture, shake the authority of the whole?" (*The Works of Rev. John Wesley* [London: Wesleyan Methodist Book Room, n.d.], vol. 9, p. 150). The present author is indebted to Timothy Wadkins for signaling several of these discussions by Wesley. See Wadkins's forthcoming M.A. thesis in Church History (Trinity Evangelical Divinity School) on John Wesley's views of biblical authority. Wadkins attempts to treat Wesley's thought in its historical context. He assesses those statements that several scholars have proposed as evidence that Wesley did not uphold complete biblical infallibility (see Robert Chiles's claim in *Theological Transition in American Methodism: 1790–1935* [New York: Abingdon Press, 1965], p. 78). In "John Wesley's Approach to Scripture in Historical Perspective," *Wesleyan Theological Journal* 16, 1 (Spring 1981): 23–50, Larry Shelton attempts to argue that Wesley did not make a close connection between the Bible's authority and its complete infallibility. Shelton's arguments are far from convincing. He entertains the same kind of false dichotomies with which Rogers and McKim operate. For example, Shelton argues that because Wesley indicates that the Bible's chief function is to reveal salvation truths, he had little concern whether or not the Bible was completely infallible. Shelton's essay is a serious piece. It deserves a careful assessment. Several Wesleyan scholars have ignored Wakefield and earlier Methodist authors in their

attempt to demonstrate that some American Wesleyans did not hold to complete biblical infallibility until they came into contact with later Princetonians. Paul M. Bassett begins his analysis of Methodist theologies in the 1870s (the works of Miner Raymond and W. B. Pope) rather than earlier Methodist authors such as Watson and Wakefield ("The Fundamentalist Leavening of the Holiness Movement, 1914–1940, The Church of the Nazarene: A Case Study," *Wesleyan Theological Journal* 13 [Spring 1978]: 68). Following Sandeen's argument, Bassett speaks of the "Princeton mutation" concerning the doctrine of Scripture. For a more nuanced analysis of the richness of the Wesleyan tradition and biblical infallibility, see William Abraham, "The Concept of Inspiration in the Classical Wesleyan Tradition" (unpublished paper). Professor Abraham acknowledges that Richard Watson, Thomas Ralston (1806–1891), Luther Lee (1800–1889), Amos Binny (1802–1878) and many others held the equivalent of the biblical inerrancy position. The present author is especially grateful to Professor Donald Dayton for providing him with recent materials regarding Wesleyan scholarship on biblical authority. This scholarship is frequently quite instructive and well conceived. It highlights the role of the Holy Spirit and Christian experience in sustaining biblical authority among Wesleyans. See also Daryl McCarthy, "Early Wesleyan Views of Scripture," *Wesleyan Theological Journal* 16, 2 (Fall 1981): 95–105.

[40]Cited in Kurt Marquart, *Anatomy of an Explosion: A Theological Analysis of the Missouri Synod Controversy* (Grand Rapids: Baker, 1978), p. 45. On Walther, see Robert Preus, "Walther and the Scriptures," *Concordia Theological Monthly* 32 (November 1961): 669–91.

[41]Balmer, "The Old Princeton Doctrine of Inspiration in the Context of Nineteenth Century Theology: A Reappraisal" (M.A. Thesis in Church History, Trinity Evangelical Divinity School, 1981). Randall Balmer and the present author have written a critique of Ernest Sandeen's interpretation of the Princetonians and biblical authority, which appears in *Scripture and Truth* (ed. D. A. Carson and J. D. Woodbridge; Grand Rapids: Zondervan, 1983).

[42]John Dick, *An Essay on the Inspiration of the Holy Scriptures of the Old and New Testament* (Edinburgh: J. Ritchie, 1800), p. 239.

[43]John Dick, *Lectures on Theology* (Philadelphia: Desilver, Thomas & Co., 1836), I, p. 124.

[44]This particular edition was published by William Collins of Glasgow. Andrew King writes: ". . . but in reference to these alleged contradictions it may be observed, that some of them are to be found only in our translations—they do not attach to the Scriptures in their original languages. You are fully aware, we trust, that we are far from maintaining that the translations of them have been made by inspiration . . ." (Ibid., p. 125).

[45]Beck, "Monogrammata Hermeneutices N.T.," *The Biblical Repertory and Theological Review* 1 (1825): 27. The fact that Charles Hodge wanted to publish Beck's article (pp. 1–122) with its review of the history of biblical interpretation indicates the breadth of the Princetonian's own interests in the field. Beck makes but few allusions to Francis Turretin in his survey. Charles Hodge developed a personal acquaintance with Beck. The next year, Hodge published Hugh Rose's "The State of the Protestant Church in Germany" *The Biblical Repertory and Theological Review* 2 (1826): 391–501, which contains an extensive critique of German biblical critics and a defense of the Bible's complete biblical infallibility. The theological horizons of Charles Hodge were extensive indeed.

[46]See, e.g., chap. 6, n. 14.

[47]"The Inspiration of the Scriptures," *Spirit of the Pilgrims* 1 (December 1828): 628–29. The author of this essay was probably Leonard Woods of Andover.

[48]"Inspiration of the Scriptures," *Christian Review* 9 (March 1844): 16. (Author's italics.)

[49]Lemuel Moss, "Dr. Curtis on Inspiration," *Baptist Quarterly* 2 (1868): 106. This review concerns T. F. Curtis's *Human Element in the Inspiration of the Sacred Scriptures* (1867).

[50]Alvah Hovey, *Manuel of Systematic Theology and Christian Ethics* (Philadelphia: American Baptist Publication Society, 1877), pp. 77–84. An article in the January 1855 number of the *Freewill Baptist Quarterly* notes: "The inspiration of the Scriptures relates to the original production of the books of Scripture, and denotes the divine superintendence of their production which secured them from error" ("Inspiration of the Scriptures," *Freewill Baptist Quarterly* 3 [January 1855]: 34). A subsequent article in the same journal reviews some of the numerical discrepancies found in Old Testament manuscripts and concludes: "These examples are enough to show how the numbers of the Bible might become confused by the copyist during the ages which have passed since they were written, and by frequent transcribing, cease to stand in perfect agreement with the original or its own several parts" ("The Word of God," *Freewill Baptist Quarterly* 14 [July 1866]: 294).

[51]A. H. Kremer, "The Plenary Inspiration of the Bible," *Reformed Quarterly Review* 26 (October 1879): 569.

[52]D. A. Whedon, "Greek Text of the New Testament," *Methodist Quarterly Review* 50 (July-October 1858): 325.

[53]Ernest Sandeen, *The Roots of Fundamentalism: British and American Millenarianism, 1800–1930* (Grand Rapids: Baker, 1978 [reprint 1970]), pp. 103–31.

[54]See the forthcoming essay by Randall Balmer and John Woodbridge on Sandeen's perception of biblical authority in nineteenth-century America in *Scripture and Truth* (ed. Carson and Woodbridge). For other criticisms of Ernest Sandeen's proposal, see George Marsden, "Defining Fundamentalism," *Christian Scholar's Review* 1 (1971): 141–51; Ernest Sandeen, "Defining Fundamentalism: A Reply to Professor Marsden," *Christian Scholar's Review* 1 (1971): 227–33.

[55]This quotation is found in Ernest Sandeen, *The Origins of Fundamentalism: Toward a Historical Interpretation* (Philadelphia: Fortress Press, 1968), p. 14.

[56]Sandeen, "The Princeton Theology: One Source of Biblical Literalism in American Protestantism," *Church History* 31 (September 1962): 314; also cited in Sandeen, *The Roots of Fundamentalism*, p. 123.

[57]Archibald Alexander, *Evidences of the Authenticity, Inspiration and Canonical Authority of the Holy Scriptures* (Philadelphia: Presbyterian Board of Publications, 1836), p. 230 (this definition clarifies his earlier discussion of superintendence on pp. 226–27). In his review "Dr. Woods on Inspiration," Alexander evidences a concern that inspiration extends to the words of Scripture: "And so, in the selection of their [biblical writers'] language, they would have been equally liable to error; and plenary inspiration, which extended only to the conceptions of the mind and not to the words, would fail of accomplishing the end designed" (*The Biblical Repertory and Theological Review* 3 [1831]: 19). On Alexander's views, see Dennis Okholm, "Biblical Inspiration and Infallibility in the Writings of Archibald Alexander," *Trinity Journal* 5 (Spring 1976): 79–89.

[58]Sandeen, *The Roots of Fundamentalism*, pp. 126–28.

[59]Ibid., p. 128. The 1881 article has been recently reprinted in book form: A. A. Hodge and B. B. Warfield, *Inspiration* (Introduction by Roger Nicole; Grand Rapids: Baker, 1979).

[60]Roger Nicole aptly summarizes Charles Hodge's use of the Parthenon illustration: "Its meaning in keeping with the context must be simply that he [Hodge] was not deterred from confessing the infallibility of the Bible by *his* inability to provide a fully satisfactory explanation in every one of the cases where a discrepancy is alleged" (A. A. Hodge and B. B. Warfield, *Inspiration*, Appendix 5, p. 95).

[61]B. B. Warfield, *The Inspiration and Authority of the Bible* (ed. Samuel Craig; Philadelphia: Presbyterian and Reformed, 1964), pp. 220–21.

[62]Randall Balmer makes a pivotal observation concerning Charles Hodge's *Systematic Theology*: "A collation of Hodge's manuscript lecture notes with his *Systematic Theology* reveals profound similarities; indeed, certain passages in the *Systematic Theology* appear to have been taken verbatim from lectures delivered as early as the 1820s. Thus it is a grievous error to detect shifts in Hodge's theology by pointing to passages in

the *Systematic Theology*, which didn't see print until 1872–1873" ("The Old Princeton Doctrine of Inspiration . . . ," p. 46, n. 63). The interpretations of Rogers and McKim, Ernest Sandeen, and John Vander Stelt stand in need of revision due to this consideration which the authors did not perceive.

[63]Archibald A. Hodge, *The Confession of Faith: A Handbook of Christian Doctrine Expounding the Westminster Confession* (London: The Banner of Truth Trust, 1958 [1869]), pp. 36–37.

[64]Rogers and McKim, *The Authority and Interpretation*, p. 302.

[65]Ibid., pp. 303–5.

[66]Archibald Alexander, "Review of Woods on Inspiration," *The Biblical Repertory and Theological Review* 3 (January 1831): 10. The review concerns *Lectures on the Inspiration of the Scriptures* (Andover, Mass.: Mark Newman, 1829) by Leonard Woods, Professor of Christian Theology at Andover. Woods, a Congregationalist, defended the complete infallibility of the Bible. Elsewhere he wrote: "For what we assert is, the inspiration of the *original* Scriptures, not of translations, or the ancient copies" ("The Inspiration of the Scriptures," *Christian Review* 33 [March 1844]: 16). Randall Balmer's thesis alerted the present author to Woods's article on inspiration (1844).

[67]Cited by Dennis Okholm, "Biblical Inspiration and Infallibility in the Writings of Archibald Alexander," *Trinity Journal* 5 (Spring 1976): 84. See also Archibald Alexander, "Review of Woods on Inspiration," *The Biblical Repertory and Theological Review* 3 (January 1831): 10.

[68]Charles Hodge, lecture on "Biblical Criticism," November 1822, File D, Princeton Theological Seminary, Princeton, N.J. In another lecture entitled "Integrity of the Hebrew Text," he advanced the view that the present Hebrew text "has neither been entirely preserved from errors . . ." (Hodge, Lecture Notes, File D, Princeton Theological Seminary, Princeton, N.J.). Hodge continued: "That the present Heb[rew] text is not immaculate is proved by the following arguments: 1. From the nature of the case and human imbecility it is impossible without a perpetual miracle that the O.T. should have been transcribed so frequently without some mistakes occurring; 2. All experience shows that every ancient work is more or less injured in its transcription from one age to another" (Ibid.). These materials are noted in a forthcoming assessment by John Woodbridge and Randall Balmer regarding Ernest Sandeen's interpretation of the Old Princetonians. Randall Balmer reviewed them in his research.

[69]See this chapter, n. 45.

[70]As we indicated earlier, the premise that only the biblical autographs possessed the trait of infallibility was widely assumed. It is true that in the seventeenth century some Christians esteemed that the Bibles they had in hand were infallible.

[71]Rogers and McKim, *The Authority and Interpretation of the Bible*, p. 288: ". . . Hodge, late in life, moved towards a theory of the inerrancy of the original autographs of Scripture." John Vander Stelt also argues that Charles Hodge began to stress the biblical infallibility of the original autographs in 1878, but that in the 1820s he had believed that the Bible "as we have it now" was infallible (*Philosophy and Scripture at Princeton Theological Seminary*, p. 141, n. 353). Vander Stelt and Rogers and McKim are apparently unfamiliar with Hodge's earlier writings on these points. In 1877 Charles Hodge wrote that his beliefs about Scripture were the same as he *had been taught in his boyhood* (Hugh Martin, *Inspiration of Scripture* [Inverness: Robert Carruthers & Sons, 1964], p. 114).

[72]Francis L. Patton, *The Inspiration of the Scriptures* (Philadelphia: Presbyterian Board of Publication, 1869), p. 112. See Balmer, "The Old Princeton Doctrine of Inspiration in the Context of Nineteenth Century Theology: A Reappraisal," pp. 36–37.

[73]Patton, *The Inspiration of the Scriptures*, pp. 112–13.

[74]Lefferts A. Loetscher leaves the impression that Patton's "defense of Scripture" *followed* the same pattern as that of A. A. Hodge (*The Broadening Church: A Study of Theological Issues in the Presbyterian Church since 1869* [Philadelphia: University of

Pennsylvania Press, 1964], p. 25). Patton did agree with Hodge. But his discussion of the infallibility of the biblical autographs *predated* A. A. Hodge's 1879 edition of *Outlines of Theology* by ten years. Patton joined the faculty of Princeton Seminary in 1881.

[75]On the biblical significance of the autographs concept, see Greg L. Bahnsen, "The Inerrancy of the Autographa," *Inerrancy*, pp. 151–93.

[76]In his 1695 Boyle lecture, John Williams argued that errors in the Bible are due to transcribers, not to the original authors. He noted that inspiration occurs "so that no error should be in the Original Copy; though he [God] left each [human author] to the liberty of their own way of expressing it" (*The Possibility, Expediency and Necessity of Divine Revelation* [London: Richard Chiswell and Thomas Cockerill, 1695], VI, p. 4 as cited in Stout, "The Place of Special Revelation in the Early Boyle Lectures," p. 10). We have already discussed the thinking of other proponents of biblical infallibility in the original autographs.

[77]See the 1881 "Inspiration" article. Roger Nicole writes: "It is interesting to note that in the present article the words *inerrant* and *inerrancy* do not occur, although the terms *errorless* and *without error* are repeatedly used by both authors and the whole intent of the article is to make it clear that the superintendence of God in Scripture guarantees the errorless infallibility of all Scriptural affirmations" (A. A. Hodge and B. B. Warfield, *Inspiration*, p. xiv). It is indeed ironic that scholars ranging from James Barr, Ernest Sandeen, to Jack Rogers and Donald McKim have indicated that this article signaled the creation of something new (inerrancy in the original autographs) when its authors did not employ that expression but ones such as *absolute infallibility* (p. 6). It is quite possible that Christians picked up the word inerrancy from the writings of Thomas Horne. Paul Feinberg writes: "Moreover, the noun *inerrancy* is said to have occurred for the first time in Thomas Hartwell Horne's formidable, four volume *Introduction to the Critical Study and Knowledge of the Holy Scriptures....* In part 2 of volume 2 of the seventh edition (1834) he states, 'Absolute inerrancy is impractical in any printed book'" ("The Meaning of Inerrancy," *Inerrancy*, p. 292). It is worthwhile to recall that Horne, a professor at Cambridge University, defended the complete infallibility of the originals in the early editions of his work. The second edition (1821) was adapted as a text at Princeton College. Horne observes: "In addition to the extensive circulation, which his work has obtained in the Universities and other Theological Seminaries in England, he [the author] has the satisfaction of knowing that it has recently been adapted as a text in the College at Princeton, New Jersey, in North America" (Horne, *Introduction to the Critical Study and Knowledge of the Holy Scriptures* [Philadelphia: E. Littell, 1825], "Preface to the Second Edition").

[78]See B. B. Warfield's reply to his conservative critics in this regard (Archibald A. Hodge and Benjamin B. Warfield, *Inspiration*, Appendix 1, Appendix 2, pp. 73–82).

[79]Randall Balmer has studied the circumstances surrounding the creation of the 1881 "Inspiration" article by A. A. Hodge and B. B. Warfield. He has found little indication of "conspiratorial thinking" in their correspondence or other writings. See Balmer, "The Old Princeton Doctrine of Inspiration in the Context of Nineteenth Century Theology: A Reappraisal," pp. 26–27.

[80]Sandeen, *The Roots of Fundamentalism*, p. 289.

[81]Leigh Jordahl, for example, notes that the nineteenth-century Lutheran theologian, Franz Pieper, agreed essentially with the Princetonian doctrine of Scripture. Jordahl observes: "What Pieper meant by verbal inspiration is exhaustively explained. His position is not significantly different from that of Charles Hodge and the Princeton Theology." Ernest Sandeen contends that the Princeton doctrine not only furnished the base for the Fundamentalist position, but also that this doctrine represented an innovation. As an interpretive hypothesis, this assertion is helpful. It is also, however, an oversimplification and not entirely accurate. That Fundamentalism adopted the view of inspiration championed by Princeton is clear. Actually, Evangelical Protestantism already believed very much what the Princeton theology affirmed. Princeton, however, provided the articula-

tion. To go on to say, as Sandeen does, that the Princeton view 'did not exist in either Europe or America prior to its formulation in the last half of the nineteenth century' is to distort the record. Nothing was even slightly new about asserting that the Bible was verbally inspired and thus also inerrant. Both Reformed and Lutheran orthodoxy had asserted the same thing, and both were also aware of the distinction between original autographs and copies" ("The Theology of Franz Pieper: A Resource for Fundamentalistic Thought Modes Among American Lutherans," *The Lutheran Quarterly* XXIII, 2 [May 1971]: 128–29). Jordahl does think that Sandeen is correct in arguing that a preoccupation with original autographs signals a "defensive apologetic." He believes that such an emphasis does damage to teachings regarding the perspicuity of Scripture.

[82]See, e.g., this chapter, n. 12.

[83]Charles Hodge, e.g., reviewed Lee's important study on Scripture in *The Biblical Repertory* (1857).

[84]Rogers and McKim proffer an interpretation of Turretin's influence at Princeton Seminary that is misleading. For example, they write the following concerning Archibald Alexander's commitment to Turretin (p. 268): "Alexander centered seminary studies in the works of Turretin and the Scottish common sense philosophy popularized in America by Witherspoon. Alexander's biographer wrote: 'Dr. Alexander . . . conceived that theology was best taught by a wise union of the text book with the free lecture. Finding no work in English which entirely met his demands he placed in the hands of his pupils the *Institutions* of Francis Turretin.' Despite the fact that the works of Calvin and the Westminster Divines were available, it was Turretin in Latin that became the standard text at Princeton. It remained so for sixty years until in 1872 Charles Hodge's *Systematic Theology* replaced it as an updated English version of the same theology. Alexander's practice was to assign twenty to forty pages of Turretin in Latin and at the next class to ask the students for an exact repetition of what they had read. He acknowledged that Turretin's work was 'ponderous, scholastic and in a dead language.' Nonetheless, he felt that if seminarians studied 'this athletic, sinewy reasoner of the faith,' they were apt to be strong and logical divines." Rogers and McKim leave out several important qualifications that James Alexander (the author of the citations they quote) made about Turretin's influence. Here is the way their source actually reads: "Dr. Alexander, herein concurring with Chalmers, conceived that theology was best taught by a wise union of the text-book with the free lecture. Finding no work in English which entirely met his demands, he placed in the hands of his pupils the *Institutions* of Francis Turretin. It was ponderous, scholastic and in a dead language, but he believed in the process of grappling with difficulties; he had felt the influence of this athletic sinewy reasoner on his own mind, and had observed that those who mastered his arguments were apt to be strong and logical divines. At this time there had been no modern edition, and copies were rare; but the classes were small, and the book was not laid aside until it became impossible to supply the demand. *It would be very unjust to suppose that the young men were charged with the tenets of Turrettine, to the injury of their mental independence. . . . Dr. Alexander often dissented from the learned Genevan, and always endeavored to cultivate in his students the spirit and habit of original investigation*" [our italics] (James Alexander, *The Life of Archibald Alexander, D.D.*, pp. 368–69). James Alexander continues his discussion by describing the innovative teaching techniques which Archibald Alexander employed; they went far beyond memorizing the writings of Francis Turretin (Ibid., p. 369). Rogers and McKim have not depicted Archibald Alexander's interaction with the writings of Francis Turretin in the same way that their principal source describes that interaction. Moreover, it should be observed that Charles Hodge's lectures constituted an essential ingredient of the curriculum at Princeton Seminary many decades before they found their way into his *Systematic Theology* (1871).

[85]The Princetonians shared with the Reformers a belief that the Bible relates the truth when it is properly interpreted. Their textual problems are often the same ones

with which Augustine and Calvin wrestled. They employed a historical-grammatical approach to their study of the Scriptures as did the Reformers. But their tendency to describe theology as a "science" led them to organize their interpretations of the biblical materials in ways which may have sometimes differed from those based on the Reformers' christological focus.

[86]Cited in John Woodbridge, Mark Noll, Nathan Hatch, *The Gospel in America* (Grand Rapids: Zondervan, 1979), pp. 40–41.

[87]See Noll, "Who Sets the Stage for Understanding Scripture" *Christianity Today* XXIV (May 23, 1980): 14–18.

[88]George Marsden's admirable volume *Fundamentalism and American Culture: The Shaping of Twentieth Century Evangelicalism 1870–1925* (New York: Oxford University Press, 1980) well deserves the plaudits it has received. However, the author's discussion of the attitudes of the Princetonians toward truth and the Scriptures is not without deficiencies. Marsden leaves the distinct impression that their viewpoint concerning the complete infallibility of the Bible was paradigm dependent upon their commitment to Common Sense Realism and Baconianism (pp. 113–15). His analysis of the Princetonian (and dispensationalists for that matter) does not do full justice to the reasons why they held their beliefs. Undoubtedly, they believed as they did because they thought the Bible taught its own infallibility and because they assumed that Christians of past centuries had held that theological stance. Many of them believed that the witness of the Holy Spirit confirmed their assessment as well. They did not self-consciously argue for biblical infallibility because they thought such was a necessary corollary of their beliefs about Common Sense Realism. Nor was it. If anything, their commitments to Common Sense Realism and Baconianism (which scholars have not yet completely untangled; see this chapter, n. 92) reinforced their belief about the Bible's infallibility; but they did not determine them. Moreover Marsden evaluates Fundamentalists in a similar fashion: "This was a Baconian model based on common sense. Almost all their apologetic and interpretation of Scripture rested on this foundation" (p. 215). This statement claims far too much. Relying upon Thomas Kuhn's competing paradigm motif (1962), Marsden attempts to explain why Fundamentalists and Liberals (including many disciples of Immanuel Kant) collided with each other. This aspect of his interpretation is quite perceptive, though overstated. Scholars are increasingly critical of the Kuhnian model upon which it apparently rests. For a contemporary's analysis of the import of Kant, Schleiermacher, and Coleridge, upon concepts of biblical inspiration, see Charles Elliott, "Subjective Theory of Inspiration," *The Princeton Review* 51 (July-December 1881): 192–204. Elliott argues that one of the first attacks on plenary inspiration was delivered by Jean Le Clerc. "The first of these theories was brought out in the controversy occasioned by the work of Le Clerc (born at Geneva 1657, died 1736), which impugned the strict infallibility of the Scriptures and asserted the existence of more or less error in them. From the Reformation until that time distinct theories of inspiration were scarcely known in the church. The assertion of the absolute infallibility of the Holy Scriptures and the denial of all error in them rendered any theory except that of plenary inspiration unnecessary" (p. 192). The author also notes the importance of Coleridge's "Confessions of an Inquiring Spirit" in introducing the "subjective" theory of inspiration (associated with German writers) into the Anglo-Saxon world.

[89]Hodge continues: "It is inconsistent with the veracity of consciousness, which is the fundamental principle of their philosophy. The theology is an incongruous combination of sceptical principles with orthodox faith, the anti-theistic principles of Kant with Theism" (*Systematic Theology*, I, p. 363). Hodge is referring to the thinking of William Hamilton, the author of *Discussions on Philosophy and Literature* and *Lecture on Metaphysics and Logic* and to that of Henry Mansel, the author of *The Limits of Religious Knowledge* (*Systematic Theology*, I, pp. 335–65).

[90]In light of Charles Hodge's teachings, we find the following comments by Rogers and McKim (p. 290) to be exaggerated: "The Princeton men were sure that sin had made

the emotions unreliable. But they held an almost Pelagian confidence that the mind was essentially undisturbed by sin's influence."

[91]In his discussion of free agency, Hodge interacts with Reid's understanding of the will (Systematic Theology, II, pp. 278–309).

[92]Steve Martin is presently studying these questions. See his forthcoming M.A. thesis (Trinity Evangelical Divinity School) devoted to Charles Hodge's anthropology and its relationship to Common Sense Realism and Baconianism.

[93]In his review of Leonard Woods, The Lectures on the Inspiration of the Scriptures, Archibald Alexander specifically criticized Woods's lack of emphasis upon the internal evidences for the Bible's inspiration and authority. He cited the Larger Catechism in this regard. "We [Alexander] believe, therefore, 'that the Scriptures manifest themselves to be the word of God, by their majesty and purity; by the consent of all the parts, and the scope of the whole, which is to give all glory to God; by their light and power to convince and convert sinners, to comfort and build up believers unto salvation: but the Spirit of God bearing witness by and with the Scriptures, in the heart of man, is alone able fully to persuade it, that they are the very word of God'" ("Lectures on the Inspiration of the Scriptures," The Biblical Repertory and Theological Review 3 [January 1831]: 8). In a lengthy letter (dated October 5, 1865) to Dr. Robert Watts, Charles Hodge explained his beliefs about the role of the Holy Spirit in confirming biblical authority: "We are clearly taught that saving faith rests on the witness of the Spirit by and with the truth. This is represented in Scripture as something different from the evidence which the word itself contains of its own truth. It is, 'an unction from the Holy One.' It is 'the demonstration of the Spirit.' The Spirit produces in our minds the infallible conviction that the Bible is true. This conviction is not the product of a process of reasoning, nor a conclusion from the facts of our own consciousness. If it were it would not be infallible, and our faith after all would rest in something human and not in the power of God. . . . In like manner the Spirit witnesses to the believer that he is a child of God" (cited in A. A. Hodge, The Life of Charles Hodge [New York: Arno Press & New York Times, 1969 (1881)], p. 489). Charles Hodge recognized the decisive role of the Holy Spirit in doing theology: "The distinguishing feature of Augustinianism as taught by St. Augustine himself, and by the purer theologians of the Latin Church throughout the Middle Ages, which was set forth by the Reformers, and especially by Calvin and the Geneva divines, is that the inward teaching of the Spirit is allowed its proper place in determining our theology. The question is not first and mainly, What is true to the understanding, but what is true to the renewed heart? The effort is not to make the assertions of the Bible harmonize with speculative reason, but to subject our feeble reason to the mind of God as revealed in his Word, and by his Spirit in our inner life" (Systematic Theology, vol. I, p. 16).

[94]See this chapter, n. 63.

[95]Theodore Bozeman, Protestants in an Age of Science, p. 209, n. 12.

[96]Benjamin B. Warfield, Calvin and Augustine (ed. Samuel Craig; Philadelphia: Presbyterian and Reformed, 1956), p. 115. Interestingly enough, Warfield claimed that he did not base his belief in Christianity on the plenary inspiration of the Bible per se: "Let it not be said that . . . we found the whole system upon the doctrine of plenary inspiration. We found the whole Christian system on the doctrine of plenary inspiration as little as we found it upon the doctrine of angelic existences . . ." (B. B. Warfield, The Inspiration and Authority of the Bible, 2nd ed. [Nutley, N.J.: Presbyterian and Reformed, 1948], p. 210). Nonetheless, Warfield was quick to affirm that the position taught by the New Testament writers could not be dismissed without undermining one's confidence in other aspects of Christian doctrine.

[97]See Andrew Hoffecker, "The Devotional Life of Archibald Alexander, Charles Hodge, and Benjamin B. Warfield," The Westminster Theological Journal 42 (Fall 1979): 111–29; Hoffecker, Piety and the Princeton Theologians: Archibald Alexander, Charles Hodge, and Benjamin Warfield (Grand Rapids: Baker, 1981). Charles Hodge met with the students at the seminary on Sunday afternoons. A reading of his outlines for these

sessions reveals the Princetonian's deep piety and emphasis upon the Holy Spirit. See Charles Hodge, *Conference Papers* (ed. A. A. Hodge; New York: Charles Scribner's Sons, 1879). A. A. Hodge described these sessions in this way: "The dry and cold attributes of scientific theology, moving in the sphere of the intellect gave place to the warmth of personal religious experience, and to the spiritual light of divinely illuminated intuition" (Ibid., p. iii).

[98]Charles Hodge wrote concerning the biblical writers and their knowledge: "As to all matters of science, philosophy, and history, they stood on the same level with their contemporaries. They were infallible only as teachers, and when acting as the spokesmen of God. Their inspiration no more made them astronomers than it made them agriculturists" (*Systematic Theology*, I, p. 165). Hodge identified an erroneous doctrine of accommodation with the thought of the German critics Semler and Van Hemert. He cites Van Hemert's remark: "If anything be taught which is contrary to reason, it is an accommodation" (*The Biblical Repertory* 1 [1825]: 126). Hodge declares: "Perhaps few causes have operated more extensively and effectually, in promoting erroneous opinions than the problems of this doctrine [a false concept of accommodation] (Ibid., p. 125). See also, Beck's discussion of accommodation (Ibid., pp. 19–21). Hodge also proposed what he thought was a proper definition of accommodation: "The sacred writers were not machines. Their self-consciousness was not suspended; nor were their intellectual powers superseded. Holy men spake as they were moved by the Holy Ghost. It was men, not machines; not unconscious instruments, but living, thinking, willing minds, whom the Spirit used as his organs. Moreover, as inspiration did not involve the suspension or suppression of the human faculties, so neither did it interfere with the free exercise of the distinctive mental characteristics of the individual.... It lies in the very nature of inspiration that God spake in the language of men;..." (*Systematic Theology*, I, p. 157).

[99]The authors do make some genuine advances on Sandeen's work, however.

[100]Rogers and McKim lapse into this rare polemical expression (*The Authority and Interpretation of the Bible*, p. 459).

[101]Several students of Professor Timothy Smith have recently done extensive research on the Bible in the nineteenth century. Professors Mark Noll and Nathan Hatch have also pursued research in this area. They are particularly concerned with the Bible's role in nineteenth-century American culture. See their co-edited volume, *The Bible in America* (New York: Oxford University Press, 1982).

[102]We need only cite Randall Balmer's thesis regarding the original autographs hypothesis as an important breakthrough in our understanding. See Balmer, "The Old Princeton Doctrine of Inspiration in the Context of Nineteenth-Century Theology: A Reappraisal" (M.A. thesis, Trinity Evangelical Divinity School, 1981).

[103]By these remarks we do not intend to minimize several important contributions that Professor Sandeen has made to scholars' perceptions of Fundamentalism.

[104]Strange as it may seem, we do not know why some Christians began to use the word inerrancy rather than the traditional word *infallibility* in the late nineteenth century. Did they do so to distance themselves from the declarations of Vatican I (1870–1871) concerning the Pope's infallibility? We do not know. We recall that A. A. Hodge and B. B. Warfield still used the expression *absolute infallibility* in their celebrated 1881 "Inspiration" article. We do know that contemporaries apparently viewed the words as interchangeable ones. See this chapter, n. 77.

[105]*The Union Bible Dictionary* (Philadelphia: American Sunday School Union, 1839), p. 256. See also the article, "Inspiration," in *A Dictionary of the Holy Bible* (New York: American Tract Society, 1859), pp. 208–9. The article notes that "the whole of the Bible was written under the unerring guidance of the Holy Ghost...."

[106]Scholars of the book trade study the number of editions through which a book passes, how many copies constituted the various editions, who bought the copies (if that can be determined), how widely a book was reviewed, and like issues. Robert Darnton's *The Business of Enlightenment: A Publishing History of the Encyclopédie (1775–1800)*

(Cambridge: Harvard University Press, 1979) is a dazzling illustration of the history of the book trade at its best. We might learn much about the popularity of views of biblical authority in the nineteenth century if we studied the dissemination of books devoted to the topic of biblical inspiration. Experts in the history of the press could also have important contributions to make in this area.

[107]Gilbert Haven, "The Divine Element in Inspiration," *Methodist Quarterly Review* 50 (April 1863): 183, as cited in Balmer, "The Old Princeton Doctrine of Inspiration," p. 57, n. 6.

[108]Louis Gaussen, *Theopneusty, or, the Plenary Inspiration of the Holy Scriptures*, trans. Edward Kirk (New York: John S. Taylor & Co., 1845), pp. 44–45.

[109]It is important to note that William Lee of Dublin cited several earlier continental authors who influenced his own views of inspiration: ". . . and among the works to which I owe the greatest obligations I may mention Olshausen's 'Commentary on the New Testament'; Hävernick's 'Introduction to the Old Testament'; Sack's 'Christliche Apologetick'; Beck's 'Propädeutische Entwicklung'; and, especially, Rudelbach's treatise on Inspiration, published in his and Guerike's 'Zeitschrift'" (*The Inspiration of Holy Scriptures*, pp. vi–vii). Francis Turretin did not figure among them.

[110]See Randall Balmer's rich bibliography concerning nineteenth-century books and articles devoted to the topic of biblical inspiration (Balmer, "The Old Princeton Doctrine of Inspiration," pp. 90–96). It is true that some Lutherans, Episcopalians, and others studied at Princeton Seminary. Their views about Scripture may have been shaped by the old Princeton theologians. The influence of the *Biblical Repertory and Theological Review* (it changes names), which Charles Hodge edited for many years, should also be considered. And yet Randall Balmer finds few allusions to the Old Princetonians in articles and books on biblical inspiration by non-Presbyterians.

[111]Robert Haldane, *The Books of the Old and New Testaments Proved to be Canonical, and their Verbal Inspiration Maintained and Established*, 4th ed. (Edinburgh: William Whyte & Co., 1832). David Dyer, *The Plenary Inspiration of the Old and New Testaments* (Boston: Tappan, Whittemore & Mason, 1849); Eleazar Lord, *The Plenary Inspiration of the Holy Scriptures* (New York: M. W. Dodd, 1857).

[112]Bruce Shelley, "A. J. Gordon and Biblical Criticism," *Foundations* XIV (January–March 1971): 77, n. 33.

[113]Professor James Barr makes this association in his *Fundamentalism* (Philadelphia: Westminster Press, 1978), pp. 260–303. Barr is apparently unfamiliar with nineteenth-century discussions of biblical authority by American Evangelicals from various denominations.

[114]See this chapter, n. 39.

[115]Washington Gladden, *Who Wrote the Bible? A Book for the People* (Boston & New York: Houghton, Mifflin, 1891), p. 357. In his review of George Marsden's volume on Fundamentalism, Timothy Smith reminds us that studies of Evangelicalism should not neglect "the thousands of Black evangelical Methodist and Baptist congregations" and the "several million members of Pentecostal denominations." See Smith's review, "Historical Fundamentalism," *Fides et Historia* XIV, 1 (Fall-Winter 1981): 68–72. For a general introduction to the Holiness-Pentecostal movement, see: Vinson Synan, *The Holiness-Pentecostal Movement in the United States* (Grand Rapids: Eerdmans, 1971).

Notes

CHAPTER VIII

[1] Rogers and McKim do correctly assess several features of that tradition. For example, they reiterate how important the work of the Holy Spirit is in confirming biblical authority to the believer. Some modern Evangelicals have neglected this teaching and made the confirmation of the Bible's authority appear to depend upon rational demonstrations and certain forms of evidential apologetics. See Paul Helm's forthcoming essay, "The Role of Faith and Evidence in Confirming Biblical Authority," in *Scripture and Truth* (ed. D. A. Carson and John Woodbridge; Grand Rapids: Zondervan, 1983).

[2] Several modern disciples of Herman Dooyeweerd seem especially assured that the "infallible" redemptive purpose of Scripture emerges unscathed from even the radical criticism of the Bible's historical narrative. For a penetrating analysis of Dooyeweerd's approach to history, see Dale Van Kley's essay, "Dooyeweerd as Historian," in *A Christian View of History* (ed. George Marsden and Frank Roberts; Grand Rapids: Eerdmans, 1975), pp. 139–79.

[3] Concerning these individuals, see chap. 5, n. 3 (Holden); chap. 5, n. 60 (Stillingfleet); and chap. 7, n. 39 (Jenyns). The influence of I. Kant's epochal writings regarding objectivity and subjectivity undoubtedly forced Christians to reconsider traditional apologetics for God's existence as well as their definitions of biblical authority. On the relationship between Kant and "Romanticism," see Ernst Cassirer, *Rousseau Kant Goethe* (Princeton: Princeton University Press, 1970). On nineteenth-century philosophy, see Maurice Mandelbaum, *History, Man, & Reason in Nineteenth-Century Thought* (Baltimore: Johns Hopkins University Press, 1971), pp. 3–37.

[4] Krentz, *The Historical-Critical Method* (Philadelphia: Fortress Press, 1975), p. 30. Krentz himself probably overestimates the revolutionary character of these developments, given developments along the same lines in earlier centuries. See Werner Georg Kümmel, *The New Testament: The History of the Investigation of Its Problems*, trans. S. McLean Gilmour and Howard C. Kee (Nashville: Abingdon, 1972), pp. 62–73 (J. S. Semler and J. D. Michaelis), 120–61 (David F. Strauss and Ferdinand Christian Baur), 281–308 (Radical Historical Criticism). Regarding hermeneutics in the nineteenth century, consult: Hans Frei, *The Eclipse of Biblical Narrative: A Study in Eighteenth and Nineteenth Century Hermeneutics* (New Haven: Yale University Press, 1974). See also Gerhard Maier, *The End of the Historical-Critical Method* (St. Louis: Concordia Publishing House, 1977); Ira Brown, "The Higher Criticism Comes to America, 1880–1900," *Journal of the Presbyterian Historical Society* 38, 4 (December 1960): 193–211.

[5]Krentz, *The Historical-Critical Method*, pp. 22–30. Niebuhr applied the solvent of rigorous critical standards to early Roman history and concluded that numerous accounts were legends. The concept of myth became very important to many students of ancient cultures in the first half of the nineteenth century. Krentz believes that Troeltsch's approach to historical method had become dominant by World War I. He describes its principles as they are exposed in the 1898 essay (p. 55): "... (1) the principle of criticism or methodological doubt, which implies that history only achieves probability. Religious tradition must also be subjected to criticism (pp. 731–732). (2) The principle of analogy makes criticism possible. Present experience and occurrence become the criteria of probability in the past. The 'almighty power' of analogy implies that all events are in principle similar (p. 732). (3) The principle of correlation (or mutual interdependence) implies that all historical phenomena are so interrelated that a change in one phenomenon necessitates a change in the causes leading to it and in the effects it has (p. 733). Historical explanation rests on the chain of cause and effect. The third principle rules out miracle and salvation history (pp. 740–742)." Consult also: Peter Reill, *The German Enlightenment and the Rise of Historicism* (Berkeley: University of California Press, 1975); Hayden White, *Metahistory: The Historical Imagination in Nineteenth Century Europe* (Baltimore: Johns Hopkins University Press, 1974).

[6]Krentz, *The Historical-Critical Method*, p. 29.

[7]For a good survey of this kind of apologetic efforts by Americans (especially Edward Robinson), see Herbert Hovenkamp, *Science and Religion in America 1800–1860* (Philadelphia: University of Pennsylvania Press, 1978), pp. 147–64. Regarding the problem of religious authority in nineteenth-century England, see Rupert E. Davies, *Religious Authority in an Age of Doubt* (London: Epworth Press, 1968).

[8]In 1885 Frederic Farrar assessed the impact of Strauss's *Das Leben Jesu*: "The ability of the book, its clearness, its mastery of the critical studies which Hegel had despised, its union of Hegelian constructiveness with ruthless criticism, its adoption of the historic method which was peculiarly suited to the tendencies of the century, all increased the shock which *Leben Jesu* caused in the minds of Christians" (Farrar, *History of Interpretation* [Grand Rapids: Baker, 1979 (1886)], p. 413). Strauss accounted for the Gospel by the theory of myths. On Strauss, see Horton Harris, *David Friedrich Strauss and his Theology* (Cambridge: The University Press, 1973); Valerie Dodd, "Strauss's English Propagandists and the Politics of Unitarianism, 1841–1845," *Church History* 50, 4 (December 1981): 415–35.

[9]L. E. Elliott-Binns devotes his attention to the crisis which affected English Christians after 1860. He chose that date due to the fact that Darwin's *Origin of Species* and J. S. Mill's *On Liberty* had appeared in 1859, and Buckle's *History of Civilization* the year before that (*English Thought 1860–1900: The Theological Aspect* [London: Longmans, Green and Co., 1956], p. 27). Nonetheless the influence of S. T. Coleridge who had forged his own interpretation of German theology was growing among clerics before 1860, and Strauss's *Das Leben Jesu* had been translated into English by 1846. Englishmen were also worried about the studies of geologists. Wrote Ruskin in 1851: "If only the Geologists would let me alone, I could do very well, but those dreadful hammers! I hear the clink of them at the end of every cadence of the Bible verses (Ibid., p. 175, n. 1).

[10]Rawlinson, *The Historical Evidences . . .* (Boston: B. Gould and Lincoln, 1875), p. 11. In his will and testament Reverend John Bampton had established lectures at Oxford University with the dual purpose of confirming and establishing the Christian faith and confuting all heretics and schismatics.

[11]Ibid., p. 36. Rawlinson declared: "Notwithstanding the personal faith of Niebuhr, which cannot be doubted, and the strong expressions of which he made use against the advocates of mythical theory, he was himself upon occasions betrayed into remarks which involved to a great extent their principles, and opened a door to the thoroughgoing scepticism from which he individually shrank with horror" (Ibid., pp. 34–35). Rawlinson was particularly critical of Strauss.

[12]Ibid., p. 38.

[13]J. W. Burgon, *Inspiration and Interpretation: Seven Sermons Before the University of Oxford in 1860–1861, Being an answer to a volume entitled "Essays and Reviews"* (Oxford: Parker, 1861), p. 123.

[14]Ibid., p. 42. In a Supplement to Sermon IV Burgon targeted for criticism a theory of inspiration very similar to the one outlined in the Rogers and McKim proposal (Ibid., p. 126).

[15]Ibid., p. 43.

[16]Ibid., p. 74. W. Neill sets the context for Burgon's lectures at Oxford in this way: "Yet the 'terror and wrath' which was aroused by such critical treatment of the Scriptures become more explicable when it is remembered that Dr. Burgon, the future Dean of Chichester, was expressing the normally held view when he delivered the classic formulation of the doctrine of the infallibility of the Bible from the pulpit of the university church at Oxford, during the controversy which followed the appearance of *Essays and Reviews*" ("The Criticism and Theological Use of the Bible, 1700–1950" in *The Cambridge History of the Bible & The West from the Reformation to the Present Day* [ed. S. L. Greenslade; Cambridge: At the University Press, 1976], p. 283). See especially, Nigel Malcolm de Ségur Cameron, "Criticism in Controversy: Conservative Biblical Interpretation and Higher Criticism in Nineteenth-Century Britain: A Study on a Conflict of Method" (Doctor of Philosophy: University of Edinburgh, 1981), pp. 115–56.

[17]On the controversy over Darwin's thought in England and the United States, see James R. Moore, *The Post-Darwinian Controversies: A Study of the Protestant struggle to come to terms with Darwin in Great Britain and America 1870–1900* (New York: Cambridge University Press, 1979); for France, see Harry W. Paul, *The Edge of Contingency: French Catholic Reaction to Scientific Change from Darwin to Duhem* (Gainesville; University Presses of Florida, 1979).

[18]The seven contributors were Frederick Temple, Jowett, Mark Pattison, Baden Powell, Rowland Williams, H. B. Wilson, and C. W. Goodwin. The *Edinburgh Review* (April 1861) noted the German influence by citing an apologist for the *Essays and Reviews* who indicated that one who "had looked ever so cursorily through the works of Herder, Schleiermacher, Lücke, Neander, De Wette, Ewald, &c., would see the greater part of the passages which have given so much cause for exultation or for offence in this volume have their counterpart in those distinguished theologians." For background on the lengthy debate about the *Essays and Reviews*, consult: Owen Chadwick, *The Victorian Church Part II* (New York: Oxford University Press, 1970), pp. 75–97. The controversy over the *Essays and Reviews* created the backdrop for the stir caused by *Lux Mundi* (1889).

[19]A reading of C. W. Goodwin's contribution to the *Essays and Reviews*, "Mosaic Cosmogony," reveals the doubts that its author had about several of the "plans of conciliation" between Genesis and science that his contemporaries were proposing. This essay is reprinted in *Religious Controversies of the Nineteenth Century: Selected Documents* (ed. A. O. J. Cockshut; Lincoln: University of Nebraska Press, 1966), pp. 136–69.

[20]Various English writers (perhaps influenced by a theory of progress) indicated that developments in philosophy, philology, comparative religions, and historical criticism would serve to make Christianity more credible. One could shuck the old doctrine of the "infallibility of every word and letter contained in the Bible" without fear and with benefit (Farrar, *History of Interpretation*, p. 421).

[21]Row, *Christian Lectures Viewed in Relation to Modern Thought* (London: Frederic Norgate, 1877).

[22]Ibid., pp. 436–37.

[23]Ibid., p. 437. In the latter half of the nineteenth century proponents of new perspectives on Scripture often claimed that they were the "inductivists" whereas the defenders of complete biblical infallibility were the "deductivists." Obviously, neither party was solely deductivist or inductivist in approach.

[24]Ibid., p. 432.

[25]Row argued that many of the objections to the Christian faith could be answered if the theory of verbal inspiration were abandoned: "Taking these objections as a whole, I feel convinced that at least two-thirds of them owe their entire plausibility to their identification of that particular form of inspiration, which is usually designated verbal or mechanical, with the divine Revelation. To this theory they believe Christianity to be pledged . . ." (Ibid., pp. 428–29).

[26]Ibid., p. 429.

[27]Ibid., p. 437. Row had earlier outlined his thinking about biblical inspiration in his *Nature and Extent of Divine Inspiration* . . . (London: Longman, Green, 1864).

[28]For the English theological scene in 1860, see L. E. Elliott-Binn's chapter, "The Position in 1860" in *English Thought 1860–1900*, pp. 1–31. In his chapter "The Biblical-Inspiration: Revelation," Elliott-Binns describes how attitudes changed toward biblical authority during the next forty years (pp. 175–91). See also, Owen Chadwick's discussion of growing unbelief and doubt after 1860 (*The Victorian Church, Part II*, pp. 112–50).

[29]Farrar especially appreciated Coleridge whom he said helped "to deliver English Churchmen from their ignorance of German literature, and their terror of German speculation" (*History of Interpretation*, p. 422). Farrar believed that Coleridge was the individual who had begun revisionist studies of the history of inspiration: "In his *Confessions of an Inquiring Spirit* he was the first to show his fellow countrymen with convincing illustrations and impassioned eloquence that the Rabbinic, medieval and post-Reformation dogma of inspiration could only lead to irreverence and casuistry. He taught them to acquire their estimate of Scripture from the contents of Scripture itself, not from the theories and inventions of men respecting it" (Ibid.). Charles Briggs sought to countermand the interpretation that the Westminster Confession taught verbal inspiration. Consult, for example, Briggs's *Whither? A Theological Question for the Times* (New York: Charles Scribner's Sons, 1889). See this essay, chap. 6, nn. 8 and 49. Although he did not favor the stance, W. Sanday, Bampton Lecturer for 1893, acknowledged that a belief in "verbal" inspiration was evident "from the very first" for some Fathers (*Inspiration* [London: Longmans, Green, 1896], p. 34).

[30]Rogers and McKim devote a lengthy discussion to Charles Briggs (pp. 348–61). They occasionally make use of Farrar's *History of Interpretation* as a secondary source. On Briggs, see Max Gray, "Charles Augustus Briggs; Heresy at Union," *American Religious Heretics: Formal and Informal Trials* (ed. George Shriver; Nashville: Abingdon, 1966), pp. 89–147.

[31]Among Roman Catholic progressives a revisionist historiography of inspiration also emerged in the late nineteenth century. The outright commendation of Richard Simon by Ernest Renan and Henri Margival is but one sign of these new perspectives. This historiography was sometimes strongly criticized during the "modernist" crisis that racked the Roman Catholic Church. On the Catholic Modernists, see A. R. Vidler, *A Variety of Catholic Modernists* (Cambridge: Cambridge University Press, 1970). Consult also: Francis J. Schroeder, "Père Lagrange: Record and Teaching in Inspiration," *Catholic Biblical Quarterly* 20 (April 1958): 206–17. F. A. Tholuck advocated a revisionist historiography in Germany earlier in the century.

[32]Jack Rogers does not perceive himself to be a Barthian nor a proponent of a neoorthodox position on Scripture.

[33]See G. C. Berkouwer, *Holy Scripture*, trans. Jack Rogers (Grand Rapids: Eerdmans, 1975). Rogers also studied with Professor Berkouwer. For background on Berkouwer's perspectives regarding biblical authority, see G. C. Berkouwer, *A Half Century of Theology* (Grand Rapids: Eerdmans, 1977), pp. 107–43.

[34]Those who would understand the later thought of Berkouwer (and therefore the thinking of Rogers and McKim) should read Geoffrey Bromiley, "Biblical Authority," *Christianity Today* 20/4 (November 21, 1975): 42–45. See also Henry Krabbendam, "B. B. Warfield vs. G. C. Berkouwer," *Inerrancy* (ed. Norman Geisler; Grand Rapids: Zondervan,

1979), pp. 413–46. Krabbendam makes particularly blunt statements: "Berkouwer and his followers are in the grip of a dialectic that arises from apostasy and can arise *only* from apostasy" (Ibid., p. 446).

[35]Loretz, *The Truth of the Bible* (New York: Herder and Herder, 1968), pp. 81–84.

[36]Ibid., pp. 88, 94.

[37]Ibid., p. 91. As we have indicated, Rogers and McKim's perspectives in this regard are generally shaped by the thinking of Berkouwer.

[38]Ibid., pp. 93–94. In a first draft schema of the Vatican II discussion of Scripture, inerrancy figured prominently as a belief that had apparently been the teaching of the church through time: "Since divine inspiration extends to all things [in the Bible], it follows directly and necessarily that the entire Sacred Scripture is absolutely immune from error. By the ancient and constant faith of the Church we are taught that it is absolutely wrong to concede that a sacred writer has erred, since divine inspiration by its very nature excludes and rejects every error in every field, religious or profane. This necessarily follows because God, the supreme truth, can be the author of no error whatever." But the final version of the document encompasses a significant shift in emphasis: "Therefore, since everything asserted by the inspired authors or sacred writers must be held to be asserted by the Holy Spirit, it follows that the books of Scripture must be acknowledged as teaching firmly, faithfully, and without error that truth which God wanted put into the sacred writings for the sake of our salvation" (*The Documents of Vatican II* [ed. Walter M. Abbott; New York: Guild Press, 1966], p. 119 and n. 31). Loretz and several other Roman Catholic scholars have attempted to find justifications for this soteriological change in focus for the expression *without error*. For background on the crafting of Vatican II's statement on Scripture *(Dei Verbum)*, consult: Bruce Vawter, *Biblical Inspiration* (Philadelphia: Westminster, 1974), pp. 143–50.

[39]Thiselton, *The Two Horizons: New Testament Hermeneutics and Philosophical Description* (Grand Rapids: Eerdmans, 1979), p. 433. Thiselton's analysis of the relationship between a "non-propositional" view of revelation and a "propositional" view should be studied with care (pp. 432–38).

[40]Vawter, *Biblical Inspiration*, p. 152. See James Barr, *The Semantics of Biblical Language* (New York: Oxford University Press, 1961), and this essay, chap. 1, n. 11.

[41]This evaluation comes from Professor Nicole's forthcoming essay, "The Biblical Concept of Truth," in *Scripture and Truth* (ed. D. A. Carson and J. D. Woodbridge; Grand Rapids: Zondervan, 1983). Consult also: Anthony C. Thiselton, "Truth Alētheia" in *The New International Dictionary of New Testament Theology* (ed. C. Brown; Grand Rapids: Zondervan, 1978), III, pp. 874–902.

[42]Loretz, *The Truth of the Bible*, p. 72.

[43]See this essay, chap. 2, n. 7.

[44]Professor James T. Burtchaell of Notre Dame writes: "Christians early inherited from the Jews the belief that the biblical writers were somehow possessed by God, who was thus to be reckoned the Bible's proper author. Since God could not conceivably be the agent of falsehood, the Bible must be guaranteed free from any error. For centuries this doctrine lay dormant, as doctrines will: accepted by all, pondered by few. Not until the 16th century did inspiration and its corollary, inerrancy, come up for sustained review. The Reformers and Counter-Reformers were disputing whether all revealed truth was in Scripture alone, and whether it could dependably be interpreted by private or by official scrutiny. Despite a radical disagreement on these issues both groups persevered in receiving the Bible as a compendium of inerrant oracles dictated by the Spirit" (*Catholic Theories of Inspiration since 1810: A Review and Critique* [Cambridge: At the University Press, 1969], pp. 1–2).

[45]Rogers, "Mixed Metaphors, Misunderstood Models, and Puzzling Paradigms: A Contemporary Effort to Correct some Current Misunderstandings Regarding the Authority and Interpretation of the Bible," Conference Papers for *Interpreting an Authoritative Bible* (June 22–26, 1981), Institute for Christian Studies, Toronto, Canada, pp. 9–10.

[46]Rogers also speaks of what amounts to a neoorthodox model (Ibid., pp. 12–13).

[47]Ibid., p. 11.

[48]Ibid., p. 15.

[49]Consult Suppe's devastating criticisms of Kuhn's approach in *The Structure of Scientific Theories* (Urbana: University of Illinois Press, 1977), pp. 643–49. As we indicated earlier, Suppe affirms that increasing numbers of philosophers of science reject Kuhn's approach as "irredeemably flawed" (p. 648). See this essay, chap. 1, n. 27. Consult also Margaret Masterman, "The Nature of a Paradigm," in *Criticism and the Growth of Knowledge* (ed. Imre Lakatos and Alan Musgrave; Cambridge: At the University Press, 1970), pp. 59–89. Masterman notes that Kuhn "uses 'paradigm' in not less than twenty-one different senses in his [1962] work, possibly more, not less" (Ibid., p. 61).

[50]Rogers and McKim never fully address the epistemological problems associated with their form/function interpretative grid for looking at Scripture. Nonetheless Rogers does think that epistemological concerns are very important. He argues that many inerrantists are caught up in a paradigm of "naïve realism" whereas defenders of his definition of infallibility are proponents of "critical realism." Thus they have a difficult time understanding each other. In point of fact many responsible proponents of complete biblical infallibility are critical realists by his definition and understand quite well the theses Rogers has advocated in his writings.

[51]These other influences probably include the writings of Professor Charles Kraft regarding cultural anthropology and more recently the studies of Professor Ian Rennie regarding the history of inspiration. Professor Rennie wisely calls for historical research that discriminates between plenary and verbal theories of inspiration. The research he envisions must be accomplished with real finesse. Some Englishmen in the nineteenth century, for example, used the words *plenary* and *verbal* interchangeably. On Protestant theories of inspiration in nineteenth-century England, see C. A. Row, *Christian Evidences Viewed in Relation to Modern Thought*, pp. 443–47. J. T. Burtchaell reviews well the fate of the Roman Catholic equivalent theory of "plenary" inspiration (a minority position within the Church vs. verbal inspiration) in *Catholic Theories of Biblical Inspiration Since 1810*, pp. 44–52. John Henry Newman's perspective on these matters is instructive: "I suppose I am not wrong in saying that there has been in the last three hundred years a growing tendency in divines to abandon the doctrine of the verbal inspiration, and to acquiesce in an inspiration *quo ad res et sententias*, without any tendency whatever to allow the errability of the sacred writers in any [of] the most minute facts of physics, history and other human sciences. What is the universal sentiment has ever a claim upon our reverence and submission; and I for one am not bold enough against such authority, and against that intrinsic difficulty of the hypotheses on which I have already dwelt, to hold that any error whatever, however slight, is admissible in the sacred writers" (Newman, *The Theological Papers of John Henry Newman on Biblical Inspiration and Infallibility* [ed. J. Derek Holmes; Oxford: Clarendon Press, 1979], p. 10). The doctrine of verbal inspiration (associated with complete infallibility) has a history which travels back through the sixteenth century and to the church fathers. Many Evangelicals argue that it represents the teaching of Holy Writ as well.

Notes

CHAPTER IX

[1] If the present author had attempted to write a book with the title that Rogers and McKim's volume bears, he would have followed a more carefully defined route, taking into consideration the methodological problems that can wreck such a bold enterprise. Moreover, he would have attempted to move beyond his own areas of specialization in order to provide a more comprehensive bibliographical backdrop to the undertaking. Actually, it would be far better for a team of scholars to set out on the journey rather than one individual.

[2] We studied the authors' own sources so that they cannot claim that our assessment is based on a historiographical tradition of "Warfieldian writers." The authors tend to dismiss the works of several fine scholars apparently on the basis that they personally held to Warfield's position on Scripture. See, for example, their comments on Ronald Nash's *The Light of the Mind: St. Augustine's Theory of Knowledge* (Lexington: University Press of Kentucky, 1969), on p. 61, n. 93.

[3] The continental Reformers stressed finding Christ in the Scriptures. They also maintained that the Bible was a rule of faith.

[4] John Henry Newman, *The Theological Papers of John Henry Newman on Biblical Inspiration and Infallibility* (ed. J. Derek Holmes; Oxford: Clarendon Press, 1979), pp. 7–8. See J. Derek Holmes, "Newman's Attitude Towards Historical Criticism and Biblical Inspiration," *Downside Review* 89 (January 1971): 22–37.

[5] The authors attempt to skirt this problem in a brief note (p. xxiv, n. 12): "The use of 'salvation' to designate the primary purpose of Scripture should not be taken to exclude, for example, social and ethical concerns. It is not meant to make the Bible only a book of personal piety. Scripture certainly deals with the relationships of persons to God, to themselves, and to their neighbors. What 'salvation' is meant to exclude is the post-Reformation scholastic notion that the Bible is a competing and superior source of technical information in the various sciences." Given this perspective, the Bible student is obliged to use his or her understanding of science and other disciplines to sort out infallible "salvation truths" from fallible materials. This operation necessitates that one's reason and personal culture judge revelation in a most unfortunate way. Many Christians believe that the Bible is completely infallible but that it is not a "scientific textbook" per se. They also use their rational capacities and personal culture to help them *interpret* the Bible after first seeking the Holy Spirit's guidance.

[6] The alert reader needs to recall that some of the later claims of Rogers and

McKim's volume are based upon misconstrued arguments found earlier in the text. He or she should also recognize the "drumbeat form" of argumentation in the book. Themes are repeated frequently as if their constant repetition will somehow finally make them true.

[7]Kenneth Kantzer's observation about the views of Augustine, Calvin, and Luther are appropriate in this regard. These churchmen believed in biblical inerrancy if inerrancy means that the Bible does not wander from the truth in anything it affirms. It should be reiterated that they, like many modern Evangelicals, believed that the Bible teaches this doctrine.

Index of Persons

Index of Subjects